OUTCOME-BASED

MARKETING

1

Jere L. Calmes, Publisher
Cover Design: Andrew Welyczko
Production and Composition: Eliot House Productions

This publication is designed to provide accurate and authoritative
information in regard to the subject matter covered. It is sold with the
understanding that the publisher is not engaged in rendering legal,
accounting or other professional services. If legal advice or other expert
assistance is required, the services of a competent professional person
should be sought.

Library of Congress Cataloging-in-Publication Data
    Leavy, John D.
      Outcome-based marketing: new rules for marketing on the web/by
John D. Leavy.
        p.   cm.
        ISBN-13: 978-1-59918-418-0 (alk. paper)
        ISBN-10: 1-59918-418-4 (alk. paper)
        1. Internet marketing. I. Title.
      HF5415.1265.L42 2011
      658.8'72—dc22   2011001349

Printed in the United States of America

15 14 13 12 11   10 9 8 7 6 5 4 3 2 1

Cyrus West Field was the force behind the first transatlantic telegraph cable, attempted unsuccessfully in 1857 and completed on August 5, 1858. On August 16, 1858, the first message sent across the transatlantic cable was:

"Glory to God in the highest; on earth, peace, and goodwill toward men."

The first transatlantic text message?

Contents

Part I
Build a Strong Web Presence

Part II
Be Found in All the Right Places

Part III
Be Social on the Web

Part IV
Generate Closable Opportunities

Foreword

by Chris Brogan

JOHN LEAVY MAKES ME TIRED. I MEAN THAT IN THE VERY BEST SENSE of the expression, however. You see, I'm sent a LOT of books to read. I'm fortunate enough to be asked to write the forewords for some of them. And you're here to learn about John and why you should read this book, but I'm going to say just one more sentence about me before I turn it over to talking about John (and it's a secret). Lots of the books I get to read these days in the world of business and marketing are more talk about talk, and not really packed with any action.

Outcome-Based Marketing made me want to take a vacation. Leavy has lots and lots and lots of information in this book. If you haven't glanced the table of contents yet, take a bit of a gander. There is TONS stuffed in here. Now, that can go one of two ways: lots of topics but not enough depth, or, "No, he has all the depth thrown in, too." Leavy shoots for B on this one.

When I did my first read-through of the book, I was thinking, "Wow, he's really gone pretty deep on websites. Maybe this book is out of touch. I mean, we're all talking about Twitter and Facebook and stuff. If John's all stuck on the website, what will this mean for the book?" But no. John had sections devoted to social networks and stuff, plus a lot (and I mean a lot) of helpful information that you need to dig into.

Before you start, and this presumes that you're actually still reading this instead of having jumped in with both feet, get two things: a notepad and a pen. Write down the page numbers where the cool stuff is taking place. Make sure you put little "!" next to the actions you're going to take when you get down with *Outcome-Based Marketing*. I'm going to bet you'll have somewhere around 27 !s when you're finished.

By the time you get down to the chapters 20-ish through 25 or so, you'll have to cancel your cable subscription. Leavy has you doing a ton of stuff that is going to blow your business up, whether you're still working for The Man, or whether you're going to do this for yourself.

Oh, and I almost forgot one more really important point: You can't just skip around in this book. Lots of business books say that's fine. Not with John Leavy. He has you doing homework. If you haven't done what you need to do before going on to the next chapters, you're screwed. There's no delicate way to put that. He's like this professor, and you've gotta get your papers in or he's going to fail you. That's how I felt. The frickin' guy has me doing homework.

I say every word of this with respect for John Leavy. I don't know him very well. We don't drink bourbon together and to the best of my knowledge, he hasn't bought me a pony or anything. Like I said at the beginning: I read a LOT of business books, and this one will really make you work. But it'll be the best kind of work.

Me? I'm going to go take a nap. Then, I'm going to go do all the stuff Leavy has added to my day. And later? I'll count the money that a book like this one is making me by following the advice.

—Chris Brogan, President of Human Business Works
and co-author of the *New York Times* bestseller *Trust Agents*

Preface

"WINNING ISN'T EVERYTHING; IT'S THE ONLY THING." YOU CAN attribute this quote to UCLA Bruins football coach Henry Russell "Red" Sanders at a Cal Poly San Luis Obispo physical education workshop in 1950. Or you can credit the passage to American football legend Vince Lombardi who is on record using the quote as early as his opening talk on the first day of Packer's training camp in 1959. I'll leave it to the football aficionados to work it out.

I never dared share this quote with my two sons and daughter while I was their little league coach because it made the hair bristle on the back of my neck. What about fair play, good sportsmanship, or trying your best—even if, at the end of the day, your team lost the game?

There's a movement afoot today that says everyone is a winner. There is no second or third place. Every child that participates in a sport should receive a trophy at the end of the season. Are they saying Lance Armstrong should share his seven Tour de France wins with those who finished behind him? Is Michael Phelps somehow hoarding his 16 Olympic swimming medals? This talk needs to be relegated to the kitchen table, certainly not the boardrooms of successful businesses, or any business for that matter.

Companies that consistently finish behind their competitors eventually go out of business. Anyone still have Enron stock in their 401(k), flown on Trans World Airlines (TWA), or had a thirst-quenching All Star Cola lately? There's a reason these companies are no longer with us. It's the law of the jungle: only the strong survive.

Thought leaders push companies to survive in good times and bad—when the economy is running lean and when times are flush. These business leaders find a way to grow when everyone else is cutting back. These companies rely on positive "results." Here is where outcome-based marketing strategies come into play.

Whether you call outcome-based marketing performance-based, results-based, or purpose-driven, the focus is just where it needs to be—on the consequence, the upshot, the outcome.

At times, some businesses are more involved in keeping the marketing activities going than in worrying about positive, lasting results. Is there anything wrong with not worrying about the results? Money is being spent. Everyone has their head down. There's hardly a free hour to rest. Let's call this marketing method the "hamster" marketing approach. Keep the wheels turning and something good is bound to happen. Unfortunately, good things seldom occur when doing the wrong activities over and over. Just ask the past employees of TWA or Enron.

Companies have wanted results from their marketing campaigns from the beginning, but somehow metrics and milestones have been left out of the marketing equation. Companies seem to be focusing more on activities than outcomes. Because *Outcome-based Marketing* is results oriented, it asks these questions: Can we accurately measure the progress the campaign is making? Did we convert more of the visitor traffic this month? Did our cost-per-conversion go down?

Notice that campaign results deal with finite numbers and not generalities or gut feelings. Oversimplifications such as the visitor traffic is up, more people are downloading the whitepapers, or we have more Twitter followers than we did last month mean little, perhaps nothing. The results of statements such as these are hard to quantify or qualify for that matter. What were the actions that caused the increases? Are the results reproducible on demand and sustainable? If not, why not? *Outcome-Based Marketing* answers these questions.

Different elements make up outcome-based marketing: inputs, activities, masses, leads, outcome targets, and outcome indicators. Here's a breakdown of each outcome-based element:

· *Inputs.* Materials and resources used during the marketing activities. The "materials" could be case studies, whitepapers, and other collateral pieces. The "resources" might be people, time, and money.

· *Activities.* Processes the business executes during the marketing campaign, such as e-mail blasts, webinars, blog postings, or podcasts.

· *Masses.* People made aware of the marketing promotion.

· *Leads.* The number of people that took some action as a result of the marketing campaign. For instance, the number of people that subscribed to the blog after reading it or the number of prospects who downloaded a whitepaper after watching a webinar.

· *Outcome targets.* The number and percentage of leads that you need to achieve the stated outcome. For example, the stated outcome might be 1,000 new attendees to the next webinar series or a 15 percent increase in visitor traffic to the company website over the next three months.

· *Outcome indicators.* Observable and measureable milestones toward the outcome target. For instance, if a marketing campaign is launched and it generates a 5 percent increase in visitor traffic in the first month, then it is likely the visitor traffic will increase by 15 percent after the third month.

The outcome indicators let you know if the outcome targets are realistic and achievable or if other activities need to be added to reach the marketing goal.

Here's how an e-mail campaign might look using the outcome-based marketing strategy:

· *Inputs.* Messaging, the e-mail sent out, and newsletter
· *Activities.* Sending out the e-mails
· *Masses.* List of recipients
· *Leads.* Those that sign up for the newsletter
· *Outcome targets.* 1,000 new subscribers (short-term goal) and 20 to 30 new partners (long-term goal), a 2 to 3 percent return
· *Outcome indicators.* E-mail service to track nonresponders, opens, bounces, click-throughs, unsubscribes, and new newsletter subscribers

Are the results created by outcome-based marketing reproducible? If certain activities increased the visitor traffic to the website by 5 percent the first month, will another 5 percent increase be generated the second month?

Granted, close attention has to be paid to all six elements of the outcome-based strategy. The inputs have to be compelling. The activities have to be well orchestrated. The masses have to be of good quality, and the leads have to be bonafide. The outcome targets have to be made up from achievable numbers, and the outcome indicators need to be closely watched, and calculated.

I hope you learn as much by reading *Outcome-Based Marketing* as I did writing it. Good Marketing!

Introduction

*O*UTCOME-*B*ASED *M*ARKETING ADDRESSES YOUR MOST PRESSING MAR-keting issues for your business. Each chapter starts out with an overview of what is discussed. You'll find a Be Strategic element at the end of each section within a chapter to get you to think strategically about what was just covered. Each part ends with Take Five, a segment to help you review the key points outlined there. Take five minutes to go over what was discussed.

The first part of *Outcome-Based Marketing*, Build a Strong Web Presence, discusses a business's web presence, the company's website and blog. These are the two locales where most companies want visitors to eventually end up. Consider websites. Visitors may stop off at podcast directories, forums, community, or social sites. But the real destination from a company's perspective is its website—the mother lode of services, solutions, offers, and information.

Not just any website is going to hold the attention of visitors, convert them to opportunities, and turn them into customers. The website needs to have compelling content, easy-to-understand architecture, and menu navigation that is intuitive. The website should create a sense of trust and confidence for anyone doing business at the site. The site also needs to have obvious decision-making paths so website visitors can make their way through the education/buying process. Decision-making paths are a mechanism to guide and educate website visitors. Let's say you run a web survey site and have two distinct visitor groups: Those that want to be educated about the online survey process, and those that are ready to buy the survey product. It makes sense to send each group of visitors in a different direction. Send those that need additional education to more information resources. And direct those that are ready to become customers to the purchasing process.

The second portion of *Outcome-Based Marketing*, Be Found in All the Right Places, considers two questions: How does a business cause itself to "be found" on the web, and where are "all those right places"? Being found on the web among the billions of web pages takes know-how. Gaining visibility to the right audiences on the web requires a calculated strategy that requires a lot of effort, time, talent, and resources. Searchers are not going to visit a company's website just because someone built it. That kind of thinking is for those that love baseball fantasy movies like the 1989 baseball movie *Field of Dreams*.

To be successful on the web, businesses need to identify their "ideal" prospect before launching their internet marketing campaigns. They need to ask themselves these types of questions about their ideal prospects: Are they looking to sell to males, females, or both? Is their age range 20 to 40? Are these prospects single or married? Do they spend a good deal of their time and energy enjoying outdoor activities? Do these candidates live in the north or southwest? Once a company can identify their "ideal" prospect, the next task is to search the web to see where these prospects hang out. What communities do they join, what blogs do they read, what information and offerings would they find compelling? Once a business has its ideal prospect identified and has a list of the prospect's gathering spots, it can develop what is called a "prospect universe," that is, every place ideal prospects gather on the web.

Now that the ideal prospects are known and their possible watering holes marked off, the next chore is to develop strategies for the business to gain visibility in those venues. Too many businesses are enraptured with the idea of attracting their first one million visitors to their own website. Doesn't it make more sense to go where your ideal prospects already gather and meet them there on their own terms? In turn, having good visibility, compelling information, and attractive offers will attract those people in droves to the company's website.

The third part of *Outcome-Based Marketing*, Being Social on the Web, deals with engaging people on the web. Social media and social networking are terms that have become interchangeable even though they have somewhat different meanings. Social media is media (music, photos, or videos) that is designed to be shared through social interaction. Social networking is linking a community of people together in some way for business or personal reasons. Here this technology is called social media most of the time. Some think social media is a time-consuming, resource-wasting fad while others hinge a good portion of the success of their business on this latest technology. It depends on the business. There's no argument social media takes time, resources, and commitment. Businesses that do not allow at least six months for their social experiment may terminate their program prematurely and thereby not realize the potential social media offers.

Businesses are finding ways to leverage these social twins. For instance, a number of businesses are putting social strategies in place to expand their reach on the web, cultivate new prospects, and deliver better customer care alternatives. Social media is the perfect vehicle to disseminate information and offers quickly. New mobile apps are hitting the airwaves every day, making the disseminating process easier and less expensive.

Companies employing social networking have a duty to develop winning marketing strategies for the web much the same way they do for marketing ground assaults. Being Social on the Web talks about how the strategy's goals need to be reasonable, attainable, and measurable.

Security is a valid concern that keeps some businesses at an arm's length from the social community. At times, it's hard to tell who the members of a group are or who's following a specific conversation on Twitter. Because a community is well-known and used by the masses does not necessarily mean it's a secure environment. Businesses should adopt security guidelines before jumping into the various social communities.

The fourth part of *Outcome-Based Marketing*, Generate Closable Opportunities, talks about strategies to generate closable opportunities. Wikipedia defines a "sales lead" as "the identity of a human or entity potentially interested in purchasing a product or service, and represents the first stage in the sales process." A lot of terms are thrown around about leads. You have hot leads, warm leads, and cold leads; qualified leads and unqualified leads; plus A leads, B leads, and C leads. For discussion purposes here, a lead is defined as someone who has shown interest in or taken action on an offer. For example, a website visitor downloads a whitepaper, takes a free trial, subscribes to a newsletter, or joins a webinar. These are all examples of leads that could potentially turn into opportunities and then sales. But how do we move these leads through the sales process to create "closable opportunities?" That's the meat of Generate Closable Opportunities.

On the web, businesses need to know how prospects are searching for them. If the company sells coffee, are searchers keying "whole bean coffee" or "coffee beans" into their browsers? Companies have to identify the key phrases potential visitors are using to find their product or service. With that information in hand, they can synchronize their messaging and their content using those key phrases. If the business is using social channels, the messages going out need to include these key phrases as well. Everything should be in harmony: the key phrases, the company's brand promise and messaging, along with all the organization's content and collateral. The company's website, blog, whitepapers, webinars, and press releases are examples. If any of these instruments are out of tune, it could spell disaster for the marketing campaign.

Statistics tell us that only 3 to 5 percent of the visitors to a website are ready to make a purchase or make a decision. What are you to do with the remaining 95 to 97 percent? This is where education and lead nurturing come into play. Companies need to move at the buyer's pace. Until the time of purchase, businesses need to build and foster relationships with those who are not ready or not sure they want to buy the company's product or service.

To help show where the responsibility might lie for certain strategies or tactics, *Outcome-Based Marketing* includes people icons (Figure I.1) to help show where the responsibility might reside. Different people in an organization have various responsibilities. Some people need to be informed about what's happening while others need to take action on that information. The first person shown in the icon quartet is the business owner, followed by the marketing person, the web person, and the SEO expert. For instance, in the section "You'll Never Be Given a Second Chance

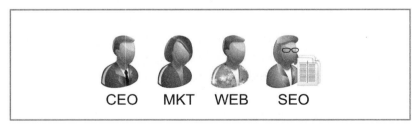

FIGURE I.1—The people icons shown throughout the book

to Make a Good First Impression," the responsibility most likely lies with the marketing person and the web designer to make sure the website has a professional look and feel.

Sample spreadsheets and a marketing calendar have been uploaded to Outcome-BasedMarketing.com/handouts. If you'd like to download and use them to give your planning a jump-start, go ahead. All we ask for is a valid e-mail address in order to send the links. You will receive no junk mail by participating in this opportunity.

If you'd like to contact me, use any of the options below.

John D. Leavy
John@JohnLeavy.com
JohnLeavy.com
LinkedIn.com/in/JohnDLeavy
Twitter @JohnLeavy

PART I

BUILD
A STRONG
WEB PRESENCE

Even though everything a business has distributed across the internet could be considered its web presence, let's just spotlight the organization's website and blog for the moment.

The website must have a professional look and feel. The menu navigation should be intuitive and easy to pilot. There must be compelling content that is well thought-out with obvious calls to action. Treating every website visitor the same is a crucial mistake too often made. Adding decision-making paths to one's homepage help separate visitors quickly based upon their needs or wants and routes them promptly to their destination.

> *"A man must be big enough to admit his mistakes, smart enough to profit from them, and strong enough to correct them."*
>
> —JOHN C. MAXWELL

Blogs are similar to websites in that they need to have a professional look and feel, good navigation, and compelling content; but blogs are different as well. Blogs are usually built from Content Management Systems (CMS) such as WordPress

(WordPress.org/com) or TypePad (TypePad.com). The blog contributors do not have to learn any HTML or other behind-the-scene software. There's also no webmaster in the loop to add the content. Blogs provide a platform for a more casual conversation with prospects and customers. Blogs can have several contributors, and new blog posts can be active within seconds. Blog postings can be bookmarked out to dozens of social communities, which mean more traffic to the company's blog and website.

Build a Strong Web Presence takes a sensible look at website or blog ingredients that will create massive awareness, attract new visitors, and generate more revenue opportunities.

Chapter 1

The Structural Elements of a Strong Web Presence

"If you don't know where you are going, you might wind up someplace else."

—Yogi Berra

TREATING EVERY WEBSITE VISITOR THE SAME IS A FATAL MISTAKE. Many of the websites being launched today show no evidence of decision-making paths. Companies have little knowledge of how to help increase their visitor conversion rate and the company's bottom line.

Think about a trip to the zoo. Everyone who enters the front gate receives a map, and each family member can head off in a different direction to see his or her favorite animals, be they lions, tigers, or bears.

Many websites create opportunities for personal choice. Anyone landing at a website's homepage might browse to see what products, services, or resources are available. Or the visitor may decide to check out the Leadership or Company History pages. These websites are built to wander. The website visitor wanders around and then leaves. The only *decision* made by the visitor was to leave the site.

Many websites seemed to be designed for visitors to wander aimlessly.

No engagement, no interaction. Guess what? No conversion. Few sites have a visitor conversion strategy in place. Only about 3 to 4 percent of visitors coming to a website are ready to purchase, join, or subscribe. That means a lot of education needs to take place before those masses are ready to buy or give personal information.

If it has been determined that three types of visitors are coming to a particular site, then three very distinct decision-making paths need to be developed to guide and educate those visitors until they are ready to make a buying decision.

If there are all kinds of hyperlinks and arrows pointing in different directions on the homepage of a site, guess what happens? Visitors head off in any direction never hearing the most important message. The buyer makes her own decision without the seller.

The Mozes.com website shown in Figure 1.1 gives visitors what they're looking for. Those new to the site can click on the green bubble and find out about Mozes. Some visitors can create new accounts and get their custom mobile experience started while existing members can sign-in to their account and manage things.

Decision-making paths make it easy on the visitor to find what

BE **STRATEGIC**

▶ Don't treat every website visitor as a buyer ready to purchase.

▶ Design each decision-making path from the visitors' perspective. Educate them. Help them come to a resolution.

▶ Make the decision-making paths obvious so no one gets lost.

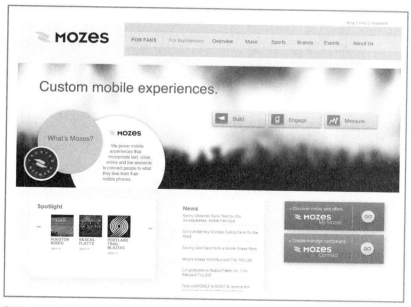

FIGURE 1.1—Mozes website homepage

they want. These paths also help move the visitor along the sales funnel.

You Only Have Eight Seconds to Grab a Visitor's Attention

"You don't want another Enron? Here's your law: If a company, can't explain, in ONE SENTENCE . . . what it does . . . it's illegal."

—LEWIS BLACK

You can use the web page example in Figure 1.2 for a lesson in web design—eye-catching taglines. Visitors need to be drawn in quickly, or they are on their way to a competitor's website. "Creating Picture Perfect Homes!" shows just what people want their homes to look like—picture perfect. The redesigned home

FIGURE 1.2—Original web homepage on the top, redesigned homepage on the bottom

remodeling website at the bottom really grabs the visitor's imagination on what the home remodel looks like once it is finished.

The tagline needs to be as few words as possible; a half-dozen choice words. The tagline should be benefit-driven. Forget the "We have been in business longer than dirt" taglines.

It is not about "the company" even though it is the company's website. It is all about the visitor and his or her perceived need or want.

"Must-have security apps," "Every legal issue one legal source," and "Find a dentist you will love" all draw the visitor into the conversation.

Just surfing by Apple.com their tagline reads, "The new iMac . . . The ultimate all-in-one . . . Now with the ultimate display." Adobe reads, "Adobe Creative Suite 4 . . . work faster with new timesaving features." ConstantContact.com says, "We're helping 300,000+ businesses and organizations . . . They use E-mail Marketing, Online Surveys, and Event Marketing to grow their business." These taglines are concise and to the point.

BE **STRATEGIC**

- Some people think the tagline should focus on what the company does or what makes it unique. Taglines should focus on the visitor's needs or wants.
- The tagline should get instant visitor agreement or approval.
- Forget about being funny, clever, or witty unless you're in the entertainment business. The tagline should be results orientated and benefit driven.

Remember, taglines do not have to be full, complete sentences or visitors may be long gone before they reach the end.

Taglines are meant to excite, capture the imagination, and promise solutions to the visitor. (The promise of a solution should be kept.) Taglines such as "30

Years in Business" and "Largest Retailer on the Web" do not motivate any visitor to stay and look around. Owners of websites are tired of hearing this but, it is not about them. It's about the visitor!

The Heat Is On

"Most people give off as much heat as a 100 watt bulb,

but not as much light."

—ANONYMOUS

Why guess where visitors are clicking on your website pages? Heat maps, a software tool from CrazyEgg.com, records the location of where visitors click on your web pages. For instance, in the blog page example from CrazyEgg.com (Figure 1.3), there are 15 potential links people can click. These locations are marked by plus signs inside circles. But, what text attracts the most attention? That's what you don't know. A heat map of the page tells the whole story. Let's look at the example that follows:

Don't make too many alterations to the web page at once. It will be difficult to determine which messages are working and which ones need tweaking.

When the mouse pointer was floated over the area "Stop paying for marketing . . ." you can see that 62 visitors clicked on that phrase. The areas are coded by color: red = the most clicks, blue = the second hottest area, and green = the least amount of clicks. You can easily see which locations receive the most concentration. This clearly tells you what messages are working and which need wordsmithing.

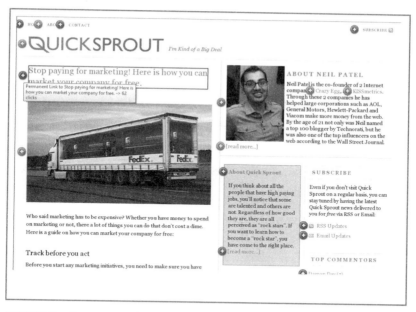

FIGURE 1.3—Heat map results on QuickSprout blog page

With heat maps you can tell if visitors are attracted more to text or images. You'll also be able to tell what position on the web page works best.

CrazyEgg's analytics also tell you what the referring websites were and what search terms visitors used to reach the web page. This information helps you determine what search phrases tie best to the page's marketing messages.

BE **STRATEGIC**

▶ Don't make wholesale changes on your web pages. You won't be able to tell what areas are working best.

▶ You don't need to run heat maps constantly unless your content is always changing.

Is the Menu Navigation Losing Visitors Along the Way?

"Don't let ambition get so far ahead that it loses
sight of the job at hand."

—WILLIAM FEATHER

There are five rules to follow when trying to make the navigation on the website as easy to use as possible:

1. Organize the menu selections with an eye on how the visitor might navigate the information.
2. Choose colors that are easy on the eyes.
3. Eliminate unnecessary menu selections.
4. Pay close attention to the number of clicks necessary to reach each web page.
5. Place additional menu selections at the bottom of long pages to make moving around the website easier.

Don't make it difficult for website visitors to find their way around. Leave navigation breadcrumbs behind so the visitor can tell what page they're on and how they got there. The menu selections should be built around what people want to learn and how they might move along in the sales process.

Ever been to a website and seen a beautiful image or perhaps a snazzy flash running? Ever stared at the motion and wondered where the menu selections are? Where is the "skip" button to shut off this self-absorption? How do I enter this site? Don't they want me to find a way? Unfortunately, some people take technology a step too far and lose a visitor in the offing.

FIGURE 1.4—Harvestime homepage

When designing a website for Harvestime.com, a nationwide church developer, a walk-on actor was added (Figure 1.4). When visitors come to the website, Ben walks on, and introduces them to Harvestime and the website layout. His opening dialogue goes like this . . .

It has often been said what you don't know won't hurt you. When it comes to building new facilities for your ministry, what you don't know can be devastating. Hi, welcome to Harvestime, the premier developer of church facilities in the United States. Our website is designed to introduce you to Harvestime and present the services we provide. As a total, turnkey solution we will demonstrate our unparalleled level of experience that will provide you with a real map for the development of your new facility. On the menu bar above you will find various options for you to explore. As you browse through the different sections I'll meet you along the way and point out some of the key features that make Harvestime such a unique company in the church development field. Thank you for visiting Harvestime.

This is a great way to engage visitors and give them a quick tour of the website's homepage.

The simplicity of website navigation is measured in clicks. Does it take more than two successive mouse clicks for a visitor to get where he or she wants to go anywhere on the website? If so, the site is losing visitors.

Does the menu structure show visitors what "Services" are offered or do they have to click and go to the Services page to find out?

In the menu bar image in Figure 1.5, one has to click on TREK LIFE to see the five options that come up; News, Events, Cycling Teams, Bike Demos, and Video. Why not show the options without the click?

On this second menu scheme shown in Figure 1.6, all that is needed to find out who the dental team members are is a flyover of the mouse pointer. The "Meet Our Team" members are Doctors, Specialists, and Support Staff.

FIGURE 1.5—TREK LIFE menu bar

FIGURE 1.6—A salon menu bar

Other weaknesses that frustrate website visitors are websites that try to look larger than they really are by using, for example, a Services menu selection that lists 10 services. No matter which service the visitors choose, they land on the same web page, in just a different location. Visitors to websites are knowledgeable today. They cannot be easily fooled with tactics such as these.

BE **STRATEGIC**

- Let users know where they are as they move from page to page (navigation breadcrumb).
- The navigation should be easy to read and understand; use names people recognize.
- When it comes to the number of navigation buttons, fewer are better.

MKT   WEB

You'll Never be Given a Second Chance to Make a Good First Impression

"Opportunity is missed by most people because it is dressed in overalls and looks like work."

—Thomas A. Edison

The likelihood of being promptly sued for libel forbids one from highlighting some websites on the web that are less than professional or just plain lousy looking.

In the consultant/client engagement, a relationship needs to be fostered before telling the customer his website (Figure 1.7) is less than professional looking. The consultant cannot just tell the client the reason no one is purchasing from his website is because the darn thing is unsightly or

It's hard to tell people their baby is ugly.

FIGURE 1.7—The ugly baby scenario

repulsive. The best approach would be to draw a comparison between the site and the competition's website. Hopefully the website owner will draw the proper conclusion before the bad news has to be broken to him.

Do you find web pages with red text on a yellow background or light gray text on a very dark one hard to read? Your eyes hurt just trying to figure out what they're saying. Some sites look like they have more moving parts than a 2007 Jeep Liberty. Then there are those sites that have music that kicks in when the visitor arrives. Their owners need to realize if they're not in the music business, skip the tunes.

A good place to start understanding what the web presence has to accomplish is by looking at the competition's websites in your business space. How do they approach the visitor? How do they offer their products or services? How much information is available for the visitor to download? Do they list their advisory board or the company executives on the site? Do they offer online chat services? Do they have a blog or offer webinars? How about the colors, text sizes, and page layouts? Are they professional looking?

So what makes a website look professional? A good color scheme. Navigation that's easy to understand and use. Text sizes and fonts that are easy on the eyes. Crisp, sharp images. Some open-page real estate (not every square-inch of the pages should be filled with photos, text, and a compelling marketing message).

Make sure the web pages are browser compliant. Not everyone is using the same browser you are using. The four biggest browser players are Internet Explorer (IE), Firefox, Apple's Safari and Google's Chrome. Before launching the website, make sure all the web pages display correctly using all the major browsers.

The topology of the website, that is, how the web pages are organized or laid out could also be mentioned. Do people have to hunt for the Contact page? Most websites have a Contact Us selection on the main menu, which makes contacting the business easy. But, some businesses hide the contact information under the Company selection. This is not as obvious and usually frustrates the website visitor.

Lay out the web pages as if you are the visitor coming to the website for the first time and either want to gain more insight or are ready to make a purchase.

Don't try and make the company look as big as General Motors by breaking every web page into as many pieces as possible. This practice is frowned upon.

The competition sets the bar. It's your job to leap over the bar and then raise it behind you for those that follow.

Once you have a good idea of what is necessary to have a website that will look professional and beat the competition, the next step is to find the right web design company.

Look over the web developer's portfolio to make sure she can produce the level of quality work that is demanded. Talk to her clients and find out what the design process was like. Did she finish on time and on budget? How did she respond when changes were solicited?

Even though the website project might be large and complicated, give the design firm a few small assignments to see how well it performs. One company gave their web design company more than $75,000, and the site is now nine months overdue. They're both in court, so it looks like the website will be further delayed.

Don't delegate the web design responsibilities to someone at the company that does not have enough to keep them busy. It's a rare breed of person who is a good graphic designer, understands the latest developments in web construction, and has a sound marketing background to craft the messaging that goes on to the website. The site may turn out looking great, but is the messaging compelling?

BE **STRATEGIC**

- Don't just create a great homepage. Make sure the site is useable from the first page to the last.
- Great site designs have these things is common: good color schemes, fonts that are easy to read, some open space, and graphics that are easy on the eyes.
- The website should be browser compliant (IE, Foxfire®, and Safari) and load quickly.

Chapter 2

Compelling Content Will Make or Break the Site

"The difference between the right word and almost the right word is the difference between lightning and the lightning bug."

—MARK TWAIN

DON'T LET THE WEBSITE FALL SHORT. CLIENTS AND WEB DEVELOPERS seem to fail here because neither is competent at writing compelling copy. The web folks are geeks, and the client may not have the marketing skills to express the messaging clearly. If a good writer or marketing person is not part of the web development team, hire one. We have all read web pages that droll on page after page. The thought here must be that the visitor is eventually worn down and convinced to purchase the product or service. We all know this practice is not an effective one.

Running statistics on how visitors navigate a site quickly tells a person whether the copy and navigation are working or not.

Web developers are not going to know the audience; this responsibility has to be in the client or marketer's hands. The copy should talk-the-talk of the audience reading the web pages. The web page content should also help move the reader along in the decision-making process.

Another thought—break up the copy with relevant images. Images add interest and give the reader's eyes time to rest.

Below are two examples of the services two accounting firms offer. They'll remain nameless. In the first example, the content misses the mark with its five uses of the word "our" and the obvious typo (no period at the end of the last sentence). The second example informs the visitor about its real-world, hands-on experience, being fully independent, and that all the partners are under one roof, eliminating delays.

BE **STRATEGIC**

- Does the content move the reader closer to making a decision?
- Does the content explain the marketing message with clarity?
- Does the content bring the reader into the story?
- Is the content written from the visitor's perspective. In other words, is it benefit driven?

Example 1: The Content Misses the Mark
At ACME Accounting, pleasing our clients is our number one goal. Our purpose for creating this website is to give you the opportunity to use it as an information tool. We invite you to explore our site and learn more about how our services can help you plan for today, tomorrow, and beyond

Example 2: The Content Is Right on Target
The services and client resources we provide have been tailored over many years of real-world, hands-on

experience and direct client need. As a fully independent firm with all of our partners under one roof, we do not suffer any delays in responding to client needs or offering services.

If the boss is doing the marketing and is not a writer, one has to be brought on board. Content is still king whether in print or in the form of text on a web page. Do not rely on the web person to get the messaging correct.

Some web designers cannot resist filling in an empty space on a web page. Resist. Crowded pages only distract from the message's meaning.

Persuading Your Visitors to Take Action Now

"I never worry about action, but only inaction."

—Winston Churchill

Calls to action should include strong, compelling action verbs such as download, buy, shop now, call, and watch. They should tell the website visitor to take some immediate action: "Call Now!" "Download Now!" "Sign-up Today!"

Think of a call to action as a conversion device. Calls to action require a higher level of commitment by the website visitor. These mechanisms also serve to move the prospect further along in the buying cycle. The call to action might be asking visitors to subscribe to a free, monthly newsletter, receive a free whitepaper, as well as make a purchase.

Keep in mind that it is just as important to have a strategy that deals with what will happen after the visitor makes the

FIGURE 2.1—Woman on the phone encouraging people to call now!

call to action. What will take place after they call the toll-free telephone number, sign up for the free webinar, or download the whitepaper? Create urgency in the mnd of the prospective buyer by giving the call to action an expiration date, real or imaginary. The call to action might expire every 24 hours.

Do not use motion, a smiling face, a waving hand, or a bouncing arrow in the call to action. It only distracts the visitor.

A picture of a call center operator (Figure 2.1) standing by for the call with a description on the image that reads "Call Toll Free Now!" is compelling. It pushes the visitor to call the number right away.

The call to action can be words, a picture, or a combination of both.

A strong call to action serves a company better than putting its toll-free telephone number in 6-point text at the bottom of every web page. Don't make the visitor hunt for the phone number. If that's the case, the phone won't be ringing any time soon.

The call to action may be in the form of a pop-up. Some people like them, others don't.

They can drive some website visitors crazy, and they leave the site. Some pop-ups motivate visitors to take action, and take it now. People have to make their own decisions about using pop-ups.

Because the call to action is such a critical part of the selling process, let's review the process:

BE **STRATEGIC**

- Have you carefully thought through what takes place after the call to action?
- Have a call to action on every web page.
- Make the call to action obvious; change the text color and move the call to the top of the page.
- Use urgent verbs such as subscribe, call, buy, and shop.
- Put an expiration date on the call to action.

- Calls to action need to be clear, concise, benefit-driven offers so the website visitor feels motivated to act.
- Calls to action should be front and center on the web page. Don't bury them at the bottom of a page where the visitor is not immediately attracted.
- Calls to action should convey a sense of urgency on the visitor's part to act now or lose out on some great deal.
- Calls to action should be placed on several different pages of the website to increase visitor participation. But, don't overdo it.

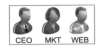

Does Your Website Create an Atmosphere of Trust and Confidence?

"I trust him to a certain extent."

—RICHARD FOSTER

When a person comes to a website for the first time, especially to do business, there needs to be a transfer of trust and confidence between the two parties. People are not going to buy goods out of some stranger's car trunk on the street or from an unfamiliar company's website. Things need to look like they're on the up-and-up. Unfortunately, the charlatans have spoiled it for everyone. Personal testimonies from current customers will go a long way in building trust in the eyes of prospective buyers. It will be their words telling the potential customer how satisfied they are with the realtionship. It's not enough today if you just say you're honest and upright, you need someone else's certification. TRUSTe is such a certification company as is VeriSign.com, TrustGuard.com, and Entrust.com.

If you're going to ask visitors for personal information, you'll want to do that through a secure web page. Most domain hosting companies provide SSL (Secure Sockets Layer) certifications. You can tell you're transacting business securely by the fact the page name in your browser starts with "https" instead of "http."

The Better Business Bureau was founded in 1912 by several private business franchises that wanted to ensure ethical business practices. The BBB logo on a company's website gives buyers confidence that they are transacting business with a reputable company.

If you do business or communicate with the ADA (American's with Disabilities Act) community, you'll want to adhere to the standards published at ADA.gov.

Many professional organizations and associations offer certification badges for websites and blogs. Make sure to display your credentials prominently on the website or blog.

BE **STRATEGIC**

▶ Testimonials from past customers help with the trust factor.

▶ Clearly state any policies the potential customer needs to be aware of before making a purchase.

Keep Your Website Visitors Coming Back to the Well

"Time is nature's way of keeping everything from happening at once."
—WOODY ALLEN

Search engines demand that page content on a website not grow stale. Some sort of content refreshment plan needs to be developed and executed. Large sites obviously need a more comprehensive plan than do smaller ones.

All the text, or website content, needs a light edit occasionally;

Have different editors do the content refreshing so that different writing styles can be utilized.

nothing else on the site has to change. The forms and images can stay the same. Some web pages should be edited every quarter. Develop a content schedule so all pages on the site are put on a yearly, revolving timetable.

Below are examples of two editors rewriting the same paragraph.

Example 1: Existing Content

ACME Document Management is the recognized market leader in enterprise-class, on-demand content management. Led by enterprise content management (ECM) industry veterans, AcmeDM delivers affordable, easy-to-deploy document management, and workflow solutions in a completely web-based environment. AcmeDM's award-winning ECM service eliminates software installations, hardware maintenance, and prolonged customization cycles associated with on-premises applications.

Example 2: Lightly Edited Content

ACME Document Management, market leader in enterprise-class, on-demand document management. AcmeDM is directed by enterprise content management (ECM) industry veterans. AcmeDM delivers a completely web-based environment that is reasonably priced, easy-to-deploy document management, and workflow solutions.

Content Freshening Plan: Outcome-BasedMarketing.com/handouts

contentFreshingPlan.xls

Web Page	January	February	March	April	May	June	July	August	September	October	November	December
company.php	x			x			x			x		
company_board.php	x			x			x			x		
company_careers.php	x			x			x			x		
company_events.php	x			x			x			x		
company_news.php	x			x			x			x		
company_locations.php	x			x			x			x		
company_press_releases.php	x			x			x			x		
company_support.php	x			x			x			x		
contact.php	x			x			x			x		
index.php	x			x			x			x		
partners.php	x			x			x			x		
products_ms_apps.php	x			x			x			x		
products_msa-qx_apps.php	x			x			x			x		
products_msa-qx_overview.php	x			x			x			x		
products_msa-qx_specs.php	x			x			x			x		
products_mx_apps.php		x			x			x			x	
products_mx_overview.php		x			x			x			x	
products_nm_apps.php		x			x			x			x	
products_nm_overview.php		x			x			x			x	
products_nt_apps.php		x			x			x			x	
products_nt_overview.php		x			x			x			x	
products_nt_specs.php		x			x			x			x	
products_overview.php		x			x			x			x	
products_pa-3g_apps.php		x			x			x			x	
products_pa-3g_overview.php		x			x			x			x	
products_pa-3g_specs.php		x			x			x			x	
resources.php		x			x			x			x	
services.php		x			x			x			x	
sitemap.php		x			x			x			x	
solutions_converged.php		x			x			x			x	

FIGURE 2.2—Content Freshening Plan spreadsheet

AcmeDM's award-winning ECM service abolishes costly hardware maintenance, timely software installations, and protracted customization cycles linked with on-premises applications.

Notice the key search phrases are still in play in the revised model (Example 2). Make sure the SEO person has an opportunity to review the editing to ensure the search terms on each page are still in play.

Download this simple example of a Content Freshening Plan from Outcome-BasedMarketing.com/handouts.

Does Your Organization Treat Content as an Expendable Commodity?

"The only thing I'm trying to duplicate is the victory . . ."
—MILT STEGALL

Well-written, compelling content takes time and money to create. A two-page whitepaper can easily price out at more than $1,000 if done by a professional. Why use it on a landing page as a one-time offering? How about repurposing that whitepaper and creating more pages for the website? Expanding the content also gives the SEO people more pages to add search terms to and to optimize.

Think about turning that same whitepaper into blog postings or fodder for an article posting. Could a case study play a duel role as well by being transformed into a series of blog posts?

Consider creating a content repurpose strategy.

Have the spreadsheet example in hand? Let's continue.

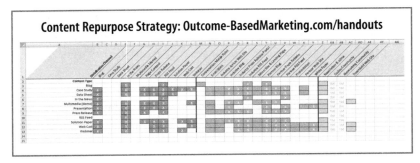

FIGURE 2.3—Repurpose Strategy spreadsheet

Three questions need to be answered when developing a Repurpose Strategy:

1. What content types are created today?
2. What potential distribution channels make sense to exploit?
3. What content rules come into play when converting a marketing piece from one layout to a new format?

The ACME Document Management Company typically produces blog postings, case studies, data sheets, press releases, webcasts, and so on. The Content Types are shown in Column A on the spreadsheet (Figure 2.4).

2	Content Type
3	Blog
4	Case Study
5	Data Sheet
6	In the News
7	Multimedia (demo)
8	Presentation
9	Press Release
10	RSS Feed
11	Solution Paper
12	Web Cast
13	Webinar
14	
15	

FIGURE 2.4—Document types shown in Column A of the spreadsheet

The next question to answer is, "what potential distribution channels make sense to exploit?"

The example spreadsheet lists these possible distribution channels:

Blog	Industry Blog
Case Study	Industry Press Release
Data Sheet	Industry RSS Feed
In the News	MicroSite or Landing Page
Multimedia	Partner Blog
Page Content	Partner Press Release
Press Release	Partner RSS Feed
RSS Feed	Presentation
Solution Paper	Partner Whitepaper
Webcast	Whitepaper
Webinar	Newsletter
Conversion Media Point	Online Community
E-mail Blast	Networking Community
Industry Article Website	Download Website

For instance, notice that a press release written by ACME could potentially be turned into a blog posting, an "In the News" item, a page on the website, or fodder for an RSS Feed (Figure 2.5).

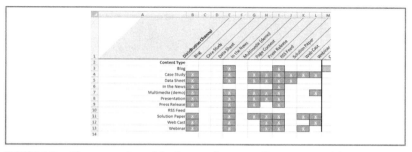

FIGURE 2.5—Blow up portion of the Content Repurpose Strategy spreadsheet

A data sheet can be used as the basis for a blog posting, an "In the News" item, page content on the website, the starting point for a press release, an RSS Feed, or a Solution paper.

Why stop at just repurposing the content for company use? Why not pass the content along to strategic business partners and then have them make it available to their segment of the internet audience.

The distribution channels shown in Figure 2.6, or alternate content types on the spreadsheet, are arranged in the order in which the website might directly benefit. In other words, adding pages of content to the website profits the site more directly than placing the content on an industry article website.

Granted, creating an article off site might create a new path for visitors to reach the website. But, what if the goals of the additional content were to increase the page content to give the SEO people more room for search terms, thus increasing the Page Rank and increasing visitor traffic?

Don't let the strategy here be overwhelming. Start small. Repurposing one piece of content three different ways immediately saves time and money and ups the percentage of searchers who will find the newly repurposed content. Every time you repurpose a piece of content, links are being created to draw visitors back to the website.

FIGURE 2.6—The Distribution Channels

Chapter 3

The Job Is Not Over Even If You Hear the Fat Lady Warming Up

"Perfection is not attainable, but if we chase perfection we can catch excellence."

—VINCE LOMBARDI

THERE ARE A NUMBER OF TOOLS ON THE WEB WHERE BUSINESSES can analyze how their website, blog, or Twitter account stacks up against the competition. For instance, you could use Google Analytics to track your visitor traffic to the website or blog. StatCounter.com and VisiStat.com also track visitor actions. Compete.com lets you compare your website against others to see what website has the best traffic. Alexa.com helps you track traffic metrics, search analytics, demographics, and more.

Think about offering options on your website that your competition does not offer. For instance, does it make sense for you to offer a 24-hour live chat service if they don't? Do they offer a free demo of their product? Does the competition have training webinars on their website? It's important to always try and stay ahead of your competitors.

HubSpot.com does a fine job of providing an analytic toolset (Figure 3.1). Here's what they have to offer:

- Website.Grader.com. Measures a website's marketing effectiveness.
- Blog.Grader.com. Scores the blog and shows its weaknesses.
- Book.Grader.com. Helps authors measure and improve the marketing of their latest book.
- PressRelease.Grader.com. Ensures your release is optimized for humans and search engines.
- Twitter.Grader.com. Measures your reach among Twitter users.
- Action.Grader.com. Optimizes your calls to action.
- Facebook.Grader.com. Measures your power and reach within the Facebook community.

The Grader tools produce a report you can use to tighten the code and hopefully receive a better score. An Acceptable grade would be in the 90th percentile.

The topics covered in the Website Grader report are:

Report Component: On-page Optimization
- Metadata. Tells search engines what the website is all about

FIGURE 3.1—HubSpot's Website Graders Score

- Heading Summary. Helps readers and spiders understand the web page
- Image Summary. Images enhance web pages
- Interior Page Analysis. How well web pages are optimized
- Readability Level. Level of education needed to read and understand the web page

Report Component: Off-page Optimization
- Domain Info. Search engines factor in domain stability
- Google Page Rank. Google's algorithm that determines individual page value
- Google Indexed Pages. Number of pages stored in the Google index
- Last Google Crawl Date. Google methodically crawls websites looking for new content
- Traffic Rank. Alexa.com tracks traffic rank
- Inbound Links. Number of other sites linking to a specific site
- DMOZ.org Directory. Site is listed in The Open Directory Project
- Yahoo.com Directory. Site is listed in the *Yahoo!* Directory

Report Component: Blogosphere
- Blog Analysis. Looks to see if the site has a blog (Blog.Grader.com analyzes the blog.)
- Blog Grade. Blog.Grader.com grades the blog
- Recent Blog Articles. Inbound links from blog posts

Report Component: Social Ecosystem
- Delicious.com bookmarks. Calculates the number of Delicious bookmarks
- Digg.com Submission Summary. Calculates the number of Diggs

Report Component: Converting Qualified Visitors into Leads
- RSS Feed. Detects whether there is an RSS Feed on the site

Section	website.grader.com
Website Grade	92
Moz Rank	5
Google Indexed Pages	n/a
Traffic Rank	12,872
Blog Grade	Not Graded
Inbound Links	11,318
del.icio.us Bookmarks	1330

FIGURE 3.2—Website Grader Summary

- Conversion Form. Looks for forms prospects or customers might fill out
- Competitive Intelligence
- Score Summary. See Figure 3.2
- Historical Data Available. Last time the site was processed by Website.Grader.com, see Figure 3.2

BE **STRATEGIC**

▶ Strive to offer more on your site than the competition.

▶ Capitalize on what the competition does not offer.

WEB

Don't Assume What You Don't Know Won't Hurt You

"Everything yields to diligence."

—ANTIPHANES

With all the spelling checkers out there, is there really a good excuse for spelling errors in the content? Nothing torpedoes a good call to action like reading a spelling error in the sales pitch.

Because websites are usually not under the control of a single person, things often go wrong over time. Images go missing, forms stop working, and entire pages are not found. No one knows why, and no one wants to take responsibility for these happenings.

Companies must take control of their websites and clean up these anomalies. It's hard enough to capture a company's share of business on the web without working against oneself.

Come up with a process (Figure 3.3) to check the site for spelling errors. Fill out your forms, and see if the information lands in the proper inbox. Download the offers to make sure everything works as expected.

Why fresh content in the first place? Google, along with the other search engines, not only ranks web pages on relevant content but also by fresh content. What this means is that even after a site has been "optimized

Consider developing a quarterly review program to keep the website accurate, professional looking, and functioning properly.

to the max," the site's rankings will increase to a certain level and then level off. To receive the best search listings, a site should deliver fresh, relevant content on a regular basis. Depending upon the nature of the business, competition, and targeted key phrases, the rate of content freshening can vary greatly.

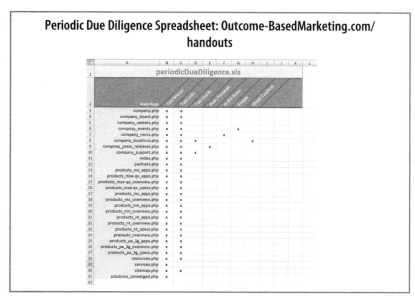

Periodic Due Diligence Spreadsheet: Outcome-BasedMarketing.com/ handouts

FIGURE 3.3—Blown-up portion of Periodic Due Diligence spreadsheet

To help get the ball rolling, a sample Periodic Due Diligence Spreadsheet can be downloaded by going to: Outcome-Based Marketing.com/handouts. Notice it doesn't take much to create an uncomplicated spreadsheet like this one.

All of the web pages on the site are listed in one column to the left. The rest of the columns highlight the items that need periodic checking: the menu items, text links, e-mail addresses, and contact forms.

Let's look at how a website content map might be a convenient way to keep track of the site as it grows and morphs over time.

Visualize Your Website's Structure

"To accomplish great things we must first dream, then visualize, then plan ... believe ... act!"

—ALFRED A. MONTAPERT

Business owners that have small to medium websites may think a website content map is overkill. Perhaps, but even a simple content map can be a useful vehicle when updating the pages and content.

Let's bring everyone into this discussion by defining a content map first and then looking at how it is used.

First, separate content maps from site maps in your mind. A site map is defined as a web page that lists all the pages that comprise a website. Site maps can aid in navigation of the website and assist search engine crawlers when indexing the website pages. Figure 3.4 shows a site map.

If a visitor to a website is unable to locate a particular page, she can go to the site map page and look for the link there.

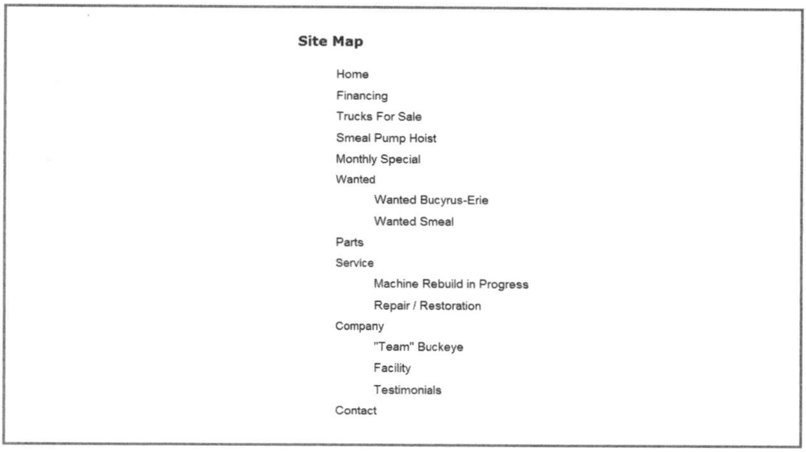

Site Map

Home
Financing
Trucks For Sale
Smeal Pump Hoist
Monthly Special
Wanted
      Wanted Bucyrus-Erie
      Wanted Smeal
Parts
Service
      Machine Rebuild in Progress
      Repair / Restoration
Company
      "Team" Buckeye
      Facility
      Testimonials
Contact

FIGURE 3.4—Typical site map page layout

A content map (Figure 3.5) is more than just hyperlinks to other web pages. Content maps are usually done in a program such as Microsoft® Excel®.

The website's homepage is tagged as Level 1 in Figure 3.5 while the major selections from the navigation menu are tagged as Level 2 and so on. Notice that each column starts out with a page name followed by all the contents, images, and links on that page. The columns to the right show whether or not the information is up to date, needs revision, or should be tossed, as well as who is responsible for getting the page up to date and what action will likely take place. Download the full-size sample to get a better illustration.

A structure such as this makes updating and tracking a website's revision less painful. Everyone knows what needs to be done and when. What a concept!

Don't underestimate the importance of the site map page. If the search engine crawler has difficulty navigating the website, it can use the site map to follow the links to all the possible web pages on the site.

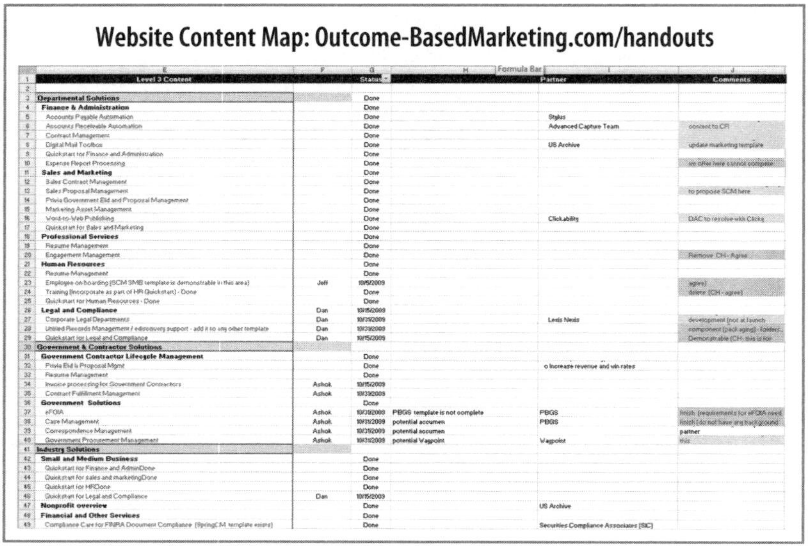

Website Content Map: Outcome-BasedMarketing.com/handouts

	E	F	G	H	I	J
1	Level 3 Content		Status		Partner	Comments
2						
3	**Departmental Solutions**		Done			
4	**Finance & Administration**		Done			
5	Accounts Payable Automation		Done		Stylus	
6	Accounts Receivable Automation		Done		Advanced Capture Team	content to CR
7	Contract Management		Done			
8	Digital Mail Toolbox		Done		US Archive	update marketing template
9	Quickstart for Finance and Administration		Done			
10	Expense Report Processing		Done			we offer here cannot compete
11	**Sales and Marketing**		Done			
12	Sales Contract Management		Done			
13	Sales Proposal Management		Done			to propose SCM here
14	Privia Government Bid and Proposal Management		Done			
15	Marketing Asset Management		Done			
16	Word-to-Web Publishing		Done		Clickability	DAC to resolve with Clicks
17	Quickstart for Sales and Marketing		Done			
18	**Professional Services**		Done			
19	Resume Management		Done			
20	Engagement Management		Done			Remove CH - Agree
21	**Human Resources**		Done			
22	Resume Management		Done			
23	Employee on boarding (SCM SMB template is demonstrable in this area)	Jeff	10/5/2009			agree)
24	Training (Incorporate as part of HR Quickstart) - Done		Done			delete (CH - agree)
25	Quickstart for Human Resources - Done		Done			
26	**Legal and Compliance**	Dan	10/15/2009			
27	Corporate Legal Departments	Dan	10/31/2009		Lexis Nexis	development (not at launch
28	Unified Records Management / ediscovery support - add it to any other template	Dan	10/31/2009			component (packaging) - folders,
29	Quickstart for Legal and Compliance	Dan	10/15/2009			Demonstrable (CH: this is for
30	**Government & Contractor Solutions**					
31	**Government Contractor Lifecycle Management**		Done			
32	Privia Bid & Proposal Mgmt		Done		o Increase revenue and win rates	
33	Resume Management		Done			
34	Invoice processing for Government Contractors	Ashok	10/15/2009			
35	Contract Fulfillment Management	Ashok	10/31/2009			
36	**Government Solutions**		Done			
37	eFOIA	Ashok	10/31/2009	PBGS template is not complete	PBGS	finish (requirements for eFOIA need
38	Case Management	Ashok	10/31/2009	potential accumen	PBGS	finish (do not have any background
39	Correspondence Management	Ashok	10/31/2009	potential accumen		partner
40	Government Procurement Management	Ashok	10/31/2009	potential Waypoint	Waypoint	this
41	**Industry Solutions**					
42	**Small and Medium Business**		Done			
43	Quickstart for Finance and AdminDone		Done			
44	Quickstart for sales and marketingDone		Done			
45	Quickstart for HRDone		Done			
46	Quickstart for Legal and Compliance	Dan	10/15/2009			
47	**Nonprofit overview**		Done		US Archive	
48	**Financial and Other Services**		Done			
49	Compliance Care for FINRA Document Compliance (SpringCM template exists)		Done		Securities Compliance Associates (SIC)	

FIGURE 3.5—Website Content Map spreadsheet

Website content maps are also handy documents when deciding to redesign the website. The content map could be passed off to the internal web team or outside web development company for recommended redesign and a quote for the effort.

The web content map can also be used to track all the incoming links to the various pages. In this way you can tell what pages have good page position in the search results when looking for the information.

The content map can also be used to measure the size and strength of the company's site against its competition.

BE **STRATEGIC**

- Create a review process, quarterly or perhaps semiannually, to look the content map over and make sure the site's content and offers are headed in the right direction.
- Create a content map of what the competition has on their sites that you don't have today.

Chapter 4

New Rules for Website Marketing

"Results! Why, man, I have gotten a lot of results. I know several thousand things that won't work."

—THOMAS A. EDISON (WHEN LOOKING FOR A SUITABLE FILAMENT FOR THE LIGHT BULB)

L
ET'S PUT EVERYTHING TOGETHER THAT WE'VE TALKED ABOUT regarding outcome-based marketing and the ingredients that make up a strong web presence. For this exercise we'll concentrate on the website itself. Keep in mind that outcome-based marketing is made up of six ingredients: inputs, activities, masses, leads, outcome targets, and outcome indicators.

Inputs. The inputs are made up of the website architecture and content:

- decision-making paths
- attention-grabbing taglines
- intuitive menu navigation
- professional look and feel
- compelling content

- strong calls to action
- atmosphere of confidence and trust

Activities. Maintain the website content in order to keep it interesting, fresh, and compelling.

Masses. The masses represent the visitors that come to the site from no matter where. They may stay for a half an hour or leave in seconds. Visitor statistics such as Google Analytics can tell us much about visitors such as how they found the site, what web pages are the most visited, and how they left the site.

Leads. Leads are seen as those visitors that take some action, visitors that downloaded an offer or signed up to receive a newsletter. Somehow they moved the relationship to the next level. Visitors that just stop by the website and take no action are not seen as prospects or leads.

Outcome targets. Let's say the outcome target you set for the newly redesigned website is to increase visitor traffic by 10 to 20 percent per month for the next six months. You'll also expect to have 10 to 15 visitors download your offers each week. A third goal would be to have 20 new visitors sign up to receive your newsletter each week.

Outcome indicators. The outcome indicators tell you whether your goal is realistic and how well you're doing on accomplishing your goals. Remember your goals need to be measurable. You can use Google Analytics or tools such as StatCounter.com or VisiStat.com to gather your numbers.

You can check the website statistics each week to see how many new visitors are coming to the website. If the outcome indicators tell you you'll never reach your goal of 10 to 20 percent, then you may need to rethink your outcome target. If the outcome target seems realistic then you need to adjust the activities you're running to attract more new website visitors.

Chapter 5

Introduce Your Clients and Prospects to Another Side of the Organization

"Everyone is wise until he speaks."

—Irish Proverbs

Now that you understand the position a website plays in an organization's web presence—the button-down, formal, straight-  laced, good-foot-forward posture—let's look at blogging, a more casual way of interacting with customers and prospects. There are various ways you can position a blog. The blog typically plays a more casual, open collar, this-is-what-the-organization-is-thinking, what-are-your-thoughts stance. The website only provides a one-way communication link "squawking the corporate line." The blog allows for a second lane of communication that draws the reader into the conversation. People can read the blog postings and make their comments. They can also read what others are saying.

Much of what was said about websites applies to blogs as well.

- The blog content needs to be written with the audience in mind; it's not just ramblings to fill up open space. What's said needs to be clear, concise, compelling, timely, relevant, and well written. There is no room for spelling and grammar gaffes.
- The organization will have to decide if calls to action are out of place. Blogs are usually not seen as sales counters. Readers have their guard down. They're looking for information or an opportunity to join in on conversations that interest them. They hope to have a voice in the discussion.
- A blog does have to grab the reader's attention, but not in the same manner a website does. Remember we're not in selling mode. What's posted on the blog has to be interesting to the reader and it has to be fresh. That said, remember to write the blog titles to catch the reader's eye. For instance, The Seven Deadly Sins of Web Marketers.
- It goes without saying that the blog should be professional looking. It might have a look similar to the corporate website; it might have the same color theme or be completely different. There are thousands of blog templates that can be adopted. Keep it clean, simple, and easy to understand.
- Blogs usually do not have a series of subpages navigated by a menu bar of countless options. Blog articles are written and posted with certain categories and tags attached. For example, a post might be categorized as Marketing with tags such as demand generation, leads, and nurturing. That way the article can be pulled up from the archives when a visitor searches for those tag names.
- Blog.Grader.com helps identify weak points in the blog. The competitors' blogs can also be scored to see if their reach exceeds that of your organization.

- Keeping visitors coming back to the well also applies to blogs. Once you start blogging, you need to keep going. People will come back expecting to see new insights, fresh materials, and new announcements. Develop an editorial schedule whereby a small group of people shares in the blogging activity.

Now let's look at what makes a blog different from a website.

The reason blogging is becoming so popular is because blog sites are easy to update and maintain. No webmaster roadblocks. (Sorry if anyone feels hurt.) You do not have to wait until the next news cycle to tell your clients or readers important information. Remember, timing is everything. A company can let readers in on their future plans and get a sounding on how their clients think.

Unlike newsletters, visitors don't have to opt-in to read your stuff.

Backlinks help raise your site's visibility in search listings. A backlink is no more than a hyperlink to another blog page location or a link back to the company website.

Seth Godin wrote an article on his blog titled "The Future of the Library." Notice the "survive" link in the first sentence in Figure 5.1. This link takes you to the CCHS website where you can read about how libraries are working to become more relevant. This practice gives the reader more information and also creates cross traffic between Seth's blog and the CCHS site.

Blogs also provide valuable backlinks to other blog postings or the company's website.

If you want to create an audience, be consistent about adding new posts on some regular basis so people coming back don't see outdated information. It goes without saying that the information needs to be timely, fresh, and relevant.

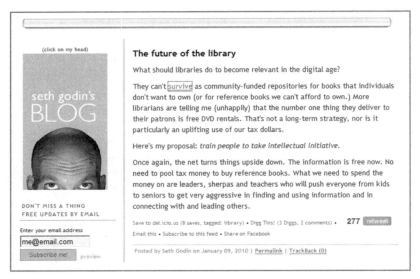

FIGURE 5.1—Seth Godin's blog page

WordPress, Blogger, TypePad, and MovableType together have thousands of blog templates so you don't have to start from scratch. Choose one you can live with and start posting. Don't get stuck with learning too much and never starting to post. You can always change the look and feel at a later date and not lose a thing.

Posting is as simple as writing an e-mail. Remember blogging is more casual than writing a business letter. But when representing your company, the post still needs to have a professional sound to it. The reader wants to get to know you as well as hear what you have to say.

The post could be private, saved as a draft until it's ready to go to publication, or time-stamped for the future.

Posts are categorized so they can be grouped together for easy indexing in the future. For instance, posts may be grouped by discussion topic: marketing, sales, website, e-mail, demand generation, and general.

Posts can even be password protected. They can also be optimized for the search engines.

You can allow people to comment on your posts or you can turn off that option.

Readers can subscribe to your blog and be notified when new posts are added.

Currently WordPress.com, a site similar to WordPress, has 7,490 plug-ins that add functionality to your blog, plus plug-ins such as Google, SEO, forms, Twitter, RSS, and thousands of others. Plug-ins are written by third-parties that desire to improve everyone's Word Press experience. No need to worry about viruses. WordPress screens these plug-in entries quite well.

There is a Twitter plug-in that displays your tweets on the sidebar area of your blog. This is a great way to send out tweets to your followers and encourage them to read your blog entries.

Another area of interest is the blogroll plug-in (Figure 5.2). Here is where you list other people's blogs that relate to yours and offer additional information to your readership. Some sites list their blogroll under the heading "Link Love."

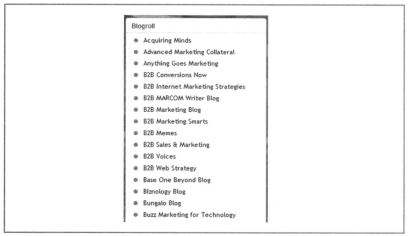

FIGURE 5.2—Sample blogroll

The blogroll shown in Figure 5.2 lists mostly marketing, search engine optimization, and entrepreneur blogs. Listing other blogs helps expand the content on your blog.

Let's touch on going mobile and micro-blogging before leaving this subject. People are mobile today. The information conduits should be mobile as well. Micro-blogging refers to blog entries of 140 characters, usually entered from a cell phone. There are phone apps that allow people to post blog entries from their cell phones. This is a great option when attending a conference or trade show. You could troll a trade show and take "man-on-the-street" interviews. After the interview is over you could post the person's comments to a blog.

BE **STRATEGIC**

▶ Don't use the blog as a second place to say the same thing. Give the readership insight into the personality and thinking of the organization.

▶ Keep the posts fresh, quick, and interesting, more like thoughts from the back room. No soliloquies, please.

▶ Have all of the thought leaders and domain experts at the organization share in the blogging activities to keep things interesting and exciting.

Unpacking the Necessary Components of a Blog

"All I'm writing is just what I feel, that's all. I just keep it almost naked."

—Jimi Hendrix

OK, so you want to put up a blog. Where do you start? From a business opportunity perspective, the company obviously wants a return on its investment. Not just revenue. Perhaps the return will be in appearing more accessible or more authoritative or in gaining insight into the company's customer base. Because companies such as WordPress, TypePad, and others offer many hosting, template, and plug-in options, blogs can be launched within days or weeks instead of months like websites. The investment in time, talent, resources, and endless meetings is considerably less.

Here's a simple plan to launch a blog. Take from it what you wish, and add elements you believe are necessary for your particular situation.

The Site Goals

There needs to be a vision, a purpose. Those in the organization need to understand why they're being asked to participate in the blog project, what will their responsibilities be, and what time, talent, and resources will they be asked to contribute. Here are several reasons a company may want to launch a blog:

1. Gives prospects and customers easier access to more news and events
2. Provide another avenue for search engines to find the company
3. Increase the company's brand awareness
4. Build community
5. Give the appearance of being thought leaders or subject matter experts
6. Reduce support or customer service calls or e-mails
7. Create an avenue to hear from customers or clients
8. Create cross traffic between the website and blog

A blog does not have to have one reason for existence. Perhaps the company has all the above-stated goals and more. Again, it's good to temper enthusiasm, start off slowly, and then build momentum. Trumpeting your blog and then falling short only leads to disappointment and customer dissatisfaction.

Think about building your blog in phases. For instance, in phase I the blog is designed and launched. Phase II represents adding news and events. Phase III corresponds to adding thought leader pieces. Phase IV deals with mechanisms to reduce support or customer service calls.

The Site Framework

The business will have to decide if it makes more sense to host the blog or allow a site such as WordPress or TypePad to do the hosting for the organization. Some blog companies charge a fee based on the services they offer. Figure 5.3 shows some blog templates from WordPress.

Many of the blog templates are quite flexible, and the cost is free. Try out several sample templates before making the final choice. Make sure it has the options you need and want going forward.

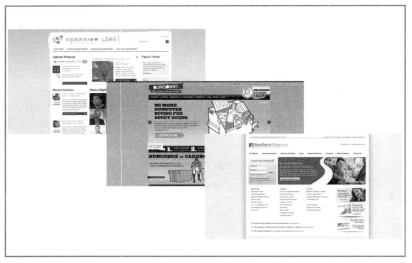

FIGURE 5.3—WordPress blog templates

The Site Audience

Will the site speak to one visitor audience or will several visitor groups be reading the blog postings and commenting? Perhaps your company sells to small service providers, mid-range companies, and enterprise businesses. If this is the case, the goals of the site, its contributors, and the content offered will need to be diverse. Each visitor group will certainly have distinct needs and wants. Each will have to be served in different ways. Each group will be looking for varying levels of information.

The Site Content

The content on the blog is what drives visitors to the site and get people talking. The content should be casual yet compelling. The writing needs to draw the visitor/reader into the discussion. Ask a thought-provoking question at the end of each post to entice the reader to comment. Here's a sample content breakdown of what might be on the blog site to get you thinking:

- higher-level posts from the executive team
- posts on new directions for the company or products
- problem-solving posts
- posts on insider tips
- offers
- resources page
- articles
- podcasts
- third-party content
- webcasts and PowerPoint (PPT) presentations
- case studies
- whitepapers
- links to other noncompeting websites

Remember to phase in each feature so the blog team is not overloaded. When a new feature is added to the site, blog about it.

Building Visitor Interest

Building interest in the various visitor groups is in all probability the one element a business will have the least amount of control over after launching a blog. Timing will be everything. When should blog posts be published, and when should the company tweet about those new articles? Tracking visitor statistics will help settle those issues. Think about how you run your day. You probably aren't likely to research new blogs to read on a Monday or Friday—you're either getting the week started or wrapping things up for the weekend. Other people are most likely in similar situations. Experience says to post new blog entries Tuesday through Thursday in the business community. If your site caters to the weekend crowd, then Saturday and Sunday may be the best days. Let's take a stab at setting up a schedule to create visitor interest in what our blog might be saying. Let's say we sell a software product that helps companies run their field service operations. We might blog one to two times per week, based on an editorial calendar, on:

- Our new mobile app
- Best practices in running a service business
- How to get paid faster
- How to use our product to solve real-life problems
- Comment on blog posts each week
- Comment on third-party blog posts
- Tweet about blog posts two days per week
- Blog about resources added to site
- Tweet about resources added to site
- Manage reciprocal blog-roll links

As you can see, we'll be posting information to our blog and then have people in the organization comment about the posts. Visitors to the blog are more likely to comment if they see other people have done that ahead of them. We'll also want to tweet about what's been posted to create as much exposure as possible. Sometimes commenting on other people's blogs draws visitors to your blog. Let's call that cross-traffic. The key to success here is consistency. There is a minimum you need to do each week to keep visitors interested in reading the blog. What's outlined here is really the minimum. Some companies blog multiple times a day and tweet every day of the week. Blogs that are updated once a month, or every other month, never seem to gain audience acceptance.

Every magazine has an editorial calendar. A recent issue of *Entrepreneur* magazine touted "Four Home Businesses in Demand." Its focus for the month highlighted four home-businesses for 2011: Catering Services, Event Planning, Virtual Assistant, and Online Retailer. *Fast Company*, on the other hand, spotlighted "The Invincible Apple." It talked about ten lessons from the coolest company anywhere. Blogs should have an editorial focus as well. One month the focus might be on customer care while the next month highlights the new software rollout and its timesaving features. Editorial calendars can build excitement and visitor expectations.

The Site Participants

Who's going to do what is the last element of the blog for us to tackle. Responsibilities have to be assigned and understood for any project to do well. Decide who's going to post blog entries and when. Assign those responsible for posting comments and tweeting. If the tasks will be shared by several team members, make sure each person understands her or his role.

BE **STRATEGIC**

- Consistency is a major part of any blog's success.
- Don't commit to doing too much too soon. Ramp things up gradually.
- Give the blog time to create community; don't pull the plug after just a few months.

Build Up Your Blog Readership

"Newspaper readership is declining like crazy. In fact, there's a good

chance that nobody is reading my column."

—DAVE BERRY

On a colleague's website (Figure 5.4), FusionMaketingPartners. com, there is an opt-in form so people can sign up to receive an e-mail once a week that lists the prior week's blog posts. It uses this strategy to be as unintimidating as possible in building its readership base. By signing up for the e-mail, people do not have to continuously come back to Fusion's blog to see what's been written. This is also an inconspicuous way to allow people to show an interest in getting one e-mail from a company without filling their inbox with unwanted spam attacks.

FIGURE 5.4—Sample e-mail subscription box

FIGURE 5.5—RSS Feed subscription example

Another business associate has a different twist on letting people subscribe to his blog. Bill has a blog titled, Bill Petro – Bridging the Gap from Strategy to Execution (BillPetro.com/blog). His strategy is to let visitors either sign up for a periodic e-mail or subscribe to his RSS Feed (Figure 5.5).

What Is an RSS Feed?

An RSS Feed, according to Wikipedia, is:

> RSS is a family of XML file formats for web syndication used by news websites and blogs. They are used to provide items containing short descriptions of web content together with a link to the full version of the content. This information is delivered as an XML file called RSS feed, webfeed, RSS stream, or RSS channel.

You have to love those technical definitions, written by geeks to keep the rest of us in the dark. In laymen's terms RSS stands for Real Simple Syndication. It's one of the coolest ways to pass information along to your blog subscribers.

Some Popular RSS Feeds

Before this dialog goes any farther, let's look at a few popular RSS Feeds on the web.

- FOXNews. World FoxNews.com/xmlfeed/rss/0,4313,81,00.rss
- DiscoveryChannel. Headlines dsc.Discovery.com/news/topstories.xml
- White House News Whitehouse.gov/rss/news.xml

- BNET. Marketing Feeds BNet. com/allRSS.html
- ESPN.com. NFL Feed. Sports. ESPN.go.com/espn/rss/nfl/news

The easiest way to know if a website or blog offers an RSS Feeds is to look for the RSS image on its homepage (Figure 5.6). It's usually found toward the top of the page or at the very bottom. So much for consistency.

To add RSS feeds to your browser, just hit the subscribe icon on someone's website or blog and you'll automatically be notified when new information is posted.

Displaying an RSS Feed on a Web Page

You know the value of an RSS Feed and how to store the feeds in your Favorites Center. How about displaying that information on a web page? You have a few choices to make. Here

The benefit of using RSS Feeds is that when subscribing to a feed, updated information is automatically downloaded to a browser. The benefit is receiving the latest content from a favorite news agency website without going to the trouble of checking those websites individually.

FIGURE 5.6—RSS Feed icon

are two: You can go to a website like Feedzilla.com. (Look, blame these funny names on someone else. Those Feedzilla guys are really out there.) Purchase RSS Feeds from $4.95 a month and up. This is like subscribing to a daily newspaper, only the feeds deliver the lastest news every hour. It's no wonder newspaper circulation is on the decline.

If you don't want to pay for an RSS Feed service, use RSSFeedReader.com. This free service allows you to pick up an RSS Feed reader that you'll need to read and display the news feeds as they come in to your website. Here are the steps:

1. First, sign up for a free account.
2. After logging into the free account, you'll use the control panel to customize the RSS Feed you want displayed on your web page.
3. Next you find a place on your web page to house the RSS code.
4. That's it.

You can also build your own RSS Feed, but that's not a topic for discussion in this book.

You can put an RSS Feed on your website and have your customers or clients subscribe. This eliminates the need of sending them updated newsletters or e-mails. When you update the feed on your website, the latest news will be available to them because of their subscription link.

BE **STRATEGIC**

- Don't have people subscribe and then stop blogging.
- Make sure the news you syndicate is "real" news and not just sales announcements.
- Place the RSS Feed in a prominent place on your website or blog. Don't make people hunt for it.

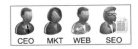

Bookmarking and Aggregating Boost Readership

*"In journalistic terms, syndication is equivalent to
ascending to heaven on a pillar of cloud."*

—JOHN SKOW

Bookmarking gives blog writers the ability to syndicate what they are talking about to multiple communities. Think of syndicating a cartoon strip to hundreds of local newspapers. A cartoonist could hardly send the same cartoon strip to hundreds of national newspapers individually and expect it to be published in all the papers on the same day. Now, think about the labor involved if you wanted to write something on your blog, have it be seen in the more popular communities where your prospects gather, and have it seen all on the same day. It would take quite an effort to post the same information in community after community. Bookmarking tools help make syndication happen with little effort.

Aggregator sites also assist in the syndication process. Let's suppose you have LinkedIn, Facebook, and Twitter accounts. Let's further suppose you want to say something in one community but have what is said picked up by the other two groups. Aggregators help make that syndication possible. Let's look at bookmarking first. Then we'll talk about aggregators.

Syndicate What You Have to Say

Figure 5.7 is a sample blog post with which to start the bookmarking discussion. Notice the "Share the Joy" icons in the lower left of the post. AddToAny.com is a free WordPress bookmarking plug-in. It gives the writer of the blog the ability to publish information about what's posted to a number of

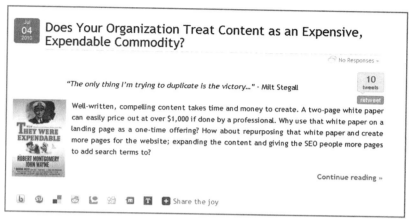

FIGURE 5.7—Sample blog post

community sites where people are trolling for news items. The eight icons represented here are YahooBuzz, StumbleUpon, Delicious, Reddit, Technorati, Digg, Mixx, and Tumblr. There are dozens more not shown and others coming online every day.

Here's what you do: Install the WordPress plug-in or a similar tool. Next, write a post on your blog and then take an extra few seconds to publish what the blog entry is about to communities where people are looking for information on that topic. In the newspaper business this would be considered syndicating your column so people across the country could see and read it.

Publishing short excerpts of what you're writing about out to communities of like-minded readers creates cross-traffic back to your blog.

When any of the bookmarking icons is selected (the second icon StumbleUpon was chosen) another window opens. As you can see in Figure 5.8 there are currently more than 12 million stumblers (readers) of the site. You can decide to publish the post in English or another language. You need to add a topic line to entice readers. The "Other" pull-down lets you select a category to file

FIGURE 5.8—Bookmarking Example for StumbleUpon

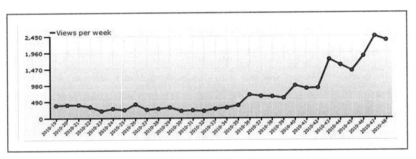

FIGURE 5.9—Visitor statistics illustrating the effect of bookmarking blog posts

the news item under such as business, marketing, or technology. You can also add an optional review to entice future readers.

Figure 5.9 shows the boost your blog can receive from bookmarking your posts. This blog owner was seeing a steady 500 visitors per week for months. After bookmarking his posts, the blog owner now enjoys 2,000 to 2,500 visitors each week.

Aggregators Makes It Easy to Reach Multiple Communities

The term "aggregate" used here means: A group of materials such as collection of items or digital objects that have similar characteristics. There are news aggregators, poll aggregators, review aggregators, video aggregators, and search aggregators. Two examples of news aggregators that may be familiar to you are The DrudgeReport.com and the HuffingtonPost.com. Both of these websites pull news stories together from various sources so the reader does not have to visit dozens of websites to catch up on current events.

Let's look at Ping.fm, a popular social media aggregation site (see Figure 5.10). For illustration purposes, let's say you belong to a half dozen social networking communities. Ping.fm is a free service that makes updating all of your social networks easy. It allows users to post from anywhere to anywhere. It can't get more

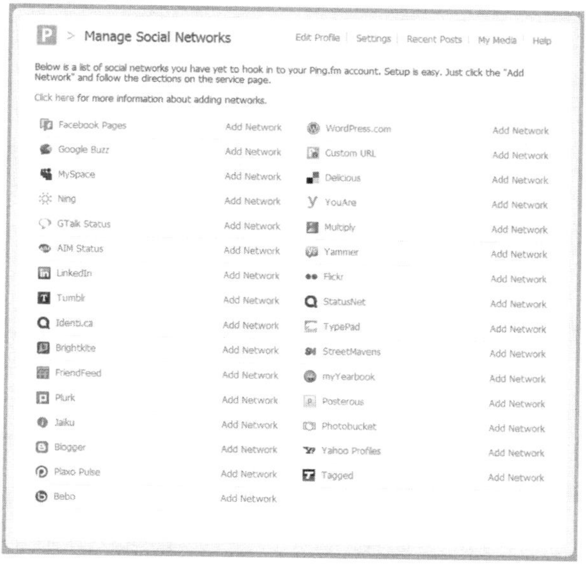

FIGURE 5.10—Ping's Manage Social Networks form

convenient than that. Ping.fm has a wide assortment of popular social networks you can tie together. Figure 5.10 shows what it has today.

Let's suppose you're a member of five social communities—Twitter, Facebook, GoogleBuzz, MySpace, and Ning—and you want to send information to all the communities at the same time. Ping.fm makes it effortless to link them together.

Now each time you use the Ping.fm dashboard to send a message, it will go out to Twitter, Facebook, GoogleBuzz, MySpace, and Ning simultaneously.

Ping.fm allows you to update your social networks by way of the web, mobile, IM, or e-mail. Ping.fm has partnered with two popular third parties—Notify.me and HootSuite.com—to help make your social media aggregation experience more enjoyable and efficient.

Using aggregators saves time and effort. Think about adding an aggregator to your social networking toolbox.

BE **STRATEGIC**

- Be diligent about bookmarking if you're going to blog. You will definitely see an increase in traffic as long as you select the right community sites.
- Explore the other aggregation methods to see if any are applicable to your business model.

Chapter 6

New Rules
for Blogging

"Hell, there are no rules here—we're trying to accomplish something."

—Thomas A. Edison

For this illustration we'll focus on the blog. In Part II, Be Found in All the Right Places, we'll learn strategies for attracting visitors to the blog by offering podcasts and webinars, sending out press releases, and publishing a newsletter, among others. In Part III, Being Social on the Web, we'll discuss ways to attract visitors through social networking techniques.

Outcome-Based Marketing: Blogs

- *Inputs.* Like websites, blogs need to convey an atmosphere of confidence and trust, and have attention-grabbing taglines, intuitive menu navigation, and a professional look and feel. Content is everything. It needs to be timely, relevant, applicable, and thought provoking. Because the content changes so often, there are more opportunities to draw new visitors. Polls and surveys can be taken to draw in new visitors.

·   *Activities.* Posting articles will be the mainstay activity. Posts can be bookmarked out to popular communities, which will increase visitor traffic. Blogs usually make it easy for the reader to pass the post along to their friends through e-mail links, RSS feeds, or retweets.

·   *Masses.* The masses that read the blog can be measured with Google Analytics.

·   *Leads.* Leads are those visitors that took some action, subscribed to the blog, or commented on the posts.

·   *Outcome targets.* For a starting point, say we expect readership to increase by 10 to 15 percent each month for the first three months. We will also target 20 to 30 people to subscribe to the blog each month.

·   *Outcome indicators.* Google Analytics helps us determine how many people visit the blog. The stats also let us know which blog articles are the most popular. The blog subscribers will be handled by FeedBurner.com, which has a popular syndication tool used by companies large and small.

Take a few minutes now to recap Part I, Build a Strong Web Presence, by scanning the upcoming Take Five. It will help reinforce what's been talked about in the first part of *Outcome-based Marketing.*

Take 5

Build a Strong Web Presence

"If you don't see yourself as a winner, then you cannot perform as a winner."

—ZIG ZIGLAR

No one could be expected to implement all of these great ideas at once. As Dr. Leo Marvin advised Bob Wiley, in Touchstone Picture's comedy What About Bob?, take baby steps. Put into practice what can be easily handled. Then ramp things up as time and resources permit. Take a few moments now to review the most important points discussed about in Part I, Build a Strong Web Presence, before moving on to Part II, Be Found in All the Right Places.

Treating Every Website Visitor the Same Is a Fatal Mistake. Develop different strategies for the various types of visitors that might come to the website. Buyers need to be directed straight to the checkout while many others need more time and education before they are ready to make a buying decision.

You Only Have Eight Seconds to Grab a Visitor's Attention. There are only a precious eight seconds to grab the visitor's attention once they arrive at the homepage. Distractions and rambling text only shorten the time they stay around. Be sure to follow the suggestions laid out here.

The Heat Is On. Heat maps give you a graphical representation of which links people are clicking on on your web pages. Heat maps tell you which marketing messages are working and which ones need tightening. These maps let you know whether visitors to your web pages are more likely to click on images on text links. Learn how heat maps can boost your marketing intelligence.

Is the Menu Navigation Losing Visitors Along the Way? The first priority of visitors is to find their way around. If the navigation is not easy to understand and operate, visitors assume the worst and head to another website, perhaps the competition.

You'll Never be Given a Second Chance to Make a Good First Impression. When measuring a website against its competition, the site should stand out to be successful. Browse the web to see what the competition is up to. Look for the best sites and follow their lead.

Don't Let the Website Fall Short. Content is king whether in print or on a web page. The marketing person needs to be heavily involved in the "wordsmithing" of the marketing message if visitors are going to be drawn into a discussion and later converted into customers, clients, or consumers.

Persuading Visitors to Take Action Now. Do not assume visitors to the website know what to do. Lead, guide, or prompt them to take some form of action, whether it be to sign up for a newsletter, fill out a contact form, or to download a whitepaper.

Does Your Website Create an Atmosphere of Trust and Confidence? Trust and confidence are factors that contribute to a buyer's decision. Websites need to create an atmosphere that removes the buyer's fears and mistrust. Using secure pages to transact business makes the consumer feel confident her personal information is protected. Having the site certified by companies such as TRUSTe or VeriSign builds trust. Posting your business's credentials and professional associations also helps remove fear.

Keep Your Website Visitors Coming Back to the Well. Search engines assume if the content on the website expands and changes, the company is on the move. Develop a content freshening plan. Do a light edit to make the search engines think new things are happening.

Does Your Organization Treat Content as an Expendable Commodity? Save time, money, and costly resources by implementing a content repurpose plan to reuse the same material in as many ways as possible. Convert whitepapers or press releases to web page content.

Find Out How Your Web Presence Stacks Up Against the Competition. There are a number of services on the web through which people can run website analysis to get an idea of how their website generally complies with the accepted guidelines of a properly constructed site. You can also run the same analyzers on your competition's websites, which gives you indications about where your website is lacking.

Don't Assume What You Don't Know Won't Hurt You. We all have the oil in our cars changed periodically and have the snow tires removed when the first sighting of a robin occurs. Websites need to be looked over from time to time to make sure everything still operates as assumed.

Visualize Your Website's Structure. We already know that site maps and content maps are different and serve different purposes. Site maps list links to all the pages on a website, whereas content maps identify the web pages and what links, content, and offers are on each page. Content maps are great for redesign purposes because they show the level of effort needed to complete the redesign. Content maps aid in periodic website maintenance and due diligence. Think about creating content maps of the competition's sites. This will give you a good indication of how the site stacks up against its competitors.

Share Your Company Talent and Expertise. Remember blogs are like websites, only for more casual conversation. They're also easier to manage and maintain. Blogs give readers a chance to participate in the discussions. Blogs create another avenue for visitors to find the business when searching for products or services. Blogs provide opportunities for creating valuable backlinks to the corporate website and are more social.

Unpacking the Necessary Components of a Blog. Uploading one of the free templates from TypePad or WordPress will save time and energy. Consistency is a necessity when launching a blog. It's important to have a plan that includes the goals, the audiences, the content, how visitor interest will be built, and an outline of who's responsible for what tasks. Editorial calendars help create excitement and foster visitor expectations.

Build Up Your Blog Readership. Offering a whitepaper or case study is a great way to entice people to opt-in to reading your periodic e-mails or blog postings. Remember not to ask for more information on the opt-in form than is necessary. Don't ask for phone numbers if you have no plans on calling them. Also remember to respect people's privacy by not sharing or selling the information they so freely give up. RSS Feeds help people stay in touch without having to come back to your website or blog.

Bookmarking and Aggregating Boost Readership. Bookmarking generates more traffic to your blog. The process builds your readership by giving you the ability to post brief clips of information about your blog posts to people in like-minded communities. This practice attracts more visitors. Aggregation is another way of building your readership by combining news sources so you can send out one message instead of dozens. People stay informed, you save time and effort.

PART II

BE FOUND IN
ALL THE RIGHT
PLACES

The shotgun approach to looking for new prospects just won't work on the web; it's too enormous. To be successful here, businesses need to identify their ideal prospects first and then develop, launch, and execute their marketing campaigns.

With the ideal prospects known and their possible watering holes marked off, the next chore is to develop strategies to gain visibility in those venues. Too many businesses are enraptured with the idea of attracting their first 1 million visitors to their own website.

> *"Efficiency is doing things right; effectiveness is doing the right things."*
>
> —PETER DRUCKER

Having good visibility, compelling information, and attractive offers will attract those people in droves.

This chapter educates readers about how to identify their ideal prospect, construct their prospect universe, and then develop strategies to gain visibility in those venues.

The venues that are identified in this section include joining blog communities to engage prospects and build a sense of community. And producing audio and video podcasts to help build relationships. Discover how to use forums as a test bed for your latest marketing campaign. Understand how to tap into the like-minded people who gather to converse in forums. Learn how writing posts for other blogs and commenting on well read blogs helps build the readership of your own blog. It also gets your product or service "out there."

iTunes.com, YouTube.com, and Tucows.com could be considered download portals. Learn how to use these portals to distribute a presentation, software demo, or webinar.

Google and Bing offer pay-per-click (PPC) ad programs. PPC can serve an early purpose in garnering predisposed visitors. This section also talks about how search engine optimization helps attract the visitors that are already looking for your services or products.

Invite customers and prospects to virtual events. There are no travel expenses or lost time incurred by either party and the ROI is better. See if virtual events are for your organization.

Webinars are inexpensive, interactive, and can be held from anywhere. Audiences can participate by asking questions during or after the presentation or by taking polls during the lecture.

Press releases serve several purposes: they help spread the word, they give a company another opportunity to be listed in search results, and they provide valuable backlinks to the website or blog. A simple, brief, concise newsletter is a great way to stay in touch with clients and customers.

Learn how to use e-mail marketing campaigns to quickly and inexpensively test marketing messages and potential audience acceptance. Learn the ingredients of proven e-mail marketing campaign tactics.

Upload pictures of upcoming product launches. Discover if image sites can increase the awareness of your company.

Why wonder if your product or service is really satisfying the masses? Discover how to leverage review and comment sites to better understand your buying public.

Why not partner with your consumers to make your product or service something they believe is the very best? Learn why not knowing what people are saying about your company can damage your reputation.

Chapter 7

Knowing Your Ideal Prospects and Their Gathering Spots on the Web

"I think I was the best baseball player I ever saw."

—WILLIE MAYS

WOULDN'T IT BE GOOD TO KNOW WHO YOUR IDEAL PROSPECT OR prospects are before sending out e-mail blasts, newsletters, tweets, Facebook fan page invites, or webinar invitations? Most of us naturally assumes that everyone wants to hear what we have to say or desperately wants to purchase the service or product we're selling. Found that to be true lately? Really?

The web landscape is full of locations that attract all sorts of prospects. Some prospects gather around iTunes and YouTube while others congregate at blogs and community websites. It is each business owner's challenge to figure out where her or his ideal prospects gather.

Nor is every single person willing to purchase our products—there, I've said it. Even though the buying public is moving to

It's time to come to grips with reality . . . not everyone wants our service no matter how good or reasonably priced.

the web in droves to make its purchases, statistics say that only about 3 percent of people who initially visit a website are ready to purchase. That means the other 97 percent are just window shopping, kicking the tires, gathering information, or are lost.

In simple terms, that means for every 1,000 people that visit a website only about 30 are actually ready to buy. Now a person might say, "Wow, that's fantastic. Thirty new customers per hour or per month." But, not so fast. Let's factor in the "bounce rate"—the percentage of visitors leaving a website within the first five seconds. It is typical for a site's bounce rate to be between 50 to 60 percent. So let's subtract 550 visitors from the 1,000 and now the 30 visitors quickly drop to 13.

The best way to know your ideal prospects is to identify their habits, their mannerisms, their wants, needs, and desires. Don't define the ideal prospect as a "male or female" living in the continental United States who likes to fish. That's way too general. The first characteristic—"male or female"—includes every one living today!

Let's try to come up with a more exact picture of an ideal prospect. Suppose you are in the seminar business and small business is your niche. Your ideal prospect might look like this:

- · self-starter
- · pioneer
- · high energy
- · their own boss
- · strong willed
- · may be a workaholic
- · competitive
- · knows they cannot do everything

These characteristics start to lead you in certain directions on the web and begin to steer you away from certain locales. For instance, small business entrepreneurs are less likely to congregate on MySpace than they are to assemble on LinkedIn, a professional network of more than 55 million business people from 200 countries. It's a great place to establish relationships with people of common business interests.

BE **STRATEGIC**

 ▶ If multiple visitor-types are coming to the website, try to identify each group with as many specifics as possible.
 ▶ Don't assume your ideal prospect does not gather at a particular web venue, make sure.

People that know they cannot handle every obstacle that comes their way are more likely to frequent bookstores, internet knowledge-bases, as well as other educational opportunities like seminars.

Businesses typically have several different prospect types. Make sure to isolate each of them with their own characteristics, wants, needs, and desires. Being too broad only attracts a general audience and a company's products and services won't appeal to a massive group of people.

Know Where Your Prospects Hang Out on the Web

"There are no shortcuts to any place worth going."

—Beverly Sills

Once the ideal prospect is profiled, you need to ferret out his favorite places to congregate on the web. Everyone on the web tends to congregate in certain spots. Financial people like reading blogs about making dough and investing other people's money. Fly fishing enthusiasts hang out at fishing forums where they can lie to each other about the last "big one" that got away.

As the illustration in Figure 7.1 shows, there are plenty of places where a company's ideal prospect might gather. It's your job to find out where your prospects congregate and develop strategies to have visibility in those venues.

Let's take a crack at chopping the web up into meeting points. There are forums and chat rooms, community download sites, social networking venues, websites, of course, and blogs. Your ideal prospects may subscribe to newsletters, read articles, or get targeted press releases. Don't forget about their favorite search

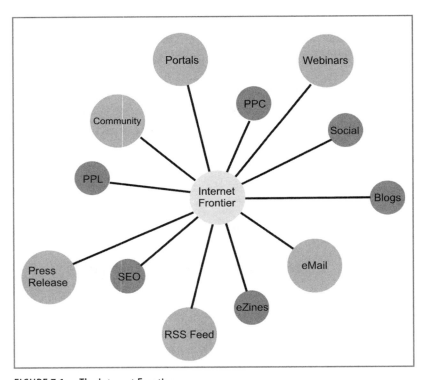

FIGURE 7.1—The Internet Frontier

engines like Google, Bing, *Yahoo!*, Dogpile, and the like. Surely the web could be separated into *several* more chunks, but this is a good starting point.

Suppose you run a marketing firm. Your marketing offerings might include on-the-ground marketing tactics like direct mail. Or perhaps you specialize in web marketing solutions with mostly electronic touches.

How could you easily tell if your ideal prospects visit community sites such as Digg, Sphinn, StumbleUpon, or Delicious? Do some searching.

If you go to Digg and search on the term "marketing," you find 345,439 results and more are coming in each day. "Internet marketing" brings up only 41,252 posts. It's easy to see that "marketing" is more popular than "internet marketing;" maybe? The analysis may be showing you that fewer people are submitting articles on "internet marketing." This means there is room for you. You could start submitting articles and attract a following of readers. Just from perusing the menu on Digg you can see that they have posts about technology, world and business, science, gaming, lifestyle, entertainment, sports, and offbeat items.

How does Sphinn compare? Its website tagline says "Internet Marketing News and Discussion Forums." Bingo! This may be just the place to get in front of your ideal prospects. Searching for "marketing" articles brings up over 360 posts. "Internet marketing" gets you more than 400 posts. You should develop a strategy to be seen in both these venues. These two spots are where "your people" gather.

Don't just have the "what's in it for me" attitude. People with that attitude are usually asked by the moderator of the community to leave.

To uncover whether or not your prospects read or contribute to certain forums, all you need do is spend a little time reading the discussion threads. Are they talking about what relates to our business? Are there problems to be solved? Can discussions be added to begin establishing relationships?

Marketing dollars are not being spent the best when the ideal prospects' whereabouts are unknown. There once was a summer camp that wanted to determine the best place to spend its marketing dollars. It spent about $9,000 a season on advertising through local radio spots and Yellow Page ads. As the new summer got underway, it

BE **STRATEGIC**

▶ Try to identify the ideal prospect gathering points. Then work on the locations that show the most promise, followed by the secondary locales.

▶ Don't think a gathering point will produce results forever. Some places will wane for no good reason. You'll just have to be flexible and develop new strategies and perhaps move to new locations.

decided to ask each family or organization coming to the camp how they had found about, let's say, Camp FunInTheSun. The answers were evenly split. Half had found the camp website, and the balance had either come to the camp as a teen, had sent their kids to the camp in the past, or knew someone who had. No one had let their fingers do the walking or had heard the local radio spots—$9,000 down a dark rat hole. Needless to say, the camp stopped the Yellow Page ads and local radio spots and launched a campaign to reach past guests and campers and strengthen its web presence.

Build an Internet Road Map So You'll Know When You Get There

"A good plan is like a road map: it shows the final destination and usually the best way to get there."

—H. STANLEY JUDD

Assume after some investigation, you learn the locations where your ideal prospects can be found:

- They gather at industry blogs.
- They join forums and start discussions.
- Many subscribe to monthly newsletters.
- Several competitors use paid search.
- Most are issuing monthly press releases.
- Some are offering webinars.

Gaining visibility in all the right places takes time, money, and effort.

During the same investigation you found no evidence of your ideal prospects or the competition at social media sites such as Twitter or Facebook, or at download sites like iTunes or YouTube (Figure 7.2). Set these venues aside.

Some venues undoubtedly will be more fruitful than others. Resources need to be spent wisely. For instance, working with a pay-per-lead company just takes money. It does all the advertising and sends prospects your way. You just have to close the deal. On the other hand, running Google AdWords campaigns without the

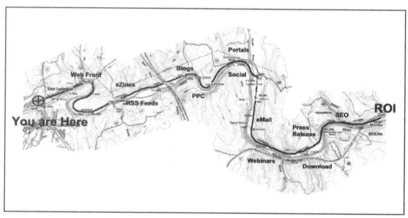

FIGURE 7.2—Internet Road Map

	A	B	C	D	E	F
1	**Watering Holes**	**Time**	**Money**	**Know-how**	**ROI**	**Notes**
2	PPL Company One		X		3	
3	PPL Company Two		X		3	
4	PPL Company Three		X		3	
5	Google PPC		X	X	1	Google looks the best
6	MSN PPC		X	X	1	
7	Yahoo PPC		X	X	1	
8	Newsletter One	X		X	3	Writing help
9	Newsletter Two	X		X	3	
10	Newsletter Three	X		X	3	
11	Blog One	X		X	3	Writing help
12	Blog Two	X		X	3	
13	Blog Three	X		X	3	
14	Virtual Trade Show One	X	X		1	Freshen Artwork
15	Virtual Trade Show Two	X	X		1	
16	Virtual Trade Show Three	X	X		1	

Watering Holes: Outcome-BasedMarketing.com/handouts

FIGURE 7.3—Internet Watering Holes spreadsheet

help of a PPC professional takes a good amount of money, time, and know-how.

Perhaps a good strategy would be to create a spreadsheet of the various places and then gauge whether gaining visibility in one location vs. another takes more time, money, or skill. Let's put together this spreadsheet of the different venues your prospects hang out at and rate whether time, money, or know-how are going to be the determining factors in gaining visibility at those gathering places.

The Microsoft Excel spreadsheet in Figure 7.3 can be downloaded to give you a jump-start on developing your own visibility chart of where your ideal prospects gather.

As you can see from this document, the ROI column shows which venue would probably give the best return on investment. These numbers are subjective until real results start coming in, but experience tells us that pay-per-click campaigns have a greater and more immediate return than sending out a newsletter.

The Money column helps identify which strategies cost marketing dollars and which simply take time and know-how.

The Notes column keeps track of special circumstances. For instance, you may need writing or marketing help in one area whereas in another area you feel self-sufficient.

There are many efforts that draw new visitors to the website that are not listed on this spreadsheet: e-mail marketing, landing pages, search engine optimization, and backlink campaigns. These tactics are outlined later in this section.

BE **STRATEGIC**

▶ Rate the gathering points according to which you believe show the best promise, and go after those first.

▶ Don't try and accomplish everything at once.

▶ If you don't have the time or talent, bring in a hired gun to get the job done.

Don't Bring Visitors to Your Site, Go to Where They Are

"Sales are contingent upon the attitude of the salesman—not

the attitude of the prospect."

—W. CLEMENT STONE

Some businesses have dreams of attracting millions of visitors to their websites. Realization of dreams such as those takes time and a sizable war chest. Not to mention a killer marketing plan and flawless execution. Is there a simpler way that's less costly, less complicated, and less time consuming?

Let's say you want to sell ball caps to baseball fans. Does it make sense to put up a website and spend months trying to attract buyers? Or should you hang outside a ballpark on game day? Why not start out where the fans are and then draw them back to the

Think about gaining visibility in the venues where your ideal prospects already gather. Someone else is doing all the work of attracting them. Take advantage of the situation.

website to make future purchases? In this way the business gets a brand established and makes money, and the least amount of effort is expended.

The same strategy can work on the web, minus the drive to the ballpark.

See if you can get opportunities to post articles on popular blogs. This will drive readers back to your blog or website. If your company builds and sells software solutions then upload a trial version of the software to download sites so people can "hold the puppy" (take a trial run). Put slide presentations up on websites such as SlideShare.net. This site sees hundreds of thousands of visitors per month.

BE **STRATEGIC**

- At first, choose a single location in which to gain visibility; don't dilute your efforts.
- It may not always profit your efforts to have visibility in the largest communities. Keep an eye on results. Ask yourself, "Is the prominence paying off?"

Chapter 8

Being Found Takes Time, Talent, and Tenacity

*"Patience and tenacity are worth more than
twice their weight of cleverness."*

—THOMAS HUXLEY

THIS CHAPTER DEALS WITH SIX WEB MARKETING TACTICS. FIRST,
BLOG communities that engage prospects and build a sense of
community. You can gain more credibility and trust by joining
the blog communities most suitable to your company on the
web. Second, audio and video podcasts that take the personal
relationship between the buyer and the seller to the next level.
Podcasts help establish you as an authority on a particular
subject. Podcasts keep the same message going over and over.
Third, forums that have been a mainstay in the social networking
communities long before we thought "tweet" was something a
bird did. Forums can be a way of saving marketing dollars because
you don't have to search where the "right" prospects hang out
on the web. Fourth, writing posts or commenting on well read

blogs helps build the readership of your own blog. It also gets your company product or service "out there." It makes more sense to go where your readership hangs out instead of trying to attract one million readers to your blog. Commenting on other people's blogs builds your readership as well. Make sure you don't upstage the owner of the blog where you make comments. Fifth, video blogging is stickier than blogging and makes a great PR (Public Relations) tool. Video blogging does take the seller / prospect relationship to the next level. Sixth, download websites make it easy for you to share the company's software demos and free trials. An interested party can download music from iTunes, videos from YouTube, and software from Tucows.

Blog Communities: Engage Prospects and Build a Sense of Community

"Our strong suit is what we do, and our audience."

—Jerry Garcia

There are venues on the web called "blog communities" where companies can list their blog to be read by others outside the organization's sphere of influence. Stacking your company blog up against others in your business space creates a reality check as to which blogs are really worth reading; that is, which blogs attract the largest readership, post the most provocative questions, and receive the most comments.

There's nothing wrong with some good old competition. Businesses can leverage blog communities to:

- Grow readership
- Entice more visitors to their website

- Broaden their sphere of influence
- Introduce their products and services to a larger audience
- Hear from people outside the company's circle
- Gain more credibility and trust
- Be seen as an expert
- Increase sales opportunities

Let's look at three of the many blog community sites that are on the web.

BlogCatalog.com (Figure 8.1). It claims to be the largest user-submitted blog in the world and has the following categories: Arts, Automotive, Blogging, Business, Education, Entertainment, Food and Drink, Geography, Lifestyle, Mom and Family, News and Media, Personal, Society, Sports, and Technology. You might be wondering how many business blogs are listed—just over 273,000 and counting. There are hundreds of discussions you can join in on or just listen in on what people are talking about and blog groups where people converse about special interest topics. The signup process is rather painless, although each blog submitted comes under editorial review.

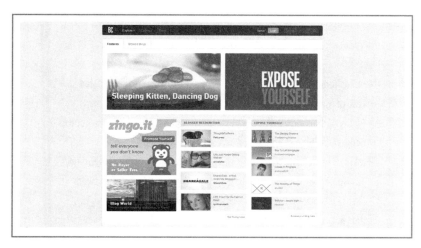

FIGURE 8.1—BlogCatalog homepage

Look over the conversations to see where you can add value.

Blogs.com. Its categories are Careers, Celebrities, Crafts and Hobbies, Economics, Fashion and Beauty, Food and Drink, Gadgets, Gaming, Health and Fitness, Home and Garden, Marketing/Small Business, Media, Mobile, Music, Parenting, Personal Finance, Pets, Tech News, Top 10 Lists, TV, US News, US Politics, Web 2.0, and World News. There are more than 25,000 business blogs. Blog submissions are subject to editorial review.

Blogged.com. It covers Art, Business, Computers, Education, Entertainment, Family and Home, Health, Internet, Music, Other Languages, Parenting, Personal Blogs, Recreation, Society, Technology, Travel, Shopping, Spanish, Sports, and United States. There are more than 23,000 business blogs at this site. Blog submissions are subject to editorial review.

Take the time to go through the prominent blog communities to see which ones suit your company's message. If your ideal prospects are present and the competition is in attendance, then there's a good chance your organization needs a presence as well.

The Pros and Cons of Blog Communities

Pros	Cons
• Builds community	• Some may feel intimidated
• Ease of use	• Transparency
• Plenty of differing views	• Audience expects frequent posts or follow-ups
• Cooperative brainstorming	
• Marketing message test bed	• Posts may not be authoritative
• Transparency	• Not useful for quick answers
• Great PR tool	• Not confidential
• Aids in customer retention	• May create competition between writers
• Great feedback mechanism	

Tread lightly at first. Don't just jump in as the unknown expert. Making a bad first impression is not soon forgotten in communities such as these.

Outcome-Based Marketing: Blog Communities

- *Inputs.* The comments to existing posts need to be thought provoking, provocative, and imaginative. Put links (back to your blog) in the posts, if permitted.
- *Activities.* Comment on a regular basis to build a following.
- *Masses.* Those reading the various blogs.
- *Leads.* Those that comment on your posts. Those that click on your links within the posts.
- *Outcome targets.* Stated goal might be to have 3 to 5 percent of those commenting on the posts click on the links within posts.
- *Outcome indicators.* Observable, measurable milestones toward the stated outcome targets. Sites such as Google Analytics or VisiStat.com can be used to take these measurements.

> ### BE **STRATEGIC**
>
> ▶ Whether you start out big or small, keep your postings consistent.
> ▶ Don't try to control the discussion . . . let them go where they go.

Podcasts: All Right, Mr. DeMille, I'm Ready for My Close Up

"Education is the ability to meet life's situations."

—Dr. John G. Hibben

If you're not familiar with the movie quote "All right, Mr. DeMille, I'm ready for my close up," it comes from *Sunset*

Boulevard, the 1950 movie nominated for 11 Academy Awards. In the movie, hack screenwriter Joe Gillis (played by William Holden) is ensnared by Norma Desmon (played by Gloria Swanson), a deranged Hollywood has-been. Put this film on your short list. Back to the subject at hand: podcasts.

Podcasts provide an opportunity for the marketer to take the relationship with the prospect to the next level. It's only a one-sided face-to-face conversation, but still better communication than a website, blog, or e-mail blast. Podcasts are simple to produce, easy to distribute, and increase a company's audience. They can be used to test a company's marketing message, for instructional purposes, or just as a means of strengthening the relationship between seller and buyer.

Of the two podcast formats, audio is much easier and less expensive to produce. Video requires a more exact technology, but the prospect gets to see the demeanor of the presenter and what he or she looks like during a video presentation, important steps in the connection process.

Here are 12 reasons why you should consider doing podcasts:

1. Podcasts are great training tools.
2. Podcasts offer a higher level of customer support and lessen support calls.
3. Podcasts are great product launch tools.
4. Podcasts are great video press releases.
5. Podcasts keep everyone in the organization on the same sheet of music.
6. Podcasts reach new audiences.
7. Podcasts make you sound like the authority.
8. Podcasts increase advertising potential.
9. Podcasts keep the message the same when responding to customer questions.
10. Podcasts give the prospect the freedom to listen when and where they want.

11. Podcasts add another dimension to your collateral.

12. Podcasts strengthen the prospect/consumer relationship.

Convinced yet? Read on.

Before you jump into the sound booth to produce your first podcast, let's take a quick glance at some pitfalls so you can save time, money, and your sanity. Eight potential pitfalls are:

1. *Interruptions.* Sound studios usually have flashing red lights, "On Air" signs, and bolted doors. You won't be so lucky. Your podcast productions will probably take place in your offices. So the order of the day will be to post a "Quiet, Podcasting" sign on your office door and let everyone on the team know quiet is needed.

2. *Technical difficulties.* There's no way to avoid technical glitches, but plenty of preparation and buying decent recording gear will lessen the occurrences.

3. *Ambient noise.* You may think the office environment is quiet, but to prove it, start recording and then listen closely to the playback. You may need to move your location or record after everyone has gone home for the evening.

4. *Bad tonal quality.* It's not your fault, but you may not have a voice suitable for recording.

5. *Unprepared.* Because stopping and starting the podcast recording session leaves gaps in the presentation, you'll have to do it from beginning to end without hesitation. Be prepared and do several run-throughs before laying down the final track.

6. *No compelling message.* Make your story compelling, interesting, and fast moving—with a call to action. Let the listener know what you expect from him or her.

7. *Reading from a script.* Everyone will know if you are just reading from a script. Their interest will wane, and they'll stop listening before you're done. Do several run-throughs until you can do the presentation with just a brief set of notes to jog your memory.

8. Poor album artwork. Do a professional job all the way through; that includes some eye-catching artwork for the podcast album cover. The image shown in Figure 8.2 is from Brian Carroll's Start with a Lead series. Think about how prospects can quickly identify your podcasts when listed with everyone else's.

There are plenty of places to upload the podcast after they're created. Let's use iTunes for our test arena. Then we'll talk about the other popular sites.

Hopefully you have an iTunes icon on your desktop. If not, you can download the software at Apple.com. To see the latest podcast entries, key "itunes podcasts" into your browser. When the podcast window (Figure 8.3) opens, click on the category that interests you.

Now you know where to go to listen or watch podcasts on iTunes. How about recording our own? We'll use Apple's QuickTime® to record our first audio podcast. Recording an audio is just a five-step process:

1. Open QuickTime.
2. Set your QuickTime recording preferences.
3. Choose New Audio Recording from the File menu.

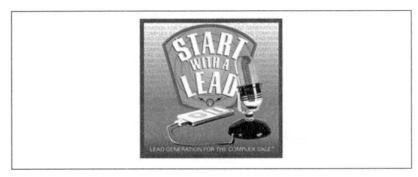

FIGURE 8.2—Brian Carroll's Start with a Lead logo

FIGURE 8.3—iTunes Podcast page

4. Record the session.
5. Rename the default output file.

Congratulations, you're ready to post your first podcast. Choose a series of websites on which to post the podcast, the more coverage the better. Post it on the corporate website and blog as well.

How about doing a video podcast on your Mac? Yes, there are other platforms (Windows and the like) other than Apple, but let's just keep things simple.

- Make sure the QuickTime software version is 7.0.3 or later.
- Connect your FireWire® camera to the Mac®.
- Open QuickTime.
- Check your recording preferences.
- Choose "New Movie Recording" from the File menu.

It's great to hear someone's voice; but watching them talk, their expressions, their reactions, and their demeanor do more to build a relationship than just listening to someone.

- Click the red Capture button to record and the black "Stop" button when finished.
- Choose "Export" from the File menu to convert the video to a format iPod understands.
- Choose "Movie to iPod" from the export drop down.
- You're ready to publish your podcast on the web.

Now that we're budding experts at creating audio and video podcasts, let's look at some of the more popular distribution websites. Notice the numbers in parenthesis. They denote how many podcasts are available for that topic. Not all podcast sites make their numbers available. The numbers do, however, give a good indication of which topics are more popular.

- *PodcastAlley.com.* Arts (2,147), Business (2,819), Comedy (4,315), Education (2,165), Environment (170), Food and Drink (289), Games and Hobbies (377), General (40,516), Government and Organizations (18), Health (1503), Kids and Family (96), Music (10,081), News and Politics (1,090), Religion and Spirituality (2,682), Science and Medicine (65), Sports and Recreation (1,392), Society and Culture (1,884), Technology (4,775), Travel (562), TV and Film (1,262), Video Podcasts (1,177)
- *iBizRadio.com.* Accounting (3), Advertising and Marketing (27), Aerospace and Defense (0), Agriculture (0), Art (3), Automotive (5), B2B Electronics and Semiconductors (1), B2B Products and Services (14), Business Management (66), Computer and Software (7), Construction (0), Consumer Electronics (1), E-Commerce (8), Education (24), Energy and Power (0), Entertainment (21), Entrepreneurship (31), Environment (1), Financial Services (36), Food and Beverage (2), Health and Family (16), Home and Garden (4), Humor (2), Industrial (0), Insurance (0), Internet Marketing (33), Legal and Law (7), Mortgage (1), Online and Internet (7),

Pharmaceuticals (0), Political (2), Public Relations (9), Real Estate (2), Religion (2), Retail (3), Science (3), Sports (2), Technology (20), Transportation (2), Travel and Hospitality (5)

- *PodBean.com*. Arts, Automotive, Business, Career, Comedy, Education, Fashion and Style, Food, Gaming, Gardening, General, Health, Kids and Family, Music, News and Politics, Nonprofit, Radio, Real Estate, Religion, Science and Medicine, Sports, TV and Film, Technology, Travel
- *DigitalPodcast.com*. Art, Audio Blogs, Audio Books, Business, Comedy and Humor, Cooking, Educational, Environment, Family, Fashion, Games, Health and Fitness, Hobbies, Info-casts, Movies and Entertainment, Music, News, Personal Finance, Podcasting, Politics and Government, Radio, Regional, Religion and Spirituality, Science and Technology, Skits, Sports, Travel, Variety shows, Video Podcasts
- *LearnOutloud.com*. Arts and Entertainment, Biography, Business, Education and Professional, History, Languages, Literature, Philosophy, Politics, Religion and Spirituality, Science, Self Development, Social Sciences, Sports and Hobbies, Technology, Travel

Podcast sites that offer sexually explicit content were intentionally left off this list. Good luck podcasting. Remember to look over the pitfalls before starting to record.

Outcome-Based Marketing: Podcasts

- *Inputs*. The podcast information needs to be timely, interesting, and applicable. The podcast format must be compelling and fast moving. Doing video podcasts will be determined by audience acceptance.
- *Activities*. The actual podcast production. The marketing efforts to broadcast the podcast's availability: (1) Notices

The Pros and Cons of Podcasting	
Pros	**Cons**
• Simple to produce	• Not easily searchable
• Easy to distribute	• May alienate a market segment
• Enriches the relationship	• Presenter may drone on . . .
• Mobile information source	• You cannot ask the presenter questions
• Convenience factor for nonreaders	
• Cost effective	
• Wide audience acceptance	
• Convenient for the viewer	

on the website and blog, (2) e-mail marketing campaigns, (3) social media, and (4) listing the podcast in popular podcast directories.

· *Masses.* The Masses will be all those people reached by the marketing efforts.

· *Leads.* The Leads will be those that sign up to view the podcast. It will be important to capture as much information about those viewers as possible for follow up.

· *Outcome targets.* Viewing the podcast may be part of the nurturing campaign. Try and convert 3 to 5 percent of those people. Viewing the podcast may be part of a measure to lower support calls. In that case, select a baseline figure such as 10 to 20 percent fewer support calls the first month. Viewing the podcast may be part of your strategy in selling your training program or new book. In that case, capture people's e-mail addresses for follow up. Try and convert 5 to 7 percent of the audience.

BE **STRATEGIC**

▶ Keep the podcasts concise, interesting, and fast moving.

▶ Keep the podcasts all about the listeners and their needs.

· *Outcome indicators.* If the podcasts are listed in podcast directories those places usually post viewing stats. Google Analytics can be used to track website or blog stats of the podcasts.

Forums: Can I Say Something?

"I love talking about nothing. It's the only thing I know anything about."

—OSCAR WILDE

Some prospects are looking for more information, and forums are filling those information and conversation gaps. Forums have been around as long as the web. They were first called "Bulletin Board System" or "BBS," a place where people could leave messages and return later to see who had answered their questions. Bulletin Board Services were touting community long before Twitter hatched or everyone's family photos were up on Facebook.

Forums are discussion platforms where like-minded people can talk about certain topics, help others, or share experiences. Sometimes forums are attached to corporate websites, or sometimes they stand alone on their own domain. Individuals host forums as do companies, associations, and industries.

Most forums require membership and decorum to join in the discussions. There may be one moderator for an entire forum or a group of moderators tasked with their own subject areas. Moderators need to be on hand when members become unruly or uncivil with other members. Someone has to keep the peace. Moderators also have to be watchful of spam or charlatans looking to take advantage of the membership.

So, how might a business leverage forums? Here are a few ideas to start you thinking:

- You can listen in on the conversations taking place.
- Like-minded forums are filled with "your people." People who are already predisposed to your marketing message and interested in the product or service you're selling.
- Forums are great test beds to try out new marketing messages.
- Why not do your product development in forums? Talk with the people who will likely be buying your next product iteration.
- Forums cost less to market to because the "right" people are already gathered in one place. You don't have to spend money looking for them.
- Forums are excellent places to be seen as experts or to build trust in the community.

Moderators need to be tactful when a member causes a ruckus or needs to be shown the virtual door.

The people that join forums need to have good people skills. Members need to be polite, courteous, social, and have something to share.

You'll likely find a forum dedicated to every industry, product, service sector, or business vertical, talking about everything under the sun. You'll even find forums that talk about nothing but other forums.

There are dozens if not hundreds of free sites where you can build and launch your company forum. Three sites that offer free forum hosting and setup are:

- Lefora.com. 10 GB free each month, Upgrade Packages, Integrate Your Existing Website, Customization, Promotion Links, Admin Panel, Automatic Spam Detection, Public, Private, and Everything in Between, Community Support, Automatic Security Patches, New Features Added Monthly,

Flash Widgets and Video, Upgrades, Newsletters, Search Engine Optimized, Facebook, Twitter, and MySpace Integration, Global Leader Boards
- Forumotion.com. Offers many of the same features and has a point-and-click interface to get you up and running within minutes.
- ProBoards.com. Offers many of the same features and has an easy-to-use interface for creation and modification.

Companies can also download free forum software and host it themselves. Tal.ki is one example. This site lets you to embed a forum much the way you might embed a YouTube video on your website. No account creation is necessary. People can log in with their Facebook, Twitter, OpenID, Google, or *Yahoo!* account information. The pricing runs from free to *$249/month* for the maximum.

Let's examine forums from two different perspectives: first when contributing to industry forums and second when being the owner-operator of the forum.

Outcome-Based Marketing: Forum Contributor

- *Inputs.* The copy used to start the discussions.
- *Activities.* Contributions (posts) made to specific interest groups or by starting a special interest group on your own.
- *Masses.* Those members and nonmembers that read the postings.
- *Leads.* Those that take some action based on your postings. Perhaps they download an offer or sign up for something.
- *Outcome targets.* The resource commitment has to be measured against the return. Say you are looking for 3 to 5 percent leads from the leads.
- *Outcome indicators.* Google Analytics along with stats from the forum.

The Pros and Cons of Forums

Pros	Cons
• Easy to launch	• Time consuming to maintain
• Boost customer devotion	• Security concerns
• Good listening post	• Someone has to be the bad cop and
• Increase stickiness	monitor posts
• Boost the amount of content	• Can't always control the conversation
on your website	• Members may lose interest
• Boost the amount of educational	• Good forums are not developed overnight
material on your website	• Good forums take a lot of hard work
• Increase traffic and repeat	• Forum content and its members need to
visitors	be monitored 24/7
• Can be used to capture	• If the forum is inactive or pulled offline
information on prospects	its members may have a negative
• Give your site credibility	impression of the company
• Help build relationships	• Not every company employee is
• Can be salted with questions	comfortable handling criticism
the company wants answers to	• Not every company employee will make
• Members can help each other	a good first impression in public
answer questions	
• Members can piggyback on	
other's ideas	
• Company staff can interact with	
customers in a more informal	
atmosphere	
• Prospects can learn what customers	
think of a company before	
purchasing their product or service	
• Prospects can ask pre-sales	
questions	

Outcome-Based Marketing: Forum Owners

- *Inputs*. The copy used for the actual posts.
- *Activities*. Moderators and support of the forum needs to be first-class. Conversations need to be kept on track. Forum owner must be seen as a driving force of the community's success. Forum owner needs to have marketing campaigns in place to advertise and expand the community.
- *Masses*. Those members and nonmembers that read the postings.
- *Leads*. Those that take some action based on marketing campaigns within the forum. Perhaps they download an offer or sign up for something.
- *Outcome targets*. The resource commitment has to be measured against the return. Say you are looking for 3 to 5 percent leads from the forum.
- *Outcome indicators*. Google Analytics along with stats from the forum.

> ### BE **STRATEGIC**
>
> ▶ Good forums have able, dedicated moderators.
> ▶ The conversations need to be relevant, timely, and speak to the membership.

Blogs: Don't Just Talk a Good Game—Be Viewed as an Expert

"Writing isn't hard. It isn't any harder than ditch-digging."
—Patrick Dennis

Blogs give companies an opportunity to share their talent and expertise along with the fact that blogs build community. What if you believe you have great things to say but you don't have a huge blog following yet? The first thought that might cross your mind is, what's the use? Nobody, okay just a few people, are going to see what I have to say. Your next thought is I can help thousands of people with this information. What should you do?

Posting comments on other people's blogs helps bring cross traffic back to a company's website or blog. It's important to be seen where the visibility is best. There's a reason those actors and actresses who are not nominated for an Academy Award show up for the presentations of the 13.5 inch tall, 8.5 pound statue. It's to be seen. Let's look at how a company can leverage other people's blogs.

You can post the information on industry blogs that attract tens of thousands of readers. Consider posting at a blog such as CustomerThink.com, which covers such topics as leadership, technology, marketing, sales, and innovation. Suppose you have some great thoughts on shortening the sales cycle or lead generation? CustomerThink would be the perfect venue to post your brilliance. It has more than 200,000 subscribers from more than 200 countries. Check out its "How to Contribute" page in Figure 8.4.

Another good site to post marketing content is B2BMarketing Zone.com. It has a library of thousands of articles on sales, marketing, social media, lead generation, and more. Its homepage is shown in Figure 8.5.

So how do you find industry blogs in your business space? Easy, use Google. Type a phrase such as "Marketing Blogs" or "Fly Fishing Blogs" into your favorite browser. Someone is bound to have compiled a list of the "Top Ten" or "Best 50" blogs in your business space. All you need to do now is check out which blogs would be friendly to your posts. Some blogs will surely be administrated by your competition. Other blogs welcome guest writers.

How about the blogs run by the "influencers" in your community? Influencers are people that have a "voice" in

FIGURE 8.4—CustomerThink How to Contribute page

your business sector, a significant following. In the marketing community it might be Seth Godin, in the PR community David Meerman Scott, for social media Chris Brogan. Some of these influencers encourage guest authors to their blogs.

There is another tack you can take to gain visibility on well-read blogs—posting comments. We're not talking spam here. Comments such as: "Great post!" or "Keep'em coming" rarely get approved for publication. How about actually adding to the discussion—without upstaging the blog owner, of course?

Outcome-Based Marketing: Commenting or Posting on Blogs

·   *Inputs.* The copy used to comment or post on the blog.

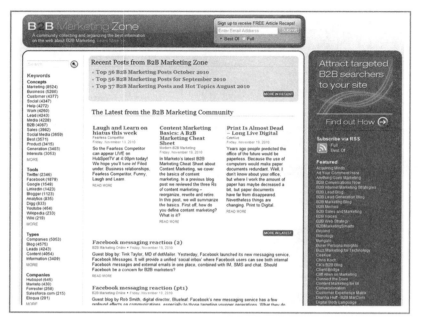

FIGURE 8.5—B2BMarketingZone homepage

- *Activities.* The commenting or posting activity itself.
- *Masses.* Number of people reached by the marketing campaign can be calculated using sites such as Google Analytics, StatCounter.com, or VisiStat.com.
- *Leads.* Number of people that took "some" action: either downloaded a whitepaper, filled out a form, subscribed to a blog, or signed up for a free trial.
- *Outcome targets.* Stated goals of the marketing campaign: increase website visitors by 10 percent, generate new revenue stream of 5 percent or grow Twitter followers by 1,000.

What better way to be seen as an industry expert that contributing to an already insightful post.

The Pros and Cons of Blogs

Pros	Cons
• Creates community	• Some may feel intimidated
• Ease of use	• Transparency
• Plenty of differing views	• Audience expects frequent posts or
• Cooperative brainstorming	follow ups
• Marketing message test bed	• Posts may not be authoritative
• Transparency	• Not useful for quick answers
• Great PR tool	• Not confidential
• Aids in customer retention	• May create competition between writers
• Great feedback mechanism	

Outcome indicators. Observable, measurable milestones toward the stated outcome targets. Sites such as Google Analytics or VisiStat.com can be used to take these measurements.

BE **STRATEGIC**

- Think about retweeting the good posts you read from others.
- Keep your posting/ commenting consistent.

Video Blogs: Can You See Me Now?

"Here's looking at you kid."

—Rick Blaine played by Humphrey Bogart in *Casablanca*

Regular text blogs are useful, but what about doing a video blog or vlog? Video blogs take the conversation and relationship to the next level. Video blogs let viewers see who's speaking. They can see the demeanor, posture, and facial expressions of the speaker. Video blogging holds a viewers' attention better than the printed word on a regular blog. They do take more time and thought to produce, but the benefits on the backend outweigh the resources spent on the front end.

While some people feel comfortable writing a blog, others enjoy filming what they have to say. Obviously more work goes into filming a blog than tapping your thoughts out on a keyboard, but video blogging offers benefits the written word does not, principally that it is more personal.

Video blogs hold people's attention longer than written blogs. They can take advantage of syndication tools such as RSS and Atom formats, and they can be played back on mobile devices, much like podcasts.

Video blogging can be used to share industry or company news, quick snapshots of sales events, or product launches. Video blogs could be used to answer support questions, demonstrate how to use a particular product, or serve as an instructional tool.

What are the steps in creating and posting a video blog? First, you'll have to come up with a catchy title for the video posting, a title that sounds interesting, one that will attract people to watch the video.

On a vlog the viewer can see your facial expressions, body language, and hear your voice inflexions, which some people prefer.

Second, you'll have to decide where the video files will reside: on the company website or at a secondary location such as YouTube (Figure 8.6). Why not both? Create the video, upload it to YouTube, and then embed the YouTube video link on the company's video blog. That way you'll cover the visitors to your blog and those searching on YouTube.

Third, develop the content, and time how long the video presentation takes.

Obama, GOP spar over new
jobs figures
3 days ago
www.cnn.com

FIGURE 8.6—YouTube political podcast

Remember less is more. No one is going to sit through an hour-long presentation. These should be like blog postings. Three to five minutes probably work the best. If you have a more involved subject, break it into smaller chunks. Having several videos to share with your readership only creates interest and excitement.

Fourth is the production phrase. You'll need some video editing software such as Adobe's Visual Communicator. Production itself is a five-step process:

1. Choose the look (theme) of your newscast.
2. Add your script to the teleprompter.
3. Add your media. This might be video, audio, or still images.
4. Record your presentation. You'll need a decent webcam or video camera to capture the action.
5. Share the video with your audience. Think about uploading it to Google Video Blog and YouTube.

There are, of course, procedures you should follow when filming:

· Know the capabilities of the camera.
· Storyboard your presentation so you stay on task.
· Check the lighting and sound.
· Be aware of ambient noise around you.
· Watch how much you move around.
· Watch the presentation with an eye toward details.

You also need to be aware of audio recording issues:

- Know your microphone.
- Do sound level checks before recording.
- Be aware of ambient noise.
- Listen to the presentation with a critical ear.

Instead of jumping right into a video blog, think about starting a regular blog first and then adding videos over time. Having a regular blog up and running gets you used to producing information on a regular basis. Once blogging fits into your schedule and it's something you believe works for your audience, then crank up the video portion. You may find that a combination of writing and video presentations works best for you.

Outcome-Based Marketing: Video Blog

- *Inputs.* The content of the video and the offers made during the presentation.
- *Activities.* The actual video presentation and the marketing efforts to attract the audience.
- *Masses.* Number of people reached by the marketing campaign.
- *Leads.* Number of people that took some form of action: watched the event, downloaded a whitepaper, filled out a form, subscribed to a blog, or signed up for a free trial.
- *Outcome targets.* Stated goals of the marketing campaign: increase website visitors by 10 percent, generate new revenue stream of 5 percent, or grow Twitter followers by 1,000.
- *Outcome indicators.* Observable, measurable "milestones" toward the stated outcome

BE **STRATEGIC**

- Pick an interesting location to stage your video to hold the audience's attention.
- Use visual aids whenever possible. Remember you're on TV.

The Pros and Cons of Video Blogs	
Pros	**Cons**
• Creates community	• Some may feel intimidated
• More personal use	• Transparency
• Ease of use	• Takes time
• Creates excitement	• Production headaches
• Increases stickiness	• Can't ask presenter questions
• Marketing message test bed	• Presenter may not be interesting
• Great PR tool	
• Aids in customer retention	
• Great feedback mechanism	
• Good for personal branding	

targets. Sites such as Google Analytics or VisiStat.com can be used to take these measurements.

Download Sites: Make It Easy to Share Your Wares

"People think that it's their sovereign right to download

music and not have to pay for it."

—JOHN KELLY (SONGWRITER AND PRODUCER)

What if your company develops and sells software? Download sites are popular venues for sharing music, videos, software, shareware, and other desktop and developer tools. These locations make it uncomplicated for a company to meet the right audience if, for instance, it sells security software and wants new spectators to give it a try. Download sites are the ideal proving ground for a company's next product update.

Movies, games, and music download sites are certainly popular. Let's set those genres aside and talk more about other business applications for download sites, using a few sites such as YouTube, Tucows, download.CNET.com, and iTunes. Of course, if your business is in movies, games, or music then rock on! And you still may find this conversation useful to your business model.

For an example of a business use of downloads, let's say our company builds high-performance add-on engine parts. Let's further assume that people reading our installation documentation make two simple mistakes that end up generating many calls to tech support staff. Why not let someone in the shop do the installation correctly, film the process, and upload the video to YouTube? You can put the proper installation video on your website and blog. Customers will find it there, and some calls to tech support will be eliminated. Tech support can also refer callers to the video to shorten the support call. It's a win-win situation for both the business and the customer.

These video sites are also perfect for uploading training sessions so they can be viewed on-demand when organizations have the time to take them in.

YouTube and iTunes are also great venues for presentations, product launches, training sessions, and discussions of special interest. Don't put hours of blood, sweat, and tears into presentations to show them once and then offload them to some file server. Upload them to YouTube and iTunes for people to find. Make sure to use a title that attracts viewers, and tag the video so people searching for the information can find you.

Download sites are also tremendous for 30-second or one-minute how-tos, tips, and insights. Say you run an online marketing firm. You could post one-minute videos on constructing a company's brand promise, developing an elevator pitch, or segmenting a market. You could follow up with clips on strategic ways to use SEO/SEM, pay-per-click, e-mail marketing, or social media. Viewers would see you as the experts and start calling.

Download sites such as Tucows and download.CNET.com are just right for uploading product demos and free trials for software products relating to security software, browsers, business software, communications, desktop enhancements, developer tools, digital photo software, drivers, educational software, entertainment software, games, graphic design software, home software, internet software, iTunes, and iPad software, MP3 and audio software, networking software, productivity software, screensavers and wallpaper, utilities and operating systems, and video software. Why make visitors come to you when they frequent the best download sites? If your competition is on the download site and you're not, it will be their software that gets downloaded, tried, and purchased.

Outcome-Based Marketing: Download Sites

· *Inputs.* Actual software or download of the trial version.
· *Activities.* Marketing efforts by the software company to bring prospects to the download site.

The Pros and Cons of Download Sites	
Pros	**Cons**
• Reach new audiences	• Poor customer service?
• Meet prospects on neutral ground	• Virus? Spyware?
• Positive reviews	• Negative reviews
• Go to where ideal prospects are hanging out	• Stiff competition
• Don't have to attract people back to your website	• Lost in the marketing noise
	• May attract too many tire kickers; not serious buyers

- *Masses.* Those regular visitors to the website and those visitors touched by the marketing campaigns.
- *Leads.* Those that download the trial version of the software.
- *Outcome targets.* Outcome targets might be a 5 to 7 percent sales increase per month or a minimum of 30 free trial signups per month.
- *Outcome indicators.* Statistics from download site along with Google Analytics to measure the success of the marketing campaigns.

BE **STRATEGIC**

- Work hard to position your product above the fray.
- Offer other enticing goodies along with the download. Offer a case study, whitepaper, or invite them to a free webinar about the software product.

Chapter 9

Paying Your Way to the Top

"Many a small thing has been made large by the right kind of advertising."

—MARK TWAIN

GOOGLE AND BING OFFER PAY-PER-CLICK (PPC) AD PROGRAMS. (Microsoft recently acquired *Yahoo!* sponsored search marketing.) Google does a better job of *targeting* ads. PPC can serve an early purpose in garnering predisposed visitors. Later on, PPC gets to be too costly for most companies' budgets.

Paid search ads show up at the top and to the right of search pages when using a typical browser such as Google, Bing, or Safari. Companies pay for these page positions hoping the searching public will click on their ads and not the links on the balance of the search results.

Utilizing pay-per-click campaigns to attract your ideal prospects can be very useful.

Launching strategic pay-per-click campaigns is a cost-effective way to jump-start your next marketing campaign.

The results of pay-per-click campaigns are known within hours. Either the business has chosen the right key phrases that will attract their ideal clients or it's back to the drawing board for some new key search terms. But pay-per-click campaigns can also be a drain on company finances if not done correctly. So let's do some homework before jumping into the pay-per-click pool.

Pay-per-Click: Compel Prospects to Click on Your Ads

"Every success is built on the ability to do better than good enough."

—ANONYMOUS

Ever come across articles or blog posts with headlines such as "Put Your AdWord Campaigns on Autopilot" or "Generate Thousands of Leads per Month"? Running effective, cost-efficient, lead-generating pay-per-click (PPC) campaigns takes nothing short of some serious dedicated time, money, and talent—and a little genius. Either the company that wants to do PPC hires an expert or it spends a good amount of time learning the ropes and literally paying its dues.

Edging out the competition that has owned certain key phrase positions in the sponsored search results arena will not happen overnight—unless you throw large sums of money at the issue by constantly overbidding the other people until they surrender. This is not a good business or budget strategy.

The folks that use Google refer to PPC campaigns as AdWord campaigns. An example of Google AdWords logo and Microsoft's Bing are in Figure 9.1.

FIGURE 9.1—Google and Microsoft pay-per-click logos

Let's get two definitions out of the way before you go any further.

- *Google AdWords.* Lets you promote your business alongside relevant Google search results. For example, if your business space is information security, it would be good if when searchers keyed in "information security," your company's ad showed up in the sponsored sections of the search results.
- *Google AdSense.* Lets a company earn money by putting targeted ads on a website.

In simple terms, an AdWord campaign is an advertising model in which advertisers pay for click-throughs to their website.

Google has great analytics so you can track when visitors come, where they come from, what pages they visited, how long they stayed, what country they came from, and what search term or phrase they keyed in to their browser.

In our illustration, Figure 9.2, paid search exists at the top and in the column to the right of the general search results. Ads are served up based on keywords or themes. But the advertiser who paid the most for the AdWord is listed first, and so on. For instance, if you run a pet store and sell pet supplies, your searchers might be using the term "pet supplies" to locate your website. So what's involved in setting up and executing a pay-per-click strategy using the term "pet supplies?"

FIGURE 9.2—Search results showing organic and paid search

· An account needs to be opened at Google. You will need to provide some personal information and a valid credit card.

· Next, investigation needs to be done to see what search terms are available in your business space and to gauge how much competition there is for the preferred ad space. Being listed at the top of the page in the search results may strain your budget. Most PPC advertisers seem to think ad positions three through five return the best for their investment.

· So how do you choose which search terms to use in AdWord campaigns? It does not matter what the people at your company think the search terms should be. What matters is what searchers are actually keying into the browser. We need to use Google's Keyword Tool to see what other search terms come up when you type in the term "pet supplies."

The first ten results generated from the Google Keyword Tool when keying in "pet supplies" are listed in Figure 9.3. (The

Advertiser Competition and the Past Month's statistics were removed to shorten figure.)

This figure tells us how strong the competition is for certain terms. It is going to be quite impossible for a small pet shop to own the first term, "pet supplies." PetSmart.com owns the first position in the search results and will likely not be unseated. A term such as "discounted pet supplies" would make it easier for a small business to be listed in the search results.

- The next decision to tackle is deciding how many campaigns to run. Instead of using "pet supplies," which is such a broad search term, it would be better to use terms such as "discount pet supplies," "wholesale pet supplies," and "online pet supplies" and set up several AdWord campaigns. This strategy of having separate campaigns makes it easier to track results.
- The remaining step of our paid advertising includes writing a powerful, eye-catching ad that compels the searcher

Keywords	Global Monthly Search Volume
pet supplies	246,000
pet supplies plus	49,500
plus pet supplies	49,500
pet supplies wholesalers	12,100
wholesalers pet supplies	12,100
pet supplies on line	9,900
pet supplies online	9,900
online pet supplies	9,900
discounted pet supplies	8,100
pet supplies discounted	8,100

FIGURE 9.3—Google Keyword Tool: Google.com/select/KeywordToolExternal

to click on the advertisement. Here's where the marketing person earns his keep. The title of the paid ad can only be 25 characters. The actual ad is two lines of 35 characters each. There is an option for creating image ads as well as text ads.

Setting the bid amount for the search term you want to use requires time and experience. How much is the company willing to spend to have a prospect click on its ad is the question that needs to be answered over time. Google, however, does supply some helpful tools that make this process easier.

Google has a Conversion Tracking tool as well. Many companies are unaware this tool is turned off by default and needs to be activated. Some businesses are able to save 30 to 40 percent of their ad budget by activating this tool and using it to sharpen their campaigns.

Campaign stats such as Clicks, Impressions, CTR, Cost Conversion, Cost/Conversion, or Conversion Rate haven't been touched here. Perry Marshall and Brian Todd put out a good book (Ultimate Guide to Google AdWords) on how pay-per-click campaigns work. Don't venture into the pay-per-click arena untrained. Let the experts do it. It's not that you cannot learn how to execute PPC well. It's a matter of running the business or becoming a PPC expert. You may not have time to devote to both endeavors.

Long term, PPC can drain your budget because there is always going to be someone with more money playing against you. PPC is, however, a good startup philosophy when waiting for SEO to take hold. Search engine optimization usually takes three to four months to kick in. SEO is the process of placing important terms, keywords, or key phrases in the headers, web page code, and web page content to improve a web page's placement in search results. SEO, or search engine optimization, will be covered in the next section. PPC campaigns could be run until the organic terms move to the top of Page 1. Then the AdWord campaigns should be turned off.

There are times when paid search makes sense. Three come to mind. First, when you cannot seem to capture a key term or phrase from the competition that you believe is vital to your web presence through organic search methods. Second, when the ROI is paying off for the time, energy, and budget you have invested. You do not need a degree from the Wharton School of Business to figure out you are spending more money than you are making with paid search. The fact will be obvious sooner than you might think. Granted, there are people who say, "I didn't know a thing about PPC. I just jumped in, figured it out, and now I'm making a fantastic return." These are rare ventures. More people have a story such as, "I didn't know how to run PPC campaigns. I jumped in with a $1,000 budget and before I knew what happened, I lost my shirt." The good paid-search people earn their money. The third reason for using paid search is in conjunction with search engine optimization. During the time natural search is kicking in, paid search can be used to attract sales and test keyword campaigns. As the terms start appearing in the natural results on page 1, the paid search for the same terms can be turned off.

To find a good paid search firm do your homework. Ask around. Get references. One company had a so-called PPC expert running the campaigns and then hired someone who really knew what to do. The client's bottom line improved after the new guy took over control of the AdWord campaigns:

· The monthly ad spend was lower by 40 percent.
· There was an almost 60 percent (57.9 percent) increase in visitor conversions.
· The cost for converting a visitor into a customer was decreased by 46.1 percent.

The Pros and Cons of Pay-per-Click	
Pros	**Cons**
• Immediate results	• Steep learning curve
• Increase audience	• Search term competition
• Sharpen marketing message	• Can be time consuming
• Temporary marketing method until SEO kicks in	• There's no end to the expense
• Target market	• Budget constraints

- The cost per click (what the company paid each time a visitor clicked on one of its ads) was lowered by 15.1 percent.
- The new guy achieved 75 percent of the conversions in one-and-a-half months that the previous one had achieved in three.
- Some budget figures will put things in perspective:
- The business spent between $6,000 and $30,000 a month for the ad spend and campaign management.
- The campaigns produced between 50 to 250 leads per month.
- The cost of converting a prospect into a customer was $120.

Outcome-Based Marketing: Pay-per-Click

- *Inputs.* The search terms, ad titles, ad content, and landing pages.
- *Activities.* The ad placement in the search listings, tuning the ad title and content, tuning the landing pages, tuning the pricing, and working to boost the Quality Score.
- *Masses.* All those that view the ads.
- *Leads.* Those that click through to the landing page and do not act are lost opportunities. Those that take some form of action based on the ad copy can be considered leads.

- *Outcome targets.* Perhaps the monthly ad budget is $10,000 to $12,000. The outcome target is 70 trial signups per month with 25 becoming new customers.
- *Outcome indicators.* Google AdWords and Analytics can be used to measure the campaign's success.

BE **STRATEGIC**

▶ Don't just concentrate on ad click-throughs, but on which AdWords produce actual conversions.

▶ AdWord campaigns need constant attention. The good ads will eventually dry up. Be ready to substitute new terms and new offers.

Search Engine Optimization (SEO): Attract Visitors Already Looking for You

"The seeking is the goal and the search is the answer."

—Anonymous

Search engine optimization is the fine art of tuning a website's content so people searching for "whole bean coffee" can find your site before they locate your competition's website. Search engine optimization takes time, talent, and patience to be successful. Successful search engine optimization is not instantaneous.

Optimizing a website takes into account both the code the reader does not see and the text on the page the reader does notice. The code that makes up the web page has to include the keywords. The page content, what the reader actually sees, also needs to include the keywords. SEO certainly includes much more: where the keywords are placed on the web page, how many times each term is used in the text, the terms in a bold font, the

*Does being
listed anywhere
on page 1
pay off?*

terms used in the page names, or paragraph titles, and so forth. Yet this cursory look at search engine optimization (SEO) gives you the main idea.

Attracting the right predisposed visitors should not be left to chance because getting listed on page 1 of the major search engines takes deliberation and know-how. A study by Search Engine Watch gives us this insight: The top three spots get a 62.66 percent share of visitor click-throughs while those "above the fold," positions 1 through 5, earn 73.55 percent of the clicks by searchers. As one can see, being listed anywhere on page 1 is not the same as being listed in the first five positions on page 1.

A search strategy might include:

· Visitor statistics
· Search term tracking
· Web page optimization
· Keyword density analysis
· Link building programs
· Website assessments
· Competitor evaluations

Organic search is all about getting the right terms to page 1 of the major search results; we might as well say Google when we think major search engines. The rest of the pack is trailing far behind. Nearly 72 percent of searchers use Google, 14 percent use *Yahoo!* and Bing comes in at 9 percent as the preferred search tool.

Most optimization experts certainly have the talent to push terms to page 1, but are the terms they push the ones that will pay off? For example, let's say 390 people search for "corporate accounts payable" each month and 6,600 searchers look for "accounts payable manager." It would be more beneficial for a company to own "accounts payable manager" because thousands more people look for that term. Of course, it takes more effort to push the most sought-after terms to the top of page 1. Before the search engine optimization strategy starts, set the goals. They might be:

· Increase current visitor traffic by 100 percent over the next six months
· Increase the number of backlinks by 2,500
· Increase the number of terms appearing on page 1 to 30
· Identify the company's top 20 terms and move all of them to "above the fold" on page 1

Watch the terms weekly. It can easily take three to four months to start to see good results on the placement of terms on page 1. Adjust the SEO strategy if necessary, but not too often. If

The Pros and Cons of SEO

Pros	Cons
• Increases audience	• Steep learning curve
• Sharpens marketing message	• Search term competition
• Gain more targeted traffic	• Can be time consuming
• Improves website position in search listings	• Results take time
• Causes content to be targeted	• At the mercy of the search engine algorithms
• Results can be measured	• Hard to predict click volumes
• Can be affordable	
• Promotion that doesn't sleep	
• Long-term positioning in search results	
• Navigable by search engines	
• Results are more permanent	

results are not forthcoming over an extended period, perhaps six to nine months, the optimization person may need to be shown the door.

Some SEO firms ask that a contract be signed for one year. Avoid those deals. If they can do what they say they can do, why are they asking for a binding contract?

Outcome-Based Marketing: SEO

- *Inputs.* The search terms, optimized web pages, and themed backlinks.
- *Activities.* The tuning of search terms, fresh web content, web pages, backlink campaigns.
- *Masses.* Visitors to the website and referred visitors.
- *Leads.* Visitors that take some action to move the relationship to the next level.
- *Outcome targets.* Increase unique visitor traffic by 20 percent per month for the next four months. Increase the number of visitors taking some action by 8 to 10 percent per month.
- *Outcome indicators.* Measurements can be taken with Google Analytics, Stat Counter.com, or VisiStat. com.

BE **STRATEGIC**

- ▶ Search engine optimization, like brain surgery, cannot be learned over a few weekends. Hire an expert. Demand results. Check references and past results.
- ▶ Don't go after the top terms to start with; you'll be fighting your competitors uphill. Pick terms that have a moderate following. Gain some ground. Own those terms and then go after the 900-pound guerrillas.

Chapter 10

Making Learning Easier on a Budget

"Money is a terrible master but an excellent servant."

—P. T. Barnum

THIS CHAPTER COVERS VIRTUAL EVENTS AND WEBINARS. LEARN HOW each of these mediums can play a role in prospecting, lead generation, customer care, training, and lead nurturing.

The days of renting white vans and dragging endless trade show paraphernalia to out-of-town hotels and conference centers is coming to an end. Why not invite customers and prospects to virtual events? There are no travel expenses or lost time incurred by either party and the ROI is better to boot. See if virtual events are for your organization.

The presenter should be interesting to listen to and well-versed in the subject being discussed.

Webinars can be presented at specific dates and times or people can attend an on-demand event at their convenience. Webinars are inexpensive, interactive, and can be held from anywhere. Audiences can participate by asking questions during or after the presentation or by taking polls during the lecture. It's important to keep the webinar presentation moving at a reasonable pace.

Learn how to use webinars to enhance the training environment.

Virtual Events: Stay Home and Attend Web Events

"We hope to attract anyone and everyone who wants to participate in our events."

—ANA GUERRIERO

Attending or launching a virtual trade show can generate leads. Traveling to conferences and trade shows are lost practices. Companies can no longer sustain the cost of presenting at these shows nor can they afford to have key people out of the office for extended periods of time. Virtual events are replacing marketing and lead generation efforts at trade shows.

Three well-known virtual event vendors are UnisFair.com, 6Connex.com, and INXPO.com (see Figure 10.1). Each vendor has similar products and services, yet they differ in the delivery of those solutions and "the visitor" experience.

A virtual event or conference is delivered over the web. Attendees stay in their office and view the happenings on their laptop or desktop computer. Think of never taking a plane to get to some distant hotel or conference center, never leaving the comfort of your office. Virtual events include the following services:

- Keynote speakers
- Exhibitors
- Special interest groups

FIGURE 10.1—UNISFAIR, 6Connex, and INXPO

- Increasing brand awareness
- Generating customer loyalty
- Social gatherings
- Knowledge transfer
- Networking

Virtual events may even have more to offer than live conferences or trade shows. Live events are a place to connect with company executives and their technical gurus, but someone is always left back at the office. In the virtual realm, no one needs to stay behind. Everyone can be available to conference attendees. Virtual get-togethers return a better ROI. A small company can have instant global or national reach. They provide a faster time-to-market as well as a reduced carbon footprint.

Vitual trade shows provide metrics: What sessions did the visitor attend? What product booths did they stop by? What speakers did they listen to? What collateral did they download? Did they record their show experience? These behavioral metrics

Real-life trade shows never provide visitor behavioral metrics.

are probably the most important factors for the organization that put on the show.

Of course, there are no opportunities to spy on the competition at a virtual show. But if your competitors put on a virtual conference and the attendance is open to the public, then let the war games begin.

Take a look at the virtual products and services these vendors offer to understand if it makes sense for your organization to go virtual:

- *Web conferencing.* If you want a more polished presentation broadcast to an unlimited audience, then webcasting is the answer. Applications such as WebEx™ or GoToMeeting® are web conferencing applications used to conduct meetings, training, or presentations over the web.
- *Virtual booth.* Think of having a show booth that is set up 24/7 across the globe—that's a virtual booth. Clients and prospects can stop by and pick up product materials (whitepapers, data sheets, podcasts, product demos) or announcements on new products or services while you're creating an engaging awareness of your company.

  Every time someone clicks on anything in your booth (a piece of collateral, whitepaper, or sales brochure), it's recorded. This means you receive big results with little investment.
- *Virtual theater.* Think of setting up a virtual theater where customers and prospects can check what's playing and stop back to view the latest webinars or presentations. You can do both scheduled and on-demand events with Q&A sessions. Use your virtual theater to generate revenue and qualified leads while your staff is busy working on other business channels.
- *Virtual corporate events.* Hold strategy sessions locally or around the world. Invite the press to your virtual event. These sessions could relate to earnings calls, key product

announcements, or annual analyst-day events. No travel to schedule. No expense reports to fill out. You can be home for dinner with your family.

· *Virtual trade shows.* Collaborate with resellers or partners to sponsor a virtual event. Attendees can listen to live or on-demand keynote presentations or workshops. In addition to speaking with booth reps and other show attendees, they can download materials and register at virtual booths.

· *Virtual career fairs.* These virtual job fairs allow people looking for a new assignment to spend their time and money wisely. The company provides an effective platform in order to talk with interested students, job candidates, and potential employee prospects.

· *Virtual communities.* Instantly connect employees from around the globe and save the cost and time of traveling to physical meetings by initiating a virtual community. Receive instant feedback on new product roll-outs or other company proposals. The community never ends and provides an opportunity for employees to enroll in educational sessions and social networking.

· *Virtual office.* Create a virtual representation of your organization's physical space. Your office door is *really* always open. Prospects, employees, customers, and partners can stop by, interact with you, drop off materials, or pick up a package left for them. Greatly reduce lost time, travel costs, office rent, and associated costs.

· *Virtual product launches.* Use these events to introduce new offerings, services, or products. Product experts can be on hand to demonstrate the features and answer questions. Product launch attendees can download technical and marketing content.

· *Virtual PR/analysts.* Hold global or regional communication events in a virtual environment with press and analysts.

Participants can talk one on one or one to many for strategy sessions, earnings calls, product announcements, or annual analyst day events.

- *Developer conferences.* Build community among your developers by offering virtual developer conferences. Use these virtual events to train and educate engineers and developers on the latest technologies and platforms.
- *Training programs/seminars.* Why send employees across the country to attend necessary training meetings? Use virtual training labs to deliver e-learning sessions on demand or at specific times.
- *Sales conferences.* Inspire your sales force and encourage teambuilding in a virtual environment for sales teams in multiple geographic regions and global markets.
- *Virtual channel events.* Use these virtual gatherings to create a high-performance sales team, provide a systematic approach to analyzing and landing opportunities, develop a balanced pipeline, boost skill deficiencies, coordinate tactics, raise collateral awareness, and share key metrics.

Now let's turn our attention to the services virtual event companies offer to jump-start us into this virtual world:

- *Event management.* "Real" event experience aside, you may want to enlist the services of a "virtual" event manager to ensure the event platform, visitor experience, event production, marketing, exhibitor areas, and audience recruitment are top notch.
- *Branding.* Branding the virtual event in the attendee's mind is all-important to corporate identity, positioning, and messaging.
- *Product services.* Many of the virtual vendors provide an event director who helps with management, configuration, and setup of the virtual event.

· *Exhibitor/sponsor recruitment.* Many exhibitors are not familiar with virtual events and need help acclimating to the new space. The virtual vendors can assist in this process to ensure the exhibitors have a rewarding experience and have positive results to show for their participation.

· *Audience/attendance generation.* Need help with attendance? Virtual vendors can help you reach millions of prospects in your business space.

· *The experience.* The overall experience determines the event's success. Designing the right environment, attracting the best audience, providing automated registration and thank-you confirmation, engaging the attendee, promoting communication, and offering exhibits and presentation that have value all come into the mix.

The process of choosing a competent virtual vendor does not differ much from outsourcing a consulting assignment. It would be best to find a virtual vendor that has been around awhile. Choose one that is a leader in the virtual industry, who offers all the services; one that has a good understanding of the technologies in use and has put on events for other companies in your business space and can show positive results.

The Pros and Cons of Virtual Events	
Pros	Cons
• No traveling	• Loss of personal contact
• Dramatic cost savings	• Learning curve
• Increased participation	• Loss of the "live" event
• Higher productivity	• Loss of networking opportunities
• Better data capture	• Presentation constraints
• Better control where the crowd goes and what they see	• Loss of audience interaction

Outcome-Based Marketing: Virtual Events

- *Inputs.* Conference speakers, demonstrations, presentations, training workshops, special interest group discussions, roundtables, etc. Of course, the visual effects of the conference will be big.
- *Activities.* Conference promotion as well as other marketing activities.
- *Masses.* Those that are touched by the marketing efforts.
- *Leads.* Those that register for the event, whether they attend or not. Those that take some action, perhaps download collateral, attend presentations or workshops, or sign up to receive more information.
- *Outcome targets.* The attendance target might be 200 attendees. Perhaps 8 to 10 percent download collateral. Another 65 percent attend presentations or workshops. Then 12 percent sign up to receive follow-up information.
- *Outcome indicators.* The virtual vendors produce excellent visitor behavioral stats.

BE **STRATEGIC**

▶ Design a virtual event that can be scaled. Start out moderately and then ramp things up.

▶ Compelling handouts will be one key to gathering useful attendee behavioral movements.

Webinars: Move Clients Down the Sales Funnel

"You can observe a lot by just watching."

—Yogi Berra

Webinars (or web conferencing or online virtual meetings) are an inexpensive way to connect with prospects and customers.

They can be one of the most cost-effective marketing tools for lead generation as well as for reaching out to an installed base of customers or channel partners. They also serve as platforms for continuing education, new product announcements, and virtual meeting venues. On-demand webinars (webinars that have been prerecorded) give audience members the opportunity and convenience of watching when it fits into their schedule.

Check out a new, free webinar service called DimDim.com (Figure 10.2). Ten people can meet at no cost, while 50 people price out at $25 per month and 1,000-person events cost $65. Its business model (100-person meetings) prices out at $396/per year.

A successful webinar is one that presents topical information in a concise, interesting, and meaningful format. It leaves the audience anticipating "what's next." It has audience members answering questions out loud from their cubicles. A successful webinar encourages audience participants to ask questions in the Chat window and to answer live questionnaires. Most importantly, a good webinar should generate opportunities and additional business for the organization.

FIGURE 10.2—DimDim free online meetings

A webinar strategy might be:

- Generate a one-hour (50-minute presentation/10-minute Q&A) webinar presentation.
- Create a topical eight-question questionnaire for inclusion in webinar production.
- Work up complete production services, including presentation, audio, and video "venue," pre-event outreach, sign-up logistics, pre-show reminders, and post-show outreach.

A good length for a webinar is 50 minutes. Forty minutes of content followed by a 10 minute Q&A session.

Estimates are that 50 percent of registrants actually attend a live webinar. Increase your attendance by offering on-demand presentations. People can watch when they want, where they want.

Webinars can also be used for training, sales, meetings, and events and to improve an organization's support functions, whether inside the company or out to its customer base:

- *Training.* Save training time, travel time, and the traditional costs of educating employees and customers. Reach more people in less time. Share your content over the web. Everyone sees the same thing and can participate in question-and-answer sessions.
- *Sales.* Present live demonstrations to clients and prospects. Everyone stays engaged, unlike during a phone conference call. Live demonstrations make a better training tool for your sales force. You can even use this tool to finalize contracts and proposals.
- *Meetings.* This online vehicle is perfect for exchanging ideas and making decisions. It also cuts down on e-mail traffic. Have your next status meeting online to move your project along faster.

· *Events*. Deliver engaging multimedia events to clients, customers, or prospects. Present your ideas in real time—globally. Interact with all the attendees and have questions and concerns answered promptly. Record the event for viewing at later dates to save time and money.

Webinar Dos

· Optimize the webinar campaign to draw interested visitors.
· Give concrete examples.
· Have goals for the webinar.
· Record the webinar so people can view it on-demand.
· Keep the webinar pace moving.
· Keep things interesting.
· Make sure there is value in the presentation content.
· Have an agenda and stick to it.
· Have a professional look.
· Allow time for questions.

Webinar Don'ts

· Don't talk in circles.
· Don't use catchy titles that are meaningless.
· Don't talk about what you don't know.
· Don't exaggerate success stories.
· Don't pitch your product or service at the beginning; the middle works best.
· Don't drone on and on.
· Don't badmouth the competition.
· Don't use graphics people can't read.

Outcome-Based Marketing: Webinars

· *Inputs*. The webinar materials and the presenters.
· *Activities*. The promotion for the webinar. Perhaps ads are

The Pros and Cons of Webinars	
Pros	**Cons**
• Inexpensive	• Presenter is seen as just a voice
• Connectability	• Participants cannot converse
• Interactivity	• Loss of synergy
• Greater participation	• Pictures and thoughts cannot convey
• Can be conducted almost anywhere	every thought
• Easy to learn	• Ambient noise
	• Probable distractions
	• Different learning styles
	• Speaker cannot tell if audience is
	listening

placed on the website and blog, an e-mail campaign is launched, and social media is used to promote the event.

· *Masses.* Those that are reached with the advertising message.
· *Leads.* Those that sign up and do not attend the webinar, and those that sign up and do attend the presentation.
· *Outcome targets.* To have 120 people sign up for the webinar with 50 people eventually attending.
· *Outcome indicators.* The sign-up process and the webinar stats tells you all you need to know about the attendees.

BE **STRATEGIC**

▶ Keep the webinar interesting ... interesting ... interesting.

▶ Partner with noncompetitive organizations to attract more viewers to the webinars. Each company sends out its own branded invites. Contact information remains confidential. It's a win-win situation for the presenters and the audience.

Putting the Word on the Street

"Life's too short to sell things you don't believe in."

—PATRICK DIXON

THIS CHAPTER DEALS WITH SENDING OUT PRESS RELEASES, DEVELOPING a newsletter that will be read, creating drip or nurturing campaigns using e-mail marketing, attracting more prospects with targeted landing pages and finally, using image sites to generate more leads.

Press releases serve several purposes: they help spread the word, they give a company another opportunity to be listed in search results, and they provide valuable backlinks to the website or blog. Learn what big companies have known for years about "dropping" press releases.

A simple, brief, concise newsletter is a great way to stay in touch with clients and customers. Newsletters can drain valuable resources—so count the cost before jumping into the publishing business. In this section, learn what it takes to publish a great newsletter that gets read. Newsletters can be informational, promotional, or relational. Find out if launching a newsletter is for you.

Learn how to use e-mail marketing campaigns to quickly and inexpensively test marketing messages and potential audience acceptance. Different prospect audiences are attracted by different offers, at different times, in different ways. Learn the ingredients of proven e-mail marketing campaign tactics. *Outcome-Based Marketing* does not encourage or condone the use of spam.

Landing pages are also known as "lead capture" or "squeeze pages." Landing pages speak to a specific topic and direct visitors to take a specific action. Landing pages increase the conversion rate of e-mail marketing and pay-per-click campaigns dramatically. Learn what it takes to build an effective landing page.

Upload photos from sales events or company picnics to let customers have an inside look at the organization. Upload pictures of upcoming product launches. Photo sites let companies reach new audiences. Make movie posters promoting your upcoming webinar series. Take photos of recognition ceremonies. Show off the corporate campus. Discover if image sites can increase your company's awareness.

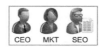

Press Releases: Publish This!

"For me, words are a form of action, capable of influencing change."

—INGRID BENGIS

Press releases can be a cost-effective way of getting your message out to your audience. Press releases level the playing field among large and small businesses. Large corporations use press releases (Figure 11.1) to notify their clients and potential customers every time a significant news or product event happens. Small companies, even one-person operations, should be using the same methodology. Each time a new service or product is added, enlarged office space is sought, or someone is added to the organization, a press release should be fired off.

Of course, the message ought to be timely. "For Immediate Release" means exactly what it says. Do not send something off when you finally have the time. Procrastinators should forget about using press releases all together. Timing is everything if you want someone's "immediate" attention. Focus on the benefits to the reader and not the fact that there is a new company car to drive around. Press releases need to be brief and to the point—both online and off.

FIGURE 11.1—Press release sample

"Dropped" is a media expression much like the saying "a newspaper edition has hit the streets." It means the press release has gone out. Once the press release goes out you'll want to track its success in reaching the "right" audience. Some PR websites offer to track press releases. It's good to know how the different services are penetrating your market.

Optimized press releases and landing pages are ways to draw more visitors to your website.

Optimizing a press release is not much different from adjusting the words on a web page to make sure as many people as possible searching for the information find that page. Media outlets that want to store large amounts of information for quick retrieval attach keywords or key phrases to the information.

If you were sending out a press release for a new accounts payable software package, you would want to make sure to use words like "accounts payable," "accounts payable process," and "purchase to pay" in the title and body of the release. When you post a release at one of the online services, a question on the input form usually deals with what keywords you want associated with the release. When people go to these information portals, they'll find your release when using search terms such as "accounts payable."

Include links back to your website or blog in the press release because if there are these links on the press release, the increase in visitor numbers can be tallied. Send visitors to a landing page for a special offer such as viewing a webinar, and those statistics can be gathered as well.

Press releases show up in the search results when using engines such as Google and *Yahoo!* This can give you more of a presence on page 1 of search results *if* your website and the press release are strong enough.

A proven press release format includes the following seven items:

1. FOR IMMEDIATE RELEASE. Always capitalized to catch the reader's eye.
2. Contact Information. Company name, e-mail address, website, postal address, phone, fax, and cell number, if necessary.
3. Headline. A single sentence in boldface, easy-to-read type.
4. Dateline. The date and city the press release is issued from.
5. Lead Paragraph. A writer would call this paragraph the "hook," an introductory paragraph that draws the reader into the news story.
6. Copy. Give the facts, and nothing but the facts. Don't ramble. Make the details interesting to the reader.
7. Recap. This space is used for product specifications or a release date. Pull out the most important benefit to the reader and restate it here.

Now you have a good understanding of how to construct a press release that will attract the reader's attention and get your message heard. How and where do you find the right readers?

You can send the press release out to your own contact list, but to get expanded coverage nationally or globally you need to use press release distribution companies.

The top ten press release distribution companies in April 2010 were:

1. PRWeb.com
2. BusinessWire.com
3. MarketWire.com
4. OnlinePRNews.com
5. 24-7PressRelease.com
6. PR.com
7. PRLeap.com
8. eReleases.com
9. PRNewsWire.com
10. eWorldWire.com

Note: This list in no way implies endorsement of these services. You're on your own to vet them yourself.

The pricing and service levels of these media outlets vary quite a bit. So look around for the best price and fit for your news.

Check out the dozens of free press release websites and save marketing dollars.

Also make sure the message is going out to the right audience. Sending out a press release to 50,000 architects does a person selling software as a service (SaaS) little good.

Optimizing a press release helps locate the news when going to services like Google News or *Yahoo!* News. News.Google.com updates its 4,500 new sources *constantly* as does News.Yahoo.com. Millions of people check these two news services daily.

Proofread the release and then proofread it again. The last thing anyone wants is a prospect or client to see that small details are not important. Do not rely solely on you own eyes. Have at least two other people read the release before it goes out.

The Pros and Cons of Press Releases	
Pros	**Cons**
• Levels the playing field	• Some of your prospects may not be on the web
• Cost effective	
• Expands the audience	• Lost in the marketing noise
• More traffic to your site	• Clients/prospects may not search out press releases
• Backlinks	
• Build the brand	• You may not have enough newsworthy items to share on a regular basis
• Targeted audiences	
• Gain credibility	
• Increase keyword rankings	
• Increase search engine visibility	

Remember technology won't solve all your problems in this area. Spelling checkers won't catch words used the wrong way. They only care if the word was spelled correctly. Grammar checkers catch most bad sentence structure but they fall short when writing certain kinds of information, such as this technical masterpiece, for instance.

So stay on your toes. Pay attention to the smallest details. It's embarrassing when someone sends an e-mail to the editor letting her know the subject being expounded upon has been misspelled.

Outcome-Based Marketing: Press Release

- *Inputs.* An optimized press release.
- *Activities.* The press release submission process.
- *Masses.* Depends upon the media outlets that are reached.
- *Leads.* Those that take action based on the release.
- *Outcome targets.* Increases in visibility can be measured with press release pickup metrics. Those press release readers that take action can also be measured.
- *Outcome indicators.* Press release pickup metrics along with Google Analytics.

> ## BE **STRATEGIC**
>
> ▶ Use PressRelease.Grader.com to tweak your release before it goes out.
>
> ▶ Optimized press releases garner more audience attention.

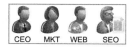

Newsletters: Write to Be Read

"Act as if you have already achieved your goal and it is yours."
—Dr. Robert Anthony

You might ask, "Do we really need another newsletter?" There are more daily, weekly, bi-weekly, and monthly newsletters out there than there are grains of sand on the beaches of the world. There are informative newsletters and sales flyers masquerading as newsletters. There are simple text and HTML-based newsletters. There are one-page newsletters and others that compete in length with the USS Constitution. Still, newsletters can and do provide a necessary link between customers and business owners.

Newsletters, first and foremost, are supposed to be timely, accurate, informative, breaking-news vehicles. Newsletters should have specific missions. There needs to be "news." A newsletter could be promotional or marketing oriented. It could be informative or relationship building. It is important to let the reader know one's intentions about the direction of the publication. If the newsletter is going to be informative, then keep it information-based and don't bore the reader with one sales promotion after another. If, on the other hand, the plan is to send out a relationship-building newsletter 11 months of the year and then publish a promotional one come spring, let readers know it's coming.

Newsletters can drain resources. Think back to the time you spent too much energy writing one more article, searching for a special quote, or mining some factoid. If the newsletter editor is not careful, the publication could be a drain on resources.

The best way to avoid exhausting assets is to focus on the "news." Not the frequency. Not the format. Not the fluff that sometimes finds its way into a publication. We've all had to endure the "quote-of-the-day," the "joke-of-the-day," or the "funny" anecdotal story that has absolutely nothing to do with the focal point of a newsletter. Keep it simple. Keep it newsworthy.

At first the decision to publish a newsletter looks easy. Competitors have newsletters, therefore I need one. Theirs come out monthly, so yours needs to be monthly. Theirs was HTML-based, so yours needs to look the same. Many first-time newsletter publishers have made this mistake. Launching a newsletter because their competition has one is not the right reason to have a publication.

Let's look at what goes into the decision to have a newsletter. It takes time, money, and energy to produce one that people look forward to reading, enjoy, and are willing to pass on to their friends and colleagues.

Before jumping into publishing a newsletter, ask yourself, "Is a newsletter for me?"

The first question to ask is, "Do I have news to share?" News is not something one person knows and the other person does not. That's knowledge. News is timely, practical, useful information a reader needs to know about.

If a company increased profits by 320 percent over the same time last year, that's news!

There are different styles of publications. If the intention of the bulletin is promotional, then it should only come out when there is a new service or product coming to market. Perhaps the new product or service is seasonal. In that case, then it makes sense to publish the newsletter at that appropriate time.

Use the newsletter to build relationships with clients. For example, if calls are coming in about specific problems with a product, then discuss the problem and solution in the upcoming newsletter. This is a win-win situation. Customers are grateful that someone is looking after their best interests and the number of support calls will certainly drop.

A periodic newsletter is a great way to stay in touch with customers and clients. It's not intrusive or time consuming. The customer can decide when to have the relationship, unlike a phone call, which can be seen as interruptive or intrusive at times.

The newsletter can be informative. You can discuss how a new technology may affect your customers' or prospects' business. Then bring customers up to speed on the new advancement. Give them honest information about how this improvement helps them deliver better service or generate more revenue.

Let's assume there are things you can share, information that's newsworthy. Let's further suppose the type of newsletter that will be published will be informative. What about the frequency of the publication?

One way to keep the reader's interest from one issue to the next is to write some two- and three-part stories. That's a good way to keep people coming back. There are also times when the information just cannot be crammed into one issue. Don't be restrictive. Give the information the space it deserves.

Newsletters need to come out on some schedule so people can anticipate receiving them. If the frequency is random, the reader's interest will wane.

A good approach is to start out slowly. Make sure there is time allocated to produce the newsletter and it's a good read, as we say in the business. Perhaps start out quarterly and then move to bi-monthly. People rarely complain about receiving useful news too often.

Maybe quarterly does the trick except when having a new service to offer. That's the perfect time for an "extra." Keep in mind, an Extra in the news business signals really big news and not an inventory reduction sale.

Suppose you decide to put the publication out monthly. Now it's time to discuss its format. If the readership likes to keep things simple, then you need to do the same. Don't make them install, download, or set any settings they do not already have established. People that read plain text newsletters are drawn in by the content not the style.

Editorial policy helps set the tone of the publication and keeps the news and readers on track. Here are some newsletter editorial issues to consider:

1. Should guest writers be invited to contribute from time to time? Don't look at their writing as competition.
2. Clients appreciate the editor going the extra mile to provide them with the very best advice and information.
3. Maybe an industry expert can be talked into sharing his or her insights.

What about advertising? Will clients or customers be able to advertise as long as their business does not infringe on your revenue stream? Advertising is a way to defray the cost of publishing the newsletter. Offering ad space to a guest writer is a goodwill gesture to people that may not want to do a newsletter but are still looking for ways to get their message out.

How about jokes or quotes? Try and resist. Keep it professional. If people want jokes, they'll visit joke websites or make a trip to Barnes & Noble.

Will sensitive business issues be openly discussed with the readership in "Letters to the Editor"? Say someone writes in and really has an axe to grind. Should the readership be exposed to that information?

Take some time to develop editorial policies that are livable and defendable.

How about doing a survey in the newsletter? A good survey early on in the publication's history can help set its direction and tone. Besides, people appreciate when asked for their opinion.

The sixth component of a good newsletter sometimes gets lost: staying on track. Be consistent. Don't put out a promotional newsletter when there is something to sell and then switch to information because there is something to say. Establish policies and follow them. If there are no editorial policies, format, frequency, or style guidelines, then the newsletter editor is likely to be swayed by the readership. Stay the course. Make significant changes only when the readers or publisher or both benefit.

Newsletters can serve their audience best by being a combination of information, relationship building, and marketing. Just make sure the reader understands where he or she is being taken by the newsletter.

Know the reader base. Don't take them for granted. Find out what the reader is interested in knowing or learning. Invite readers to respond. Ask for their opinion. Let the reader know the editor of the newsletter. Give them small bits of personal information from time to time. A person should let their personality show through the writing. It is much easier to build a relationship if each party shares information about themselves.

Don't make the reader search high and low for the unsubscribe process. Make it as simple as possible for someone to decline receiving any further mailings. It's good to put an "unsubscribe" link at the beginning as well as at the end of the newsletter. Don't be offended if someone opts-out. It happens.

Think about creating an archive of past issues. This is a good idea for two reasons. First, the reader won't have to worry about saving old issues; it is done for him. The second reason for archiving past newsletter issues is that it creates a need for people to come back to the website where the archive resides. Remember traffic, traffic, and traffic is what makes a website successful.

If a newsletter cannot be read within 15 minutes, it's destined for the recycle bin. It hurts, but it's the truth. This world is moving fast. People tend to segment their time with 15 minutes for this and 10 minutes for that. A good newsletter fits into how people structure their time. An 8-page newsletter will probably hit the Deleted Items folder faster than someone can say "Good Morning."

Let's assume the newsletter is the perfect length. How can one be sure people are reading it? A few people might send in a complimentary e-mail or ask a question, but that is going to be a very small percentage of the audience. What about the balance of the subscribers? Just because readers subscribe does not mean they're actually reading what was published.

There are services on the web that give insight into readership. Are the e-mail addresses valid? Are people opening the e-mail or deleting the newsletter? ConstantContact and iContact are services that help answer those questions.

As long as we're talking about sending out e-mails, let's chat about asking the recipient's permission before sending them your offer.

Seth Godin wrote a great book in 1999 titled *Permission Marketing*. As a matter of fact, he coined the phrase "permission marketing." Seth's point is that it makes more sense to ask someone's permission to send them something rather than filling their inbox or interrupting their day.

We might say permission marketing is asking our readers to opt-in or subscribe to the newsletter before assuming they want to be added to the circulation database.

The Pros and Cons of Newsletters	
Pros	**Cons**
• Increases customer retention	• Can be time consuming
• Increases customer loyalty	• Can be resource draining
• Regular contact	• Publishing deadlines
• Builds community	• Limited space
• Easy to deliver	• Fresh material
• Inexpensive	• Hard to keep going
• Easy to start	

People that don't ask readers to "opt-in" may be afraid of the truth. They don't want to know that only 13 percent of the e-mail addresses they are sending to are valid or actually care about what is being received. Doesn't it make more sense to talk to the people that want to hear from you or read what a person has to say? If only 200 customers want to hear the message, then talk to just those people. A person that does not want to hear does not want to buy as well.

Send out the inaugural issue and ask the interested parties to "opt-in" to continue receiving future installments.

Outcome-Based Marketing: Newsletters

- *Inputs.* Feature stories, tips and tricks, interesting articles, promotions, insights, surveys, polls, upcoming events, or guest writers.
- *Activities.* Writing the newsletter and the promotion to secure readership.
- *Masses.* Current customers, past customers, prospects, purchased e-mail lists, and partner lists.
- *Leads.* Leads are those newsletter readers that make a move to take the relationship to the next level. They may download an offer or sign up for a free trial. Just receiving and reading the newsletter won't do.
- *Outcome targets.* The newsletter needs to serve one or more specific, quantifiable (measurable) purposes: move the reader along the sales funnel, lessen support calls, increase website visits, boost free trials, or take advantage of downloadable offers.

BE **STRATEGIC**

- Be committed to publishing your newsletter before asking customers to commit to being faithful readers.
- Concentrate more on substance and content than format, fonts, and colors.

· *Outcome indicators.* Visits to newsletters on websites or blogs can be measured with Google Analytics. Newsletters delivered through e-mail marketing services can be measured by their service stats. Newsletters sent by direct mail can be measured by the actions readers take.

E-mail Marketing: The Drip, Drip, Drip of Your Marketing Message

"Did you ever feel like the whole world was going to a party and
your invitation got lost in the mail?"

—Anonymous

E-mail marketing is an inexpensive way to reach large and small audiences. The ramp-up time for an e-mail campaign is short. E-mail marketing gives an organization the opportunity to sharpen its marketing message until it finds the one that works best. E-mail campaigns can be personal and help strengthen customer relationships. E-marketing does not infer spam.

There are at least three variations of e-mail marketing campaigns (Figure 11.2) that companies tend to enlist:

1. Some companies purchase e-mail software such as EMS Bulk Email, Email Sender, Spryka Email, or 32-Bit Email Broadcaster and then launch and track their own campaigns.

2. Other organizations use e-mail services such as ConstantContact, iContact, BenchmarkEmail, or MailChimp to store their contact databases and e-mail templates. These services usually charge a monthly fee based on how many contacts are in the databases. They also

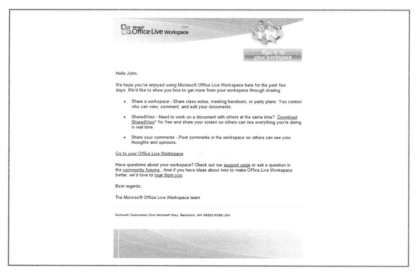

FIGURE 11.2—E-mail campaign sample

tell their clients how many e-mails bounced, were opened, and acted upon.

3. Still other businesses outsource their e-mail campaigns in their entirety. They hire a company and give them access to their contact databases. As a rule, companies pay a setup fee to the e-mail contractor and then so much per lead. A lead is usually someone who opens an e-mail and then takes an appropriate action—downloading a whitepaper for instance.

It is imperative that e-mail campaigns are professionally designed, launched, and tracked. Organizations should adhere to the CAN-SPAM Act of 2003 by giving prospects/customers the option of opting out or unsubscribing to the e-mail.

Look at two different e-mail campaigns to see what we can learn.

The first e-mail campaign is designed around a free trial offer from a SaaS (software as a service) software company. Prospects sign up for a 15-day free trial before deciding whether or not they want to subscribe. The company offering the free trial sends out eight e-mails during the free trial process. The prospects can opt-out of the e-mail campaign at any time. It does not affect their ability to complete the free trial. Here's how the eight e-mails are structured:

- E-mail 1. Sent out upon subscribing to the free trial. Confirms sign-up.
- E-mail 2. Sent out on Day 1. Welcomes user to the free trial process.
- E-mail 3. Sent out on Day 3. Focus on a major feature that benefits the prospect.
- E-mail 4. Sent out on Day 7. Focus on a major feature that benefits the prospect.
- E-mail 5. Sent out on Day 11. Focus on a major feature that benefits the prospect.
- E-mail 6. Sent out on Day 13. Focus on a major feature that benefits the prospect.
- E-mail 7. Sent out on Day 15. Lets prospect know the free trial is expiring.
- E-mail 8. Sent out on Day 17. Tells prospect of a special offer if purchase is made.

This e-mail campaign strategy is nonthreatening because the prospect can opt-out at any time. The e-mails keep the prospect engaged with compelling information about important benefit-driven features of the software product. At the end of the trial people can either subscribe to the software product or not.

Based on what you may be trying to accomplish, you could decide to send out fewer e-mails. If your company offers a 30-day trial, you may want to add an e-mail or two to keep the prospect engaged.

In the second scenario, the same SaaS company decides to send out a newsletter. It does not want to attach a newsletter to an e-mail because of the many stories people tell these days about viruses being attached to e-mails. The company decides to do the newsletter in HTML and embed it in the e-mail. To save readers time, it decides to send out a brief version of the newsletter in the actual e-mail and places the bulk of the newsletter copy on the company blog, allowing readers to scan the stories for what interests them and then click on the "see the full story" links to be taken to the blog.

The SaaS vendor wishes to reach three different audiences. It has a dead trial file, the Lazarus file, of 5,000 contacts. (These were people that either signed up for the free trial and never took it or started the trial and never finished.) The company wishes to see how many of these people can be re-engaged. The company's second list is of past customers, people that at one time subscribed to its software service but have since left. We'll call this the Past Customer file. The third list of contacts is of current customers and will be called the Current Customer file.

E-mail marketing campaigns give a business the ability to prototype, prototype, prototype at a very low cost, and little effort.

The newsletter will need to have slightly different messages because the audience relationships vary. The Lazarus contacts will receive the newsletter with a special free trial offer in which the first month of service is free. The Past Customer file people will receive the same newsletter with a special reactivation offer to see if they would come back. The current customers will receive just the newsletter.

An e-mail service such as VerticalResponse, iContact, or ConstantContact will be used to send out and track the campaign e-mails. The service will flag which e-mails are returned, unopened, opened, and which prospects clicked-through to the newsletter landing page.

There are some simple, but highly effective, e-mail strategies that can greatly affect the return on investment.

Most studies say the best day to send out e-mails is Tuesday through Thursday. This schedule gives people a chance to start their week on Monday, and it also leaves them free to wrap things up on Friday before the weekend.

Let's assume a percentage of the e-mails are not opened after being sent out on a Tuesday, Wednesday, or Thursday. Try changing the subject line in the e-mail to be a little more enticing. Some of the people that did not open the first e-mail will open the one with a more intriguing subject line. For those prospects that still have not opened one, send e-mails on different days, at different times, and with varying subject lines. Eventually there will be a group of prospects that just do not want to open your e-mails. So be it.

Now let's say people are opening the e-mail but not taking the offer for, perhaps, a whitepaper. Whitepapers will attract some people while repelling others. So change the offer to a case study, free webinar, or podcast. You'll have to find out what works for each individual group of prospects.

The Pros and Cons of E-Mail Marketing	
Pros	**Cons**
• Inexpensive	• May be lost in the crowd
• Short ramp-up time	• May be seen as spam
• Targeted audience	• May limit originality
• Sharpen marketing message	• May be seen as intrusive
• Builds customer loyalty	• May not be the right vehicle
• Builds customer retention	• May be difficult to keep going on a
• Personalization	regular basis
• Results can be measured	• May lack good information to share

A single e-mail with one offer will not appeal to the entire audience, nor will every campaign. But because e-mail campaigns get immediate results, either positive or negative, you'll know within a day or two what works and what does not. Change what's not working. Resist changing what is working.

Outcome-Based Marketing: E-Mail Marketing

- *Inputs.* The e-mail subject line, the content, landing page, and the offer.
- *Activities.* The e-mail campaign itself.
- *Masses.* Those reached by the e-mail campaign.
- *Leads.* The leads would be in different categories; those that open the e-mail, those that click-through to the offer, and those that take the offer.
- *Outcome targets.* Leads vary by industry. In the insurance industry, for example, 21 percent of e-mails are usually opened, with a click-through rate of 3 percent. (Stats compiled by MailChimp.com)
- *Outcome indicators.* Statistics will be compiled by e-mail campaign provider. Google Analytics may also be used.

> ## BE **STRATEGIC**
>
> ◗ Prototype, prototype, prototype
> ◗ Successful e-mail campaigns eventually stall out. Make moderate changes until the results start to turn around.

Landing Pages: Tightening Up the Marketing Message

"Your seat cushion can be used for flotation, and in the event of an emergency water landing, please take them with our compliments."

—AIRLINE ANNOUNCEMENT

E-mail campaigns and landing pages go hand-in-hand. Custom landing pages continue the tailored message of the e-mail campaign. This marketing tactic produces higher conversion rates than sending the prospect to a generic page on the company website. There are fewer distractions when using a landing page than sending a prospect to the homepage of the corporate website.

A landing page should have "one" function—to get the prospect to take action; to download the whitepaper, sign up for the virtual event, or subscribe to the newsletter.

When businesses run e-mail or pay-per-click campaigns or invite prospects to webinars or virtual events, they use what are called landing pages. A page dedicated to the event being promoted. Landing pages are sometimes called squeeze pages. It's best to route visitors to a single page to keep their attention on what's being talked about and to lessen distractions.

Landing pages (Figure 11.3) that have mixed messages garner poorer results. Landing pages that have links to other resources along with the offer cloud the discussion. The visitor to the page

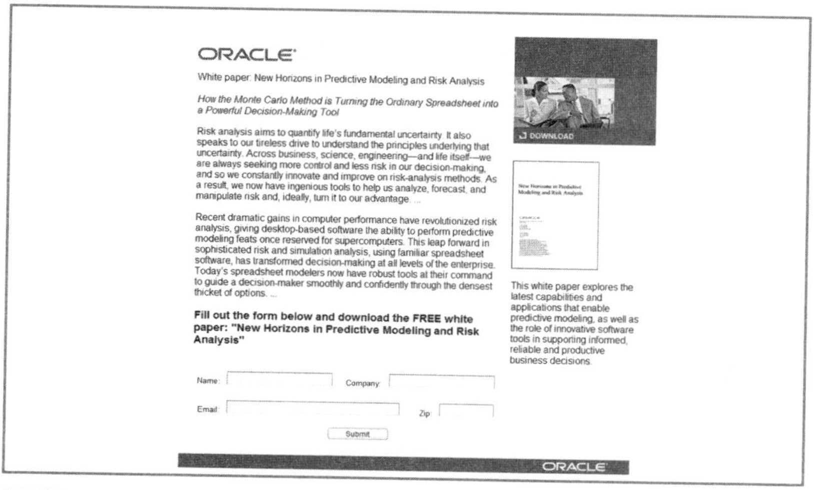

FIGURE 11.3—Landing page illustration

becomes confused or distracted and does not take the desired action.

Figure 11.3 is an example of a landing page that asks the prospect to enter some personal information in order to download a specific whitepaper.

The headline on the landing page should be what the visitor is expecting. If she clicked on a pay-per-click ad that talked about Predictive Modeling and Risk Analysis then the landing page header had better highlight that topic.

The information on the landing page should be clear, concise, and to the point; not more than one-half page. The personal information asked for in the form should only be that which is necessary. If you do not plan on calling the person, do not ask for her phone number. If her title at the company has no bearing on the campaign then leave it off the form. The more information asked for the higher the objection is raised against giving any information.

Personalizing the e-mail with the prospect's name increases the response rate.

The Pros and Cons of Landing Pages	
Pros	**Cons**
• Simple set up	• Hard to get good Quality Score from Google
• Allows preselling	• Tuning content and offers takes time
• Creates more flexibility	• Insufficient data collection
• Tightens the marketing message	• Limited elements can be tested
• Fewer distractions	
• Keyed toward specific audiences	
• Captures attention	
• Captures more responses	
• Provides a good test bed for A/B testing	

Landing pages are perfect for what is known as A/B testing. Two versions of the landing page are created and visitors are randomly sent to one page or the other. This is a quick and easy way to tell if the content is compelling enough and if the offer is what prospects are looking to acquire.

Outcome-Based Marketing: Landing Pages

- *Inputs.* The landing page messaging and the offer.
- *Activities.* How visitors are driven to the landing page. They might come from e-mail campaigns, PPC, or social media tactics.
- *Masses.* Those people reached by the marketing efforts.
- *Leads.* Those people that take some action to move the relationship forward.
- *Outcome targets.* Based on the click-through rate to the landing page suppose you want to convert 8 to 10 percent of those arriving at the page.
- *Outcome indicators.* Google Analytics will tell you what you need to know.

BE **STRATEGIC**

- ▶ Focus on asking the landing page reader to take one action.
- ▶ Remember landing pages are there to bring the prospect along in the informational process—not the selling process.

Image Sites: A Picture Is Still Worth 6,173 Characters— or 1,000 Words

"Pictures are for entertainment, messages should be delivered by Western Union."

—Samuel Goldwyn

Image and photo sites work well to showcase award ceremonies or company events. Organizations can display their campuses and highlight their facilities. These sites give businesses the opportunity to brag about their new product lines. Businesses need to leverage these venues where it makes sense.

The photo cloud from Flickr shown in Figure 11.4 gives you an idea of the types of images being uploaded these days. As you can see, the uploaded pictures are tagged with names of people, places, or things.

Dave Rosen posted 44 reasons (on his blog B2BFormula.com) why companies should consider using photo sites. He split his reasoning between which photos should be posted and which strategies should be employed by the businesses. A few of his suggestions follow. Upload pictures that show:

· Executives giving speeches with links to the transcript
· Movie posters promoting your webinars, podcasts, and YouTube channel
· Product photos

animals architecture art asia australia autumn baby band barcelona beach berlin bike bird birds birthday black blackandwhite blue bw california canada canon car cat chicago china christmas church city clouds color concert dance day de dog england europe fall family fashion festival film florida flower flowers food football france friends fun garden geotagged germany girl girls graffiti green halloween hawaii holiday house india iphone ireland island italia italy japan july kids la lake landscape light live london love macro me mexico model mountain mountains museum music nature new newyork newyorkcity night nikon nyc ocean old paris park party people photo photography photos portrait raw red river rock san sanfrancisco scotland sea seattle show sky snow spain spring street summer sun sunset taiwan texas thailand tokyo toronto tour travel tree trees trip uk urban usa vacation vintage washington water wedding white winter yellow york zoo

FIGURE 11.4—Flickr photo cloud

- Company events
- Customer recognition ceremonies
- Maps showing corporate offices or campuses
- Covers of thought leadership pieces, whitepapers, and case studies with links to the actual reports

Approach photo sites strategically by:

- Using press release photos
- Highlighting conferences, tradeshows, or other important gatherings
- Using geotag photos of company locations, facilities, or projects
- Keeping a watchful eye on the competition
- Sharing for prospects and stakeholders
- Encouraging customers to take pictures of themselves using your product

The photo cloud from Flickr shown in Figure 11.4 gives you an idea of the types of images being uploaded these days. As you can see, the uploaded pictures are tagged with names of people, places, or things.

Each site offers a different level of service, community, and support. Some of the features offered are free while others incur a cost.

Properly tag all the images on your business website or blog so they show up in QWiki.com or images.google.com.

- *Features.* Pro, premium, and upgraded account levels, free accounts or free trials, safe filters, spam filters, create your own web page, batch photo uploading, single photo uploading, viewer comment posting per photo, file a complaint, invite history, and photo printing service.
- *Community.* Control public viewing; create photosets; form private groups; have most commented photos section,

The Pros and Cons of Image Sites	
Pros	**Cons**
• Reach new audiences	• Poor customer service?
• Meet prospects on neutral ground	• Virus? Spyware?
• Positive reviews	• Negative reviews
• Give prospects a conference snapshot	• Stiff competition
• Share company events with the public	• Lost in the marketing noise
	• Loss of branding

most recent photos section, most visited members section, and tags or keywords, and support weblog, blog, or online journal.

· *Support.* Phone support, FAQ, tutorials, user forum, e-mail address, contact form, table of contents, and e-mail newsletter.

You'll need to look over the features, functions, support, and pricing to make the choice that suits your needs and budget.

To start, look around at the more popular images sites and see if your ideal prospects are there. If they are, then you belong there. You might also look to see if similar products are present. It does not matter if the competition has a presence if your ideal prospects are not there. Let the competition waste the effort. You only need to be where your ideal prospects congregate.

BE **STRATEGIC**

▶ After uploading pictures make sure to blog or tweet about them.

▶ Seed as many sites as practical to expand your audience reach.

Chapter 12

Which Companies Are Being Talked About, Trashed, or Touted?

"Nothing is swifter than a rumor."

—Horace

C OMPANIES NO LONGER CONTROL THE "MESSAGE." WITH THE ADVENT of Review and Comment sites, consumers can go to these sites and rave or rant about a product they just purchased. If companies turn a blind eye to these conversations, there may be damage done that cannot be easily nullified. Companies should fess up to their mistakes and reassure consumers that they have their best interests at heart.

Epinions.com and Yelp.com, two of the more popular review and rating sites popping up on the web, are places where you may or may not want your company to be found. Customers and clients can drop by these sites and either praise or pan a company's product or service.

So companies are no longer totally in control of their own brand simply because people can speak out and be heard at these sites.

These sites do cater more to the B2C crowd. Epinions's consumers can talk about cars, books, movies, music, computers, electronics, home and garden, office supplies, sports, travel, and more. Figure 12.1, for example, is a sample review of Apple iPad (16 GB) Wi-Fi (MB292LL/A) Tablet PC. No one needs an account to read the current postings on the site, but an account needs to be created to add posts. The profile requires a username, e-mail address, and password. (Yelp has the same posting requirements. Creating a profile requires a first and last name, password, e-mail address, zip code, and country. Birth date and gender are optional fields.)

Don't use these sites to berate a company or post false accusations. That's just plain unprofessional. If you need to let off steam, write the company a letter.

Epinions deals with services as well as products: shopping, restaurants, health and medical, food, beauty, home services, event planning, arts and entertainment, nightlife, automotive, hotels and travel, education, real estate, pets, financial services, and more. Figure 12.2 shows a sample review of Denver's Music Venues.

A business review site is surely in the offing for professional

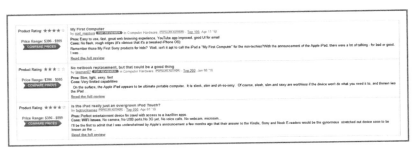

FIGURE 12.1—Review of Apple's iPad

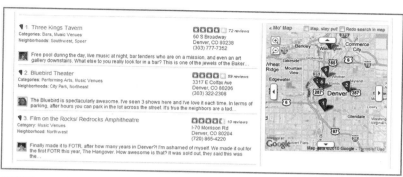

FIGURE 12.2—Review of Denver's Music Venues

services such as consulting, project management, business development, sales, marketing, search engine optimization, and public relations.

It does little good for a company to salt these sites with glowing reviews of its own services or products. Let the product or service stand on its own. If there's problem with a service or product, fix it. If there are unsatisfied customers, work to satisfy them. In truth, these sites can be a great way for companies to gain

The Pros and Cons of Review and Comment Sites	
Pros	Cons
• Reach a new audience	• Information may not be accurate
• Find out what consumers are thinking	• Someone may have an axe to grind and put up false reviews
• Handle bad reviews that may not be posted on the corporate site	• Cannot control the conversation
• Competitive advantage	• The company may not be able to stay ahead of the story
• Unbiased endorsements	
• Credible reviews	
• Less skepticism by the buyer	

an understanding of customers. People are honestly expressing how they feel about a product or service. Decide to learn what there is to learn and make improvements from there.

BE **STRATEGIC**

▶ Don't try and control the conversation—be transparent and sincere.

▶ Work with trusted clients who would be willing to give your product or service a positive review.

Take 5

Be Found in All the Right Places

"An advertising agency is 85 percent confusion and 15 percent commission."
—FRED ALLEN

The most important message to remember from Part II is to be specific when defining your ideal prospect. Then investigate to understand where those people gather on the web. Finally, choose the best gathering spots that will return the best results.

Knowing Your Ideal Prospect and Their Gathering Spots on the Web. By identifying your ideal prospect, you are not limiting your audience but qualifying it. Doesn't it make sense to market to those people who are looking for your service or product? That way, half the sales process is already complete. Remember to classify your ideal prospect as precisely as possible. If you have multiple visitor types coming to your website, keep your ideal prospects in separate groups. Don't try for a one size-fits-all solution. It won't work.

Know Where Your Prospects Hang Out on the Web. The only way to find out where your ideal prospects hang out on the web is to go there. You can't know if your prospect likes viewing certain webinars until you see what's available. Does the webinar speak to their needs or wants? Are those in attendance at the webinar asking the kinds of questions your prospect would ask? If the webinar offers materials for free, are those materials that would be of interest to your prospects? The only way to determine where your ideal prospects hang out is good old detective work. In this case, no shoe leather will be required.

Build an Internet Road Map So You'll Know When You Get There. Road maps are great for showing the starting point and final destination. Once you have identified the waterholes where your ideal prospects gather, it makes sense to develop a strategy to go after the web locations that show the most promise. If you can't do the job yourself, hire an outside contractor to get the job done. Keep updating the Watering Holes spreadsheet so you won't have to rely on gut feelings as to whether the waterholes are paying off.

Don't Bring Visitors to Your Site, Go to Where They Are. Why not identify your ideal prospects and then go to where they congregate on the web? It takes a lot less time, energy and effort. It makes more strategic sense to work on gaining visibility in the venues where your prospects gather. Learn how to develop strategies to gain a presence in those communities.

Blog Communities: Engage Prospects and Build a Sense of Community. Listing the company blog in blog communities helps syndicate the company's reach. It also gives the company the opportunity to reach people outside the business' universe. Being listed in blog communities also builds credibility and trust. Choose blog communities where your ideal prospects congregate.

Podcasts: All Right, Mr. DeMille, I'm Ready for My Close Up. Audio podcasts are easier to pull off while video podcasts present some challenges. Podcasts help build relationships that e-mail campaigns and whitepapers cannot. Podcasts help establish you as an authority on a particular subject. Podcasts keep the same message going over and over. Don't forget to review the list of podcast pitfalls before heading to the sound studio.

Forums: Can I Say Something? Before launching your own company forum, join a few forums to find out what it takes to pull off a successful community. Forums need attention. They need moderators and fresh discussion material. More forums languish than flourish. Forums are a great place to listen in on what's being said about a particular company, product, or service. Forums are the perfect venues to test marketing messages. Think about rewarding the participants for their involvement in surveys.

Blogs: Don't Just Talk a Good Game—Be Viewed as an Expert. Blogging creates community. It strengthens the relationship between buyer and seller. Make sure you post on a continuous basis. People that read blogs often come back for more information. If posts on a blog look stale, people won't return. Blogs give you the opportunity to hear what other people are thinking. Blogging is simply a great tool for public relations.

Video Blogs: Can You See Me Now? Try a mixture of blogging and video. Your audience may prefer that combination. Make sure you look at the videos with a critical eye and listen with a critical ear. The video content should be fresh, timely, and interesting. Remember, less is more. Take more complex subjects and break them into bite-size videos. This will boost excitement about upcoming videos.

Download Sites: Make It Easy to Share Your Wares. Download sites allow sellers to reach new audiences. Positive reviews on the sites let sellers know what buyers think about their products. Negative comments need to be dealt with swiftly and in a positive manner. Pick download sites where you believe your ideal prospects collect. Some sites specialize in downloading software, movies, music, presentations, and images.

Pay-per-Click: Compel Prospects to Click on Your Ads. Rewarding pay-per-click campaigns take time, patience, and the right key phrases. Pay-per-click results are immediate. PPC campaigns give you the ability to sharpen your marketing message to ensure the right prospect groups are taking action. PPC campaigns can, however, be expensive if not watched closely. PPC campaigns should be a short-term solution while search engine optimization and other marketing efforts take hold.

Search Engine Optimization (SEO): Attract Visitors Already Looking for You. Search engine optimization offers promotion that does not sleep. It takes time to see the effects of the optimization in the organic search results. It's hard to predict the click volume from SEO. Do not go after the most popular terms at first. Start out with search phrases you believe you can own. Search engine optimization is more cost effective over time than pay-per-click.

Virtual Events: Stay Home and Attend Web Events. Virtual events offset the cost of putting on or travelling to conferences. Virtual events are excellent mechanisms for data capture. Companies putting on events can track what presentations attendees go to, which booths they stop by, and what sales materials they find interesting enough to download. Virtual events are cost effective, can be staged more often, and can be open for business 24/7.

Webinars: Move Prospects Down the Sales Funnel. Webinar presenters need to find ways to keep the audience engaged. Presentations that drag on discourage attendees from staying. Record the webinar so the people that missed the presentation can watch it later at their convenience. Upload your webinar presentations to other community sites and expand your audience. Make sure you have "take-a-ways" for the audience and a plan to nurture the newly formed relationships.

Press Releases: Publish This! Press releases increase a company's visibility, expand its audience, and boost traffic to your website or blog. Press releases are a cost-effective way to get your message out and gain credibility. The information in the press release needs to be newsworthy. Optimize the press release to gain the best possible search results. Press releases also provide valuable backlinks to the website or blog.

Newsletters: Write to Be Read. Remember to consider costs before launching a newsletter publication. Newsletters increase customer retention and customer loyalty and help build community. Electronic newsletters are inexpensive to produce and deliver but take real effort to keep going. A newsletter with a growing readership requires a constant supply of fresh content.

E-Mail Marketing: The Drip, Drip, Drip of Your Marketing Message. Keep in mind your e-mail campaign messaging needs to be prototyped until you hit the desired results. E-mail marketing works best when targeted at specific audiences that have identified needs or wants. They work well to nurture prospects that need more information and have not yet made a buying decision. E-mail marketing can be used for customer retention and to build customer loyalty.

Landing Pages: Tightening up the Marketing Message. Design the landing page to have a singular purpose—a call to action. Resist including other links back to your website or blog. Resist offering more than one deal. Multiple links and offers only confuse and distract the prospect. Make sure the marketing message is brief, succinct, and compelling. Ask only for the personal information that is necessary.

Image Sites: A Picture Is Still Worth 6,173 Characters—or 1,000 Words. Use photo sites to keep a watchful eye on the competition. Have geotag photos of company locations, facilities, and ongoing projects. Share photos with stakeholders. Encourage customers to take photos of themselves using your product.

Review and Comment Sites: Is Your Company Being Talked About, Trashed, or Touted? Offer credible advice to fix any issues people are complaining about. Don't try and sidestep them. Don't try to tell the respondent that there is no problem. Use these venues to strengthen the company's position on offering the best possible customer care.

PART III

BE SOCIAL
ON THE WEB

Social media is media that is designed to be shared through social interaction, and social networking is linking people together in some way. Some companies think social networking is a time-consuming, resource-wasting fad while others credit a good portion of their success to this technology. Like any other web activity, it's a business choice.

> *"Social media . . .*
> *The key is to*
> *listen, engage,*
> *and build*
> *relationships."*
>
> —David Alston

There's no argument social networking takes time, resources, and a commitment, but it can be a positive for many businesses. Unlike other online business strategies, however, it is not necessarily quick to produce results. Businesses that do not allow at least six months for their social experiment to develop may terminate the program prematurely and thereby not realize its potential.

Businesses are finding ways to leverage these social twins. For instance, a number of web businesses are putting social strategies in place to expand their reach on the web, cultivate new prospects, and deliver better customer care alternatives. Social networking is the perfect vehicle to disseminate information and offers quickly. New mobile apps are hitting the airwaves every day that make the disseminating process even easier and less expensive.

Companies employing social networking have a duty to develop winning marketing strategies for the web much the same way they do for marketing ground assaults. This section, Be Social on the Web, talks about how the strategy's goals should be reasonable, attainable, and measurable.

Security is a valid concern, and one that keeps some businesses at an arms-length from the social community. Businesses should adopt security guidelines before jumping into the various social communities. Because a community is well known and used by the masses does not necessarily mean it's a secure environment.

Chapter 13

Fundamentals of Social Networking

Social Media Team

"Leverage your brand. You shouldn't let two guys in a garage eat your shorts."

—Guy Kawasaki

SOCIAL NETWORKING IS ABOUT ENGAGEMENT, SHARING INFORMATION, ideas, and trust. In short, it's about building relationships. Organizations can use social networking channels to lower their customer support costs by solving some problems quicker. Social networking aids in customer retention by keeping the company brand in the customer's consciousness. Because social networking conversation is happening in real time, businesses can use it to spot trends and new developments more quickly.

Organizations that jump on the social networking bandwagon thinking of nothing but widening their revenue stream will be disappointed. They will soon find that social networking interactions mean more than exchanging a virtual handshake in hopes of selling some merchandise.

Businesses can exploit social networking in a number of ways.

Consider the following approaches when applying social networking as part of your business mix:

- GetSatisfaction.com collects and organizes all social knowledge (questions, feedback, concerns, and praise) into a unified platform that can be shared and leveraged across both internal and customer-facing channels (Figure 13.1).
- CrowdSound.com gives businesses the opportunity to open up a suggestion box for everyone to see. It works with customers to improve the company, its products, and the lines of communication. Why not make the feedback social?

Social networking is a nonthreatening way of engaging prospects in the knowledge transfer process. It is also a way of strengthening a company's brand awareness and a covert way of keeping an eye on the competition.

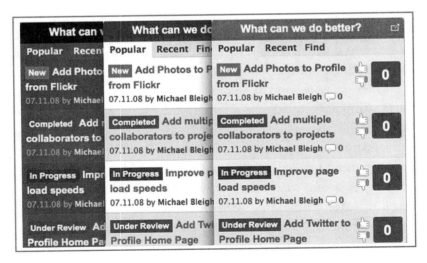

FIGURE 13.1—CrowdSound.com feedback

Increase Your Standing of Expertise

SlideShare.net is the largest business community for sharing slide presentations, PDFs, or documents. An organization can upload a presentation to SlideShare.net and then embed a link to the presentation on its corporate website or blog. From there, visitors can watch the presentation. Visitors to SlideShare.net that do not know about the company can also search, find, and view the presentation. The presentation can be viewed publicly or shown privately. Audio can be synched to the presentation to add to the stickiness of the presentation. Company events can also be highlighted. SlideShare.net encourages the formation of groups of like-minded individuals who want to discuss topics of interest. Always keep an eye out for ways to build community.

LinkedIn allows you to show a link from your LinkedIn profile to three presentations.

Blogs are another great way to share the expertise of a company, give customers inside looks at the operation, and involve them in the conversation.

Foster More Community

Start talking with your customers by creating a Facebook fan page or a LinkedIn company page. Create a special interest group to narrow the conversation. LinkedIn has Groups where the conversation can be more to the point. Because these social networking vehicles are more removed from the corporate website, people on both sides of the conversation feel more at ease and are willing to open up.

Using Twitter to drive community is like inviting customers to a backyard barbecue. The conversations are direct, short, and to the point. Much can be gleaned in a very short period of time.

Blogging is still a community staple in which key people from organizations can direct what's talked about and at the same time listen in as the customer-conversation develops.

LinkedIn gives its members the ability to launch either private or public events. It promotes the events through its DirectAds program and handles the event registration as well. Facebook offers a similar service for private and public occasions.

Create New Revenue Streams

Airlines and hotels use Twitter to clear out their unused inventory by offering last-minute deals at reduced fares. They are also integrating social networking with travel applications and reviews.

LinkedIn, Facebook, and Twitter can certainly be used to create new visitor streams to a company's website and blog. More visitors mean more conversions if the website is doing its job.

The job-hunting process has exploded on Twitter by people texting their desired position and referring followers to their resume. Search firms that use Twitter can find out within an instant if there is a viable candidate anywhere in the immediate area or across the country.

Build Trust

A company needs to be honest, upfront, and transparent on its blog with its customers when issues come up, such as the annual recalls that seem to plague the automotive industry from time to time. Negative situations will come up. It is how the company handles the situation that matters most to people. Try a cover up, and the company's social networking days may quickly come to an end. Admit the company knows about the problem, and outline the steps being taken to solve it.

Trust can also be boosted through blog communities, blogs, comment and reputation sites, customer service sites, forums, livecasting audio and video sites, reviews and ratings sites, and Twitter.

Gather Competitive Intelligence

The web makes it easy to snoop on the competition. Other than reading their websites and blogs, companies can use social networking tools to keep track of what their competitors are doing. An organization can check LinkedIn and Jigsaw to gather company information and see the key players. It's easy to stay anonymous on Twitter and follow the companies you're interested in knowing more about. Signing up for webinars and other virtual events are also ways to keep an eye on what companies in your business space are bringing forward.

Some organizations opt to use Google Alerts to stay abreast of the competition. You can set up Google Alerts to inform you when new links are established to domains. You can be alerted to blog entries, news, videos, etc. Google will alert you daily, weekly, or whenever something is posted. You can set up 1,000 alerts per account.

Learn What People Are Saying about Your Products or Services

Yelp and GetSatisfaction provide that opportunity. These social vehicles also provide companies and customers with the opportunity to share ideas, gain assistance, and extinguish rumors before they can gain steam.

Learn from How Others Use Social Networking

YouTube with its one billion downloads per day is one of the 900-pound social networking gorillas on the web. It is a great place to post instructional videos to make sure customers are following the directions when installing or putting your product together (Figure 13.2). Presentations and workshops also find their way to the video giant. YouTube is a great platform for informal discussions by subject matter experts and key people in an organization and can serve as a convenient place for people to listen to debates and roundtable discussions without leaving the comfort of their offices. YouTube also lets companies host their own information or entertainment channels, much like a cable TV station.

If a company needs help in producing its video channel with a more professional look, they may want to look at Blip.

FIGURE 13.2—YouTube video

tv's offerings. Blip.tv helps creative people be more imaginative. Companies can usually create good content. It's applying technology that's the rub. Blip.tv is great at technology, business development, distribution, marketing, and advertising sales. It has more than 48,000 independently produced web shows that reach over 22 million people.

Take Your Company Global

Social networking gives organizations the ability to have their tweet heard around the world. The social networking stratosphere knows no bounds, at least not yet. Companies can localize their social networking reach by joining local groups and communities. But if someone wants to find you, they will. Why be shortsighted? Let new buyers find you. If you can service their needs and strike up a new relationship, why not?

LinkedIn gives you the ability to look for new connections by continent or country. At this writing there are over 37,000 connections in mainland China, 98,000 in Australia, and almost 114,000 in Japan. There are also special interest groups that talk about international issues. Facebook has similar features.

GeoFollow is a location tool that gives you the ability to find new followers by city, state, country, tag, name, Twitter username, and keyword.

Raise Your Company's Brand Awareness

Blog Catalog is the premier blog catalog on the web. Companies can list their blog on it to make it easy for the businesses looking for their products or services to find them. If your company is not listed, they'll find the competition instead.

Blogs.com is another good community to list your blog.

BlogPulse, run by Nielsen, allows a company to gauge its presence on the web as well as see how its competition is doing. You can review the Top Links, Key People, Top Videos, Top Blog Posts, Top Blogs, Key Phrases, Top News Stories, and Top News Sources.

Technorati helps the technical/business community by gathering and highlighting the best stories across the web. If someone in the company has written a great post on "demand generation," it could be bookmarked to Technorati. In this way, interested parties can find the article and then be enticed to visit your website. In other words, this action creates another visitor stream.

Manage Your Business' Reputation

BackType is a real-time, conversational search engine. It indexes and connects millions of conversations from blogs, social networks, and other social networking. In this way, you can find out what people are saying about the topics that interest you. Companies can eavesdrop on customers to find out what they really think about a particular service or product.

Disqus is a comment system and moderation tool for your site. This service lets you add next-gen community management and social web integrations to any site on any platform. With Disqus a writer would not have to leave her blog to find out what the readership is thinking.

Research Your Current Customer Base

Social networking monitoring helps organizations create more human personas instead of general stereotypes.

Act.ly gives you the ability to launch surveys on Twitter and track responses.

Sites such as Yelp and Epinions allow people to talk about what's great and not so great about products, services and places. If your company is in the service sector, it makes sense to be aware of what people are saying. Remember, straightening out the problem is better than mounting a defense.

Track Industry Trends

Create surveys with SocialToo and track media trends. Act.ly gives you the ability to launch surveys on Twitter and track the responses.

Trendpedia tracks the buzz on blogs. Find out what bloggers are talking about: B2B marketing, demand generation, or the sales process.

SocialSeek tracks trends and brands through social networking.

ViralHeat helps brands monitor 200 plus video sites, on top of Twitter tracking and real-time search and monitoring for brand mentions across the web.

Gather Market Research

One of the beauties of the social networking explosion is the niche sites that are cropping up, sites that deal specifically with pets, women's issues, hunting, cars, and political views.

Forums are still going strong. Members can discuss topics of interest and bounce ideas back and forth with those who have similar interests.

Twitter gives real-time information on products, services, people's views, what's being talked about or complained about, and emerging trends in any industry across this planet.

LinkedIn is especially good for garnering news and information on the B2B community.

StumbleUpon lists sites on interesting topics and those passionate about the same. You can find out demographic, gender, age, and location data as well.

The social networking stratosphere is a great place to monitor a company's brand, analyze trends, gather customer/prospect data, and learn about unmet needs.

Avoid the Security Risks

Social networking like any other computer platforms has its worms, viruses, infections, trojans, restless juvenile delinquents, and charlatans. Be careful out there. Take the necessary precautions to keep your information and identify safe. More than 1.2 million people filed a complaint of fraud, identity theft, or a related act to law enforcement or regulatory agencies in 2008, up 16 percent from the year before, according to the Consumer Sentinel Network, a branch of the Federal Trade Commission. Financial losses came to $1.8 billion, or about $3,400 per victim reporting a financial loss. Losses of $1 million or more were reported by 257 people.

Cautiously share information about business trips, proposals, strategies, competitors, and vacations and limit out-of-office replies or sensitive company business topics. Remember, sharing the locations of where you are at any moment also lets people know where you are not. Keep personal information out of conversations where everyone and anyone could be listening. Take the time to develop a social networking security policy and stick to it. Expect an attack . . . it's on its way.

Measure Social Networking's Effectiveness/Results

More social networking monitoring tools are being launched every day. Keep your eyes open. Of course, Google Analytics is a good place to start measuring incoming traffic to your website and blog. One can find out what social communities visitors are coming from, what search terms they're keying in to find you, and what pages are receiving the most views. Those that like to drill down in the information can do so to garner more details. Twitter supplies your Follower count; Twitterholic lets you know who the big tweeters are in your area. A person can also track retweets and links. Twitalyzer measures impact, engagement, and influence. Figure 13.3 shows the Wall Street Journal's statistics from Twitalyzer.

Of course businesses are not interested in the number of tweets done by an employee or the number of followers one might gain in a one-month period. Organizations are interested in establishing their prowess in a business sector, having their company awareness increased, gathering data on their competition, expanding their market reach, and increasing revenue. If those metrics are not calculated early and a winning strategy developed and deployed, social networking is meaningless to the business.

Exploit The Viral Features Within Social Networking

The funny videos of people doing ridiculous stunts are the king of viral on platforms such as YouTube. Good comedy in story

FIGURE 13.3—Twitalyzer Profile Statistics

form seems to run a close second. If advertisers can capitalize on these fads, then their messages can go out to millions. But what if a company is selling information security software or a medical center dealing in heart bypass surgery? Perhaps humor is not the best advertising avenue to explore. Potential clients would find the practice pretty tasteless. Viral marketing relies on immediate action. People see a picture or hear something interesting and make an instant determination that their friends would or would not find this information useful. If businesses are to appropriate this technology, the information should be interesting, time-sensitive, and unique. The message cannot be just another 10-percent-off sale or the umpteenth feature of a new product. The best place to be viral is where community is the strongest.

Twitter is certainly viral with its instantaneous communication platform. Facebook may hold promise for businesses that deal in products or services procured by families or the younger set. In a down economy, recruiters are finding their open position announcements becoming viral because unemployed people tend to look out for each other. If an opportunity does not appeal to them, they are more likely to pass it along to an out-of-work colleague. Hotels and airlines are taking advantage of people's frugality by seeing their discount deals passed along to friends and family.

The Hidden Secrets (Pitfalls) of Using Social Networking

Potential pitfalls are loss of control; what's said stays in the social networking stratosphere for eternity. Mistakes will happen. Results may be hard to measure at first, and friends or followers may have hidden agendas. Mistakes may crop up, but how the problem is handled by the company means everything to the consumer. Don't think the social networking stratosphere can be controlled. It can't be. People are already talking about your products or services. Why not join in the discussion and set things right. If there are problems, fess up and get them fixed.

Pay close attention to your social networking metrics. You don't want them to be hidden secrets. Once you're comfortable, take on more social networking responsibilities. Trust the people in the organization to be creative. Remember to show personality. Listen. Listen. Listen. Use social networking to boost website traffic.

Of course, this list is not meant to be exhaustive or comprehensive. It is here to aid businesses and organizations in their strategic thinking about social networking. Can you leverage it to offer a higher level of customer care? Is it a vehicle to help you understand the direction your customers would like to see a certain product or service head? Is social networking a viable opportunity to introduce another revenue stream? These are all fair questions that need to be answered.

There are numerous opportunities for businesses to leverage social networking to lower support costs, strengthen relationships with customers, build brand awareness, mine new prospect venues, and create trust.

BE **STRATEGIC**

- Don't try and implement all of these methods at once. Take your time to understand which ones benefit your business the most.
- Using social networking to accelerate your customer care may help you out-position your competition.
- Social networking allows you to hear what customers are really saying about your product or service. Use this social networking feature to short-cut problems.
- Use social networking as a global listening post to see where your products or services might be most needed.

The Roles People Play in the Social Networking Stratosphere

"My role in society, or any artist's or poet's role, is to try and express what we all feel. Not to tell people how to feel."

—JOHN LENNON

If the social networking duties are assigned to one person because he has free time on his hands, the social networking experiment will surely fail. Instead talk with those employees who are under 30 and thus most likely to use social networking in their lives outside the corporate compound. Their acumen can help jump-start the organization's social networking plans.

A variety of talents are necessary to make the social networking endeavor a success. People can surely be assigned more than one task depending upon an organization's situation. It's pretty easy to see that a business cannot delegate the social networking experiment to one person in the organization. There isn't one person in the business that can answer all the questions that may be asked or perform the various tasks.

- Upper management needs to sell the social networking vision throughout the company.
- The marketing people will be in charge of wordsmithing the messaging.
- The web person jump-starts the social networking effort by constructing the blog and setting up other social channels such as Facebook, Twitter, and LinkedIn.
- The SEO expert can show everyone the search phrases necessary to draw the right visitors into the discussions.
- Domain and subject matter experts need to be identified within the company and assigned to participate by posting on the blog and texting through the various social channels.

· Someone within the organization will have to keep an ear to the ground as the social networking ecosystem evolves and more features and functions become available.

Social Media Team

Do You Really Have Time to Be Social?

"Real men don't use emoticons."

—ANONYMOUS

Every organization will have to decide if it has the time to be social. Don't jump in the social networking environment and create time constraints that burden the company. Companies that start and abruptly stop their social enterprise or let their blog languish are not seen in a positive light by people in the social community. There is little patience for companies that do not count the cost before making the investment.

Start out slow with few commitments. Don't promise to post information to a blog weekly or to Twitter several times a day if the resources are not there. Start to post or text on an as-needed basis and then ramp things up slowly as it makes sense.

Being social cannot be one person's assignment. It needs to be a group effort. One person cannot be the voice of everyone in the company. Each person has a different view of things, an individual personality, and speaks with a distinct voice. Marketing people speak from their perspective while engineers from their point of view. Mix things up.

A content syndication plan helps define people's responsibilities and gives everyone a good indication of the time commitment required to keep the social sphere afloat. Figure 13.4 shows a simple content syndication outline.

The spreadsheet in Figure 13.4 is a three-month plan that shows content being added to the website as well as being published through social networking channels. Notice some activities such as creating a new whitepaper, case study, press release, or In the News item take place once a month. Social space activities are executed on a more frequent basis.

Building business relationships through soical networking will not happen overnight. It will take time, dedication, and consistency.

As you can see in Figure 13.5, which is a blow up of a content syndication plan, a case study on ACME Software will be produced the first week of January. A webinar on CRM will be developed the third week, and additional web content will be created the last week of the month.

The social networking commitment involves more participants and an accelerated schedule. Chris, John, Bill, and Sunny will each blog once per week. There are hooks to Facebook and Twitter so that all blog posts get noticed by those communities as well. John and Bill need to contact the influencers in the software and CRM communities directly to continue to build the relationships.

Guy Kawasaki, a social networking luminary, suggests these ten reasons for being social on LinkedIn:

1. Increase your visibility.
2. Improve your connectability.

Content Syndication Plan: Outcome-BasedMarketing.com/handouts

	A	B	C	D	E	F	G	H	I	J	K	L	M	N
1	Content Channels					Content Syndication Plan								
2		4-Jan	11-Jan	18-Jan	25-Jan	1-Feb	8-Feb	15-Feb	22-Feb	1-Mar	8-Mar	15-Mar	22-Mar	29-Mar
3	White Paper or Case Study	X				X				X				
4	Press Release			X				X				X		
5	In The News		X				X				X			
6	Additional Content				X				X					X
7														
8	Blog Posts	X	X	X	X	X	X	X	X	X	X	X	X	X
9	Facebook	X	X	X	X	X	X	X	X	X	X	X	X	X
10	Twitter	X	X	X	X	X	X	X	X	X	X	X	X	X
11	Bookmarks	X	X	X	X	X	X	X	X	X	X	X	X	X
12	Influencers	X	X	X	X	X	X	X	X	X	X	X	X	X

FIGURE 13.4—Sample Content Syndication Plan spreadsheet

	A	B	C	D	E
1	Content Channels	Content Syndication Plan			
2		4-Jan	11-Jan	18-Jan	25-Jan
3	White Paper or Case Study				
4	ACME Software	X			
5	Press Release				
6	Webinar - How to Use CRM to Bridge the Gap Between Sales and Marketing			X	
7	In The News				
8	Annouce webinar		X		
9	Additional Content				
10	Marketing Minute - Sunny				X
11					
12	Blog Posts				
13	Chris	X			
14	John		X		
15	Bill			X	
16	Sunny				X
17	Facebook	X	X	X	X
18	Twitter	X	X	X	X
19	Bookmarks	X	X	X	X
20	Influencers				
21	John & Bill	X	X	X	X

FIGURE 13.5—Blow up of Content Syndication Plan

3. Improve your Google Page Rank.
4. Enhance your search engine results.
5. Perform blind "reverse" and company reference checks.
6. Increase the relevancy of your job search.
7. Make your interview go smoother.
8. Gauge the health of a company.
9. Gauge the health of an industry.
10. Track startups.

Most of these ideas certainly apply across other social communities as well.

Businesses need to consider the costs before jumping into the social networking pool. Start slow and build momentum. Don't go in a half dozen directions at once. Start in one community, get established, and then move to your second choice. Develop a content syndication plan.

BE **STRATEGIC**

▶ Social networking cannot be successfully handled by one person in an organization.

▶ Any social networking strategy ought to include consistency of message.

▶ Give any social networking program six months to succeed. Building relationships takes time.

Chapter 14

Social Networking
Parts and Pieces

Social Media Team

"To be social is to be forgiving."

—Robert Frost

THERE ARE A NUMBER OF PIECES THAT MAKE UP THE SOCIAL NETWORKING puzzle. Consider, for example, LinkedIn. (It could just as well be Facebook, but let's stick with a pure business community example.) LinkedIn is a full-featured, business-oriented community that shows the different aspects of a typical social networking kinship. It has 55 million members from 170 industries in over 200 countries—not a small player.

Most social networking communities are made up of the same elements: a Profile that describes the member to the others in the community, Contacts that this individual has some relationship with, Groups that have a common interest, and Discussion platforms where every member can share their ideas, thoughts and concerns. These communities are also great places to give and receive advice.

Profiles

As Figure 14.1 indicates, profiles on LinkedIn can be simple or exhaustive—it depends on how much information you believe is worth sharing. The LinkedIn Profile allows for Current and Past Employment Positions, Education, Specialties, Interests, Groups, Honors, and Awards, Interested In, as well as a Summary section. Each entry can be turned on or off from view.

Contacts

On LinkedIn, two members make a connection. These relationships are with trusted friends, people you know directly, people you have worked with, or people you have done business with in the past.

Figure 14.2 gives a snapshot of a LinkedIn network. LinkedIn members use these connections for advice, consul, interview opportunities, job search, a sounding board, and plain old camaraderie. You can chat directly with your contacts or ask your connections to talk to theirs on your behalf.

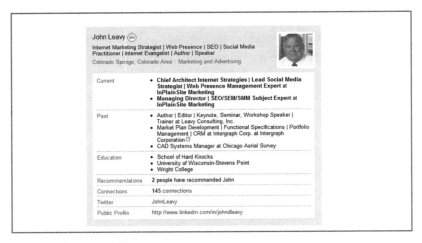

FIGURE 14.1—Sample LinkedIn profile

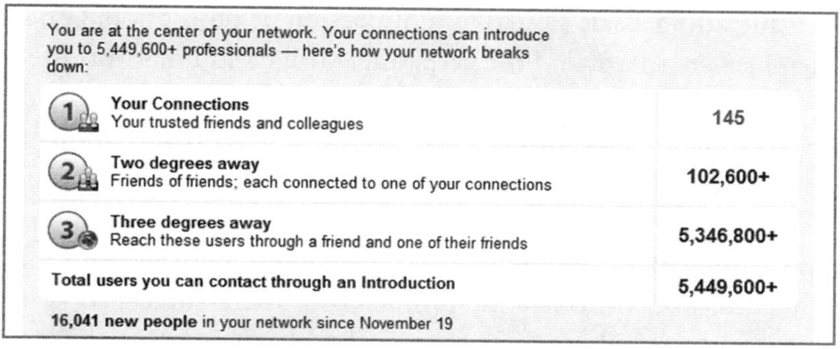

You are at the center of your network. Your connections can introduce you to 5,449,600+ professionals — here's how your network breaks down:

1	**Your Connections** Your trusted friends and colleagues	145
2	**Two degrees away** Friends of friends; each connected to one of your connections	102,600+
3	**Three degrees away** Reach these users through a friend and one of their friends	5,346,800+
	Total users you can contact through an Introduction	5,449,600+

16,041 new people in your network since November 19

FIGURE 14.2—Number of LinkedIn Connections

Groups

There are close to a half million Groups on LinkedIn from HR Resources, Sales, Marketing, Executive, Startups, Consulting, Alumni, and Non-Profit to highlight a few categories. A LinkedIn member is allowed to join up to 50 Groups at one time. The Groups provide a way to get closer to like-minded individuals. Perhaps you want to share a marketing strategy and want to know if anyone has done something similar before and what the success rate was. Groups are also great places to perform unscientific surveys or opinion polls or to gather marketing research.

Discussions

Within each Group members can start discussions, enter a promotion, look for job opportunities, or start subgroups within the main group. A person can just listen in on the discussions or join in the fray. Resist

Notice as you move between communities such as Facebook and LinkedIn that some names of features stay the same while others change. For instance, in Facebook connections are seen as "Friends" while on LinkedIn "connections or contacts" can be labeled: "Colleagues, Classmates, We've done business together, Friends, or Other."

masquerading a sale's pitch as a discussion or promotion. Group members are smart, and the perpetrator will be summarily ousted.

LinkedIn is also a good resource for posting an open position or looking for employment. Don't use LinkedIn like Monster and join the community just to spam everyone with your resume. That's not LinkedIn's intention in helping its members find employment. The job search goes more like this: You join LinkedIn. You fill out your profile. You invite some people to connect to you. You join and contribute to a few Groups. You build some relationships. Then perhaps you let it be known to your trusted contacts that you're looking for a marketing position on the East Coast and ask if anyone knows someone you can connect with to discuss a possible engagement.

There's really a lot more to LinkedIn. Take a look at it when you have time. Build relationships with past and present friends and business colleagues. The effort will pay off many times over.

Facebook is slightly different. It deals mostly with personal connections between people—usually family, friends, and relatives. There are some 6,700 fan pages for celebrities, celeb wannabes, and most likely quite a few who are delusional. There are also business pages. But don't think your engineering firm, chemical plant, or marketing firm is going to tap into this 53-million-member base. Members on Facebook like to chat with friends and share vacation stories and photos of the kids and pets. Companies are misdirected if they think they'll be able to attract this audience. A T-shirt shop—yes. A music store—sure. But not every business.

BE **STRATEGIC**

▶ Take a look at the profiles of the rock stars in the community you plan on joining to glean ways to build your profile. Profile content is extremely important.

▶ Join only these Groups and Discussions where you believe you have something to offer.

Chapter 15

Social Media Netiquette

Social Media Team

"You can't be truly rude until you understand good manners."

—RITA MAE BROWN

WE ALL SAY DUMB THINGS OUT LOUD FROM TIME TO TIME. LUCKY for us we're not in the movie business, sports industry, or political arena. The dim-witted things those people say end up on the evening news or on the front page of the morning papers. Writing one's thoughts on a blog or in a Comment to a post is akin to carving what's said into stone—forever travelling the airwaves of the web. Social networks are not the place for strong criticism, unkind words, or gossip. Keep your comments constructive and tone down your attitude or you'll be seen as uncivil or just plain rude. Communities ban people who are negative. Learn why it's better to keep criticism to yourself and how being civil will attract more readers.

*Don't play the part of a horse's ass in one community
such as Facebook thinking your LinkedIn business
colleagues or future boss or client won't go there
to look you up.*

Social Media Team

If You Don't Want to See It in Print Forever, Then Don't Say It

*"We have two ears and one mouth so that we can
listen twice as much as we speak."*

—EPICTETUS

*Be careful what
you say to friends
and connections.
Friends have
connections who
have connections
and so on. You
may not want
what's said to be
sent around the
world.*

There are people on the web who think they have the right to malign anyone who does not believe in their point of view. Issues aside, for them attacking people personally is what they enjoy. No person has the right to yell "Fire!" in a crowded movie theater. Nor can a person play the radio as loud as she wants at 3:00 in the morning with no consideration of the neighbor's children who are asleep.

In any community civility should be championed. Everyone needs to have equal rights. We all have to coexist for the community to stay together and survive. People who cannot keep their personal attacks to themselves will find themselves on the outside of the community looking inward.

Be social, be civil, be courteous, and be careful out there.

Social Media Team

Don't Drop Your Drawers on the Web

"If you want total security, go to prison."

—DWIGHT D. EISENHOWER

Just because a community site profile asks for 10 or 15 pieces of information does not mean every line on the form has to be filled in. For example, Twitter wants to know your full name, username (@johnleavy), password, and e-mail address. There are other profile decisions that are optional: time zone, URL, one-line bio, geographic location, language, and geotagging. A mug shot or favorite image can also be uploaded.

Facebook asks for first name, last name, e-mail address, password, sex, and birthday. Once the account is created, a person can add a photo, religion and political views, education and work information, along with what groups she has joined.

Some people see letting strangers view their personal information as a privacy issue or security risk. Having a few pieces of personal information on someone can aid in the search for more facts on that person. Sad to say, there are most likely charlatans

BE **STRATEGIC**

- When you get frustrated, the best practice may be to write what you want to say to that person who has you bugged and then delete it before sending. Then write a courteous response. Flame mail does neither party any good.

- If you find readers leaving less-than-civil comments on your blog, delete them and ask the person to be civil. Privately owned communities can take stronger action by banning the person from further participation.

Think about what the community members need to know about you. When joining a business community, think about giving pertinent information that relates to business experience, past performance, successes, or challenges.

in every community and forum on the web looking to misrepresent themselves or to rip off some unsuspecting mark.

Most members assume that every community they belong to has taken every step possible to secure their account. Sorry to say that's not true. They are making an effort but so are the criminals.

A recent study indicated that 13 percent of Facebook members befriend people they don't even know and 92 percent of Twitter users connect with complete strangers. Members discuss sensitive business plans and vacation arrangements in communities as well as announce they will be away from their office or home for extended periods of time, forgetting that not everyone listening is a friend or business colleague.

Businesses are also naïve to think their competitors are not among their fans on Facebook or their followers on Twitter.

BE **STRATEGIC**

▶ Would you just hand your wallet to a stranger on the street? Some unscrupulous people might be following you on LinkedIn, Facebook, or Twitter. Keep as much information private as you can.

▶ Organizations should develop a social networking privacy policy.

Social Media Team

Create Different Social Networking Personas

"Personality is an unbroken series of successful gestures."

—F. Scott Fitzgerald

No one would seriously think of visiting the president of the United States in the Oval Office in jeans and a favorite rock concert T-shirt. The Office of the President itself commands respect. There is a protocol to be followed.

The different social communities on the web have their own protocols as well. Think of socializing on LinkedIn. Some professionals in the LinkedIn community are known to you while others are not. Think of meeting the boss for dinner at a fine restaurant downtown—formal, button down, reserved. One would dress well for the dinner engagement and leave the running clothes on a hook in the bathroom. Some formality is involved with engaging on LinkedIn as well.

Spend some time listening to the conversation in a community before joining. This helps to understand the tone of the conversation before stepping on people's toes.

The conversations on LinkedIn revolve around business issues and practices. Conversation topics might be starting a business, forming partnerships, marketing, sales, accounting, legal situations, and so on. On the other hand, the Facebook community is more casual. Think of having a social gathering of family and friends at your home. Everyone knows each other and is sharing stories and photos, much like what happens on Facebook. Families and friends get together online and share birthdays, weddings, vacation photos, and daily happenings. Yes, business is also conducted on Facebook, but mostly human-interest transactions take place. Twitter is similar to attending a neighborhood block party. Some of the people attending would be friends while others look unfamiliar. The kids are running around. There are too many dogs in attendance, and the women are off in small groups conversing while the guys are standing around the BBQ pit lying to each other as the steaks sizzle.

The dialog in these different communities might be:

1. LinkedIn
   - There is a Network Updates box of 140 characters on each member's homepage where brief messages can be sent out to first-level connections.
   - Anyone visiting another person's profile will see the Network Updates at the top of the page.
   - Messages of 7,000 characters, or about 1,000 words, can be sent out to first-level connections—50 at a time.
   - There are other options to send messages to one's second- and third-level connections.
   - Videos and pictures can also be swapped.

2. Facebook
   - There is a "What's on your mind?" section on each Facebook member's homepage.
   - Twenty Facebook friends at a time can receive a 1,000-word message.
   - Videos and pictures can also be exchanged.

3. Twitter
   - Messages are 140 characters in length. The message needs to be clear, concise, and to the point. A lot of thought needs to go into the message before sending it out.
   - Videos and pictures can also be traded.

So conversations in these communities are similar, yet they vary. The timing and the tone of conversations also vary:

1. *LinkedIn.* As regular messages are received from LinkedIn members, they drop into your inbox and also are routed to your personal e-mail client if that is the way your settings are arranged. The only gap in communication occurs when you don't log into your LinkedIn account on a regular basis.

2. *Facebook.* Facebook works much the same way. Messages are received and routed to your Facebook inbox and your personal e-mail client. Again, the only gap in communication comes from not logging into your Facebook account on some regular basis.

3. *Twitter.* Three different types of Twitter messages can be sent or received. (1) DM or Direct Messages with the Twitter syntax: D + handle + message; Direct Messages are sent to specific people, so no one else can see or read the message. (2) Mentions are where other Twitter followers include your handle somewhere within the messages they send. (3) Regular Twitter messages are sent out to the world, so you will see that person's messages if you are following him on Twitter.

If you have a Twitter account you know a standard Twitter page holds 20 messages. When the twenty-first message (tweet) is received, the last message at the bottom of page 1 falls to page 2. If you have a few followers that chat occasionally, the chance of not seeing a message on page 1 is small. But think of having thousands of followers and receiving hundreds of tweets per day. If you do not have time to scroll to the back pages, things people are talking about won't be seen. Don't worry about being out of the loop on some conversations. No one can keep up on every conversation at a business forum either. For instance, people typically walk from group to group listening to what the conversations are about. When they hear something of interest, they may hang around for some time. They may even join in a discussion. That's the way the conversation on Twitter works. If a Twitter account is only accessed once or twice a week, much of

BE **STRATEGIC**

- Keep business and personal friends and colleagues separate.
- Don't create phony personas. You'll be found out sooner than you think.

what followers are talking about will not be seen by that account owner.

Chapter 16

Planning Your Business' Social Networking Presence

Social Media Team

"Life is what happens to you while you're busy making other plans."

—JOHN LENNON

YOU NEED TO DEVELOP AND EXECUTE A SOCIAL NETWORKING STRATEGY. The strategy can be simple or complex depending upon the amount of detail you believe fits your organization. Your business will need to answer a series of questions such as "Why social networking in the first place?" and "Will social networking fit into your overall communication and marketing plan?" From there you'll want to decide what people-types you want to engage and what social networking channels make the most sense to pursue. Your social media strategy will also have to deal with how your company will be involved in the social communities and who will manage the company's social networking presence. Your commitment to social networking can not be casual or limited. Building relationships take time. You need to know about the different media components, how to implement them, and how to measure success or failure.

Some people might say any networking strategy should have seven steps while others say ten steps. For this discussion, there are 12 steps. If you want to break the plan down to more granular stages, have at it.

Social Media Team

Building Your Social Networking Strategy

*"All men can see these tactics whereby I conquer, but what none can see
is the strategy out of which victory is evolved."*

—SUN TZU

Before outlining your social networking strategy, there are some questions you need to consider:

1. What's the point of your social networking strategy?
2. Why social networking in the first place?
3. How does social networking fit into your overall marketing/ communication plan?
4. What people-types (technoids, engineers, or C-level) do you want to engage in conversation?
5. What social networking channels will you use?
6. What are community participants talking about today?
7. How can you add to the conversations already underway without being overly promotional?
8. How will you involve the social networking community?
9. Who will maintain your social networking presence?
10. What is the length of your commitment to social networking?
11. Can your company culture adapt to the demands of social networking?

12. How will you measure success or failure?

The Point of Your Social Networking Strategy

If the reason for adopting social networking is because your competition is using that tactic, the strategy is built on a pretty shaky foundation. Better reasons would be to boost brand awareness and engagement, customer loyalty, and revenue generation. These are goals that you can measure.

The reason behind any social networking strategy is to have goals that produce positive results for the company and its customers.

Try not to put too many demands on the social networking strategy if this is your first foray into this venue. The more complicated things are, the harder it will be to clearly measure how well the strategy works.

The Point of Social Networking

Answer these questions: Are your ideal prospects using social networking? Is this the best way to spend your marketing dollars? Will you receive a greater return on your investment using social networking? Are you trying to generate word-of-mouth about your products or services, or listen in on what your customers are saying? The same investigation needs to be done as when defining the internet assembly points where your ideal prospects hang out.

The Place of Social Networking in the Overall Marketing/Communication Plan

The social networking strategy cannot exist by itself. It needs to be part of the company's overall marketing/communication plan. There needs to be cross-platform integration. The media messaging should support the other marketing pieces and vice versa. The clients or customers ought to hear a consistent message.

Determine Who You Want to Engage in Conversation

Who are the participants in the social group you're contemplating joining? Are the participants technoids, engineers, or C-level people? Are the conversations underway sales related or marketing focused? Don't join just to be in the group. Play the role of an observer until you know whether or not the group can benefit by your membership and/or there is potential revenue to gain. Revenue gains aside, hopefully the group will benefit by your being a part of it.

Determine What Social Networking Channels to Use

Some social channels require immediate interaction. One tweet per week just won't do it. Others using that channel will quickly understand your commitment is not serious. If you cannot commit the time to Twitter, perhaps writing your own blog or commenting on other people's blogs would be better. Blogs and networking sites do not require an instant response and might work better with how your company operates. Take the time to understand how the various media channels work and what demands they will put on time and resources.

Similar Communities Talk about a Variety of Subjects

Belonging to a group on LinkedIn titled Internet Marketing might be too general for some while others would say it's right on target. It depends what type of conversation you're looking for in the group. Here are six titles for discussions currently ongoing in the group:

1. Headline Writing: Four Essential Attention Grabbing Elements
2. Article Marketing Finally Exposed
3. New Year's Resolutions: The I'll-Start-in-January Syndrome
4. The Truth About Pre-launches and Ground Floor MLM Opportunities Exposed
5. Successful Time Management Strategies

6. Twitter Marketing: Eight Simple Steps to Follow

As you can see, the six people who started these discussions all have a very different idea of what should be talked about in a group focusing on internet marketing. This is one good reason for being an observer to the group until you believe there will be value in joining.

Add to Conversation Already Underway without Being Overly Promotional

Don't think that all social networking people try to sell each other something. There are certainly plenty of social groups that were created just for being social, for plain, old, friendly conversation. There are also good Samaritans in most social networking groups, people who like to help other people. For instance, a successful entrepreneur might like to spend time giving novices a hand up. Some companies launch social networking programs to strengthen their branding or shore up customer care. Think about what value can be added in terms of knowledge, opinion, or content. Then there are those that know what buyers will surely do—buy. So why not buy our company's solution? It's an admirable goal; just do the solicitation with grace and panache. Don't join a group and launch six discussions that masquerade as information while the intent is to sell something. The other members are bound to get upset and withdraw your group membership. And because members usually belong to more than one group, your name will be passed along and everyone will know you're up to no good.

Involving the Social Networking Community

If you build it, they will NOT come. That's the way things work on the internet. Just because someone puts up a blog does not mean visitors will start flocking to read the latest post. Visitors need to be drawn in. It's no different than opening a retail store in a new location. How will people know the new store is open for business? Advertising, that's how. So the questions are: How will visitors be engaged in the social activity? Is there a budget to make that happen?

Maintaining Your Social Networking Presence

Building a social networking presence takes time—it just won't "happen." Don't assign the task to people who are either too busy or who have too little to do. The best fit is someone who already has a social media bent. The marketing team can feed the social individual or individuals brief, concise, compelling content to converse with when chatting with community members. The goal here is not to keep someone texting all day or visiting social sites to see what's happening. The social networking strategy is to generate brand awareness, revenue, or both.

The Length of Your Commitment

When someone starts a blog, the readership thinks the blogger will be there forever. Forever is a long time. How long will the company commit to the media strategy? Is it just for a specific product launch or a mainstay of the marketing/communication plan?

Adapting Company Culture to the Demands of Social Networking

A social networking strategy fits a nimble business much better than it does an organization that needs to have endless discussions before taking action. Social networking is happening now . . . all around that organization as it meets. If the company is not talking to its customers, the competition is or surely will be.

Can the business react quickly to a situation that needs attention? If someone slams the company's product will the company respond, and how? Or will it overlook it? Circumstances such as these require mapping strategies out ahead of time. The company cannot answer the claim weeks later. The die is already cast. What the person said about the product is now part of that product's lore, never to be erased. It would be good for most companies to produce a series of social networking guidelines: This is what we talk about online. This is what we avoid talking about. This is how we answer questions. The ones involved in the social networking frontlines should understand the company's value proposition, brand promise, elevator pitch, and target audience segmentation. These talking points will be woven throughout the online discussions.

Measuring Success or Failure

What success metrics will be developed? Will you succeed based on the number of leads generated, the number of comments or subscribers to your blog, or the number following you on Twitter? What constitutes failure, and what will you do about it? In the social networking space a lot of people get excited about numbers. As long as those numbers stand for the new revenue generated, then all is well.

BE **STRATEGIC**

- Here's a strategic step everyone is familiar with— put the plan down on paper.
- Start out small and adjust the plan as time goes by and as more resources are available.

Social Media Team

12 Ingredients of a Winning Social Network Marketing Plan

"If winning isn't everything, why do they keep score?"

—VINCE LOMBARDI

Now that the questions relevant to mapping out our social networking strategy have been evaluated and answered, the next logical step is execution. For an example, let's take each topic from the mapping section and attach tactics. Our company name will be CoolTools Software. Its compliance and accessibility products work in conjunction with Microsoft's SharePoint®.

Our example focuses on five verticals: education, health care, pharmaceutical, finance, and government. The key phrases are sharepoint accessibility, sharepoint governance, sharepoint compliance, share-point risk management, and sharepoint privacy. Factors to avoid in

No plan is a real plan unless it's written down on paper.

the plan are misdirected effort leading to irrelevant exposure, wasted time and effort, backlash, and missing the best opportunities.

The social media marketing plan (SMM) is to start off slow and gain momentum as successes are achieved and conversion methods are refined. The most popular social networking channels will be investigated, developed, and measured first.

The Point of Our Social Networking Strategy

There are five goals we'll try to accomplish with our social networking marketing strategy. Because the goals vary and the messaging differs, the actions against each goal will be executed separately. The five goals are:

1. Maximum exposure with minimal effort
2. Generation and nurturing of new leads
3. Increased brand awareness and buzz
4. Positioning CoolTools Software as a thought leader
5. Establishing the CoolTools Software brand in appropriate business verticals

The Point of Social Networking

We brought the key people at CoolTools together, and they came up with eight reasons why it made sense for the organization to extend its reach into the social networking stratosphere:

1. Social networking saves time and money if used correctly.
2. Time to execution is short.
3. Learning curve is small.
4. People (customers/prospects) want honest conversation.
5. Pull marketing bears more fruit than push marketing.
6. The prospects you want to do business with are already online.
7. Engaging people in conversation is cheaper than advertising.
8. Social networking can create lasting relationships.

Social Networking Needs to Fit into the Overall Marketing/Communication Plan

CoolTools produces software that works with SharePoint and offers packages to enterprises that do not use SharePoint. The first campaigns focus on integrating SharePoint. The social networking, marketing, and communications will all be synchronized.

Determine Who You Want to Engage in Conversation

Following is the audience (Target Audiences and Target Titles) CoolTools Software is most interested in reaching and engaging:

Target Audiences
- Federal government
- State and local government
- Healthcare, including pharmaceutical companies
- Education
- Financial
- Publicly traded corporations

Target Titles
- Compliance officers
- Privacy officers

- Sec 508 coordinators
- Chief information officers (CIO) or other senior technical managers
- Webmasters
- Marketing departments: branding protection, social networking
- Line of business managers (HR, marketing, e-commerce)

Determine What Social Networking Channels to Use

After preliminary investigation, the following social networking channels are deemed most appropriate: SlideShare.net, YouTube, Facebook, Twitter, and LinkedIn.

Investigation showed the following presentation topics were available:

SlideShare
- SharePoint (4,886 results)
- SharePoint Accessibility (606 results)
- SharePoint Governance (231 results)
- SharePoint Compliance (191 results)
- SharePoint Risk Management (181 results)
- SharePoint Privacy (93 results)

YouTube
- SharePoint (4,400 videos)
- SharePoint Governance (17 videos)
- SharePoint Accessibility (2 videos)
- SharePoint Compliance (0 videos)
- SharePoint Risk Management (0 videos)
- SharePoint Privacy (0 videos)

Facebook
- SharePoint (171 Groups)
- SharePoint Governance (6 Groups)
- SharePoint Compliance (2 Groups)

- SharePoint Risk Management (2 Groups)
- SharePoint Privacy (0 Groups)
- SharePoint Accessibility (1 Group)

Twitter (Twellow.com)
- SharePoint (1,756 Matches)
- SharePoint Governance (1 Match)
- SharePoint Compliance (0 Matches)
- SharePoint Risk Management (0 Matches)
- SharePoint Privacy (0 Matches)
- SharePoint Accessibility (0 Matches)

LinkedIn
- SharePoint (635 Groups)
- SharePoint Governance (4 Groups)
- SharePoint Compliance (0 Groups)
- SharePoint Risk Management (0 Groups)
- SharePoint Privacy (0 Groups)
- SharePoint Accessibility (0 Groups)

With this data we can start to draw some conclusions. Further examination is required to determine if the competition is present at any of these venues. Some time will have to be put in to see what SharePoint topics are being discussed in the different channels.

- *SlideShare.net.* Is the most delineated between the various SharePoint topics.
- *YouTube.com.* Has a number of videos; but time is needed to see what topics are discussed and where there might be gaps to exploit.
- *Facebook.* Has a number of Groups. Time is needed to understand which Groups are the most active and what is being discussed.
- *Twitter.* Has almost 2,000 profiles, a small number considering the popularity of SharePoint. Time will tell if the Twitter community will produce any positive results.

· *LinkedIn.* Has 635 SharePoint Groups. Time will be spent understanding which Groups are the most active and what is being discussed.

Community Participants' Issues Today

Many times the name of the group gives us a hint about who the members are. The 10 most popular Sharepoint groups on LinkedIn are:

1. Microsoft Business Intelligence (27,273 members)
2. SharePoint Users Group (22,037 members)
3. SharePoint Experts (13,624 members)
4. PartnerPoint—An Online Community of Microsoft Partners (12,965 members)
5. The IT Developer Network (13,124 members)
6. Microsoft Office SharePoint Server (12,783 members)
7. SharePoint 2007–2010 (11,044 members)
8. Worldwide Intranet Challenge (8,019 members)
9. SharePoint 2010 (6,599 members)
10. Programmers and Developers (5,960 members)

From the names of the Groups, it's obvious that a wide variety of users are talking about every aspect of SharePoint. It will take time to determine which Groups may bear the most fruit.

Add to the Conversation Already Underway without Being Overly Promotional

The best approach may be to just listen to the group's discussion before jumping in. Keep the comments brief. Never be "salesy." Keep the discussion benefit-driven. Answer people's concerns without being overly promotional. Resist taking control of the conversation. Look for gaps you can fill. Share tips and tricks.

Involving the Social Networking Community

Different social networking campaigns identifying the pain points for each segment will be developed for the various subject areas: SharePoint Governance, SharePoint Compliance, SharePoint Risk Management, SharePoint Privacy, and SharePoint Accessibility.

We will work closely with our SEO expert to gather the best key phrases to use in creating compelling messaging in the community.

A broader campaign focusing on SharePoint in general will be used to draw visitors in and direct them to the delineated campaigns.

Landing pages with case studies, data sheet, and whitepapers will be developed for each subject area.

Maintaining Our Social Networking Presence

Social networking responsibilities will be divided among several people. The CEO will handle the overall messaging related to the direction of the company. The IT folks will cover the support functions and interface with HR when new social networking tools are introduced. The various engineering groups will handle the subject matter expert duties for posting and texting. One person will oversee the social networking project management duties.

The Length of Our Commitment

A successful social networking marketing plan cannot unfold and produce fruit in just a few weeks. Relationships take time to develop. Trust with prospects and customers is not built overnight. CoolTools Software is determined to give the SMM six months. It will be monitored closely in order to measure the results—good or bad.

Adapting Our Company Culture to the Demands of Social Networking

Because CoolTools is a relatively new venture with a large number of younger employees, it was easy for CoolTools to sell the idea of moving to the social networking stratosphere. CoolTools will integrate social networking education into its new employee orientation program.

Measuring Success or Failure

Measurements will be taken from a variety of sources. Numbers are important, as are metrics.

- Benchmarks will be taken on the website, blog, LinkedIn, Twitter, and Facebook.
- New and returning visitor's actions will be tracked on the website and blog, as well as the campaign landing pages. We'll be able to see what campaign tactics had the best results. LinkedIn, Twitter, and Facebook visitors will be separated to see which campaigns garnered the best outcomes. The analytics will also show what times of the day and days of the week were most successful bringing in visitors.
- The LinkedIn, Twitter, and Facebook discussions will be checked to see what results were produced and how much engagement was created.
- Landing page messaging and the offers presented will be examined to see which produced the best results.

BE **STRATEGIC**

- Prototype. Prototype. Prototype.
- Launch one campaign at a time so metrics and measurements will be easier to understand.
- Shut down the campaigns that are not producing results. Retool the campaigns once they start to languish.

Chapter 17

Social Networking
Best Practices

Social Media Team

"Conversations among the members of your marketplace happen whether you like it or not. Good marketing encourages the right sort of conversations."

—SETH GODIN

DEVELOPING BEST PRACTICES IN YOUR BUSINESS SAVES TIME, MONEY, and resources. Cultivating social networking best practices results in the same benefits. Backlinks boost the prominence of any web or blog page. Having text links pointing from one page to another page helps extend the story or information being relayed. Backlinks also give the web or blog page importance in the search listings.

Getting noticed in the social networking communities is a good thing. Developing a bad reputation in these communities will be hard to shake off. Learn what it takes to develop the best possible reputation as you move from one social networking community to the next.

Best practices deliver the best results.

Connecting, following, or befriending just anyone dilutes your influence and standing among those in your audience. Connect with like-minded people who can help your business and whose business you can assist. Learn how to expand your social networking audience.

If you don't have time to be social at least take the time to be consistent. Trying to be social minute by minute or day by day may present too many distractions. Deciding to only attend to your social networking duties over the weekend will leave your connections wondering why they are not hearing from you for days on end. Create a simple schedule that you can live with while still getting your job done. You may find that you have to skip a day once in awhile but most times you'll be on schedule and able to reply to friends and colleagues.

Social Media Team

Send Someone Some Link Love

"Our most basic common link is that we all inhabit this planet."

—JOHN F. KENNEDY

Some would say "link love" is equivalent to Google's Page Rank. One of Google's measurements in determining Page Rank is the number and quality of links pointing at a certain web page, website, or blog posting.

These love links are called "backlinks," and are hyperlinks from one web page or blog page to another web page or blog page. Links coming to a web page are called "inbound links" and links going out to another page are called "outbound links." These links continue, or flesh out, a story or give the reader more information. In Figure 17.1, the blog entry from BillPetro.

com/blog has two links pointing to other sites (the arrows). The first link points to a historical site which talks about the great reformer Martin Luther. The second link points to a Google video of Martin Luther King's memorable "I Have a Dream" speech during the March on Washington, August 28, 1963.

History of Martin Luther King Jr.

by BILL PETRO *on* JANUARY 15, 2010 · 0 COMMENTS

in AUDIO, HISTORY, HOLIDAYS, US

HISTORY OF MARTIN LUTHER KING, JR

Born on January 15, 1929, we celebrate a holiday in honor of a man who was not a president, nor an explorer, nor a saint, rather he was a Baptist minister and an American leader of the 1960s civil rights movement who was named after the Protestant Reformer Martin Luther. Though he was awarded by President Carter the Presidential Medal of Freedom posthumously in 1977, it was not until 1986 that a day was established on his birthday as a federal holiday.

The only other American federal holidays that honored *individuals* have been for Jesus, Presidents Washington and Lincoln, and Christopher Columbus.

Though **Martin Luther King, Jr.** had an earned doctorate degree, he was also an ordained minister, the son and grandson of ministers. From his biblical roots came many of the metaphors of his talks, the text of his presentations, and the cadence of his speech. He served as a minister starting in 1954 in Alabama, where after he led the boycott against segregation on buses that lasted 382 days. During this time he was arrested, his house was bombed, and he suffered personal abuse.

It was his involvement in the **American Civil Rights Movement** that gave him his greatest visibility, as he began in 1957 non-violent civil disobedience, not unlike **Ghandi**'s in India. Marches and protests were an effective means of accomplishing many of his goals, culminating in 1963 with the "March on Washington for Jobs and Freedom" and most famous speech, entitled "I Have A Dream" which he delivered from the Lincoln Memorial in the Mall of Washington, DC.

FIGURE 17.1—Blog posting honoring Martin Luther King Jr.

You can send someone some link love by having a text link or hyperlink on your website or blog that points to a page on another website or blog. Links give people the option to drill down in a subject that matters most to them.

These links expand on the subject being talked about in the blog posting. In this instance the links reference Martin Luther and the bio of Martin Luther King, Jr. and his now-famous speech.

Backlinks also help boost the prominence of any page in search listings. The pages with the most links and the links with the highest Page Rank are listed at the front of the search results. If you had two blog pages about the same topic and one page had no backlinks and the other page had dozens, the chances are the page with the most backlinks would be listed before the page with no links.

Linking from one page on your website to another page on your site is also encouraged. This practice helps the website visitor drill down in the information without being lost. Think about linking between your website and blog as a way of creating cross-traffic.

Ethical link love states that if one blogger uses content from another person's website or blog, he gives a link back to the original website content or blog post.

Remember, the number of links back to your website or blog increases its Page Rank and therefore its placement in the search listings.

BE **STRATEGIC**

- Be generous in giving links where link love is due.
- It's quite acceptable to give yourself link love between your website, blog, Facebook page, and tweets.

Social Media Team

Get Noticed in a Good Way

"Get someone else to blow your horn and the sound will carry twice as far."

—WILL ROGERS

Let's talk about being noticed in the social networking community, noticed without being obnoxious or looking desperate, that is. Getting noticed in a good way is good for business.

Some quick ways to begin to establish credibility in the social networking stratosphere are:

Organizations work hard to position themselves as the experts in a certain field, the authorities, the go-to guys, the thought leaders.

- Identify the influencers in your business sector and comment on their blog posts. Posts such as "Great post!" or "This information really helps me" are worthless. These posting tactics are used by spammers looking for backlinks. They're usually deleted and never approved by the owner of the blog. Take the time and energy to post something useful. If you leave cogent posts, readers following this blogger will start following you.
- Video podcasts are a great way for people to see more of you or your team. Podcasts are the next best thing to a face-to-face meeting. They can be posted on your website, blog, YouTube, iTunes, PodcastDirectory, PodcastAlley, or a hundred other points across the web. Keep the podcast interesting, timely, and fast-paced, and never lose eye contact with the viewer.

- Webinars extend the podcast conversation by making it two-way. People joining a webinar can talk with the presenter and ask questions. Webinars hold more value as a tutorial instrument. Organizations can host their own webinars or use a free or paid service. Check out WebEx, GoToMeeting, ConnectPro, and DimDim.
- Join or start your own discussions on LinkedIn. There are already 480,000 Groups and growing. Your organization is bound to find a place to fit. Question traditional thinking. Push the envelope of conventional wisdom. Ask thought-provoking questions.
- Check out what's being talked about in your business sector on Twitter and join the discussion. Use Trendistic to see what Twitter conversations are hot. Twitter also provides a search tool to look up phrases.
- There are free article submission websites popping up each day. A few of the more popular sites are ezinearticles.com, articlesbase.com, goarticles.com, and articlecity.com. These sites are used by two groups on the web: those individuals writing articles and looking for a place to publish their work, and those looking to boost the content of their website. For instance, a person launching a website selling pet supplies could go to free article sites and pick up articles dealing with pet training, pet health, and breeding. These articles would create interest on the retailer's site and give search engines more content to index for better placement in the search results. Choose the sites that best fit your business model and then scan the site to see what people are reading. This gives you a good idea of what's there and any gaps in the conversation, which could be a great opportunity for you to say what you have to say.
- Sites such as SlideShare.net are a perfect platform for those presentations companies work so hard to produce.

After the conference is over, after everyone leaves the sales and marketing meeting, or after the new product announcement take the presentations and upload them to SlideShare.net. Now they are available to millions of viewers and can create new visitor streams to your website or blog.

BE **STRATEGIC**

▶ It can't be said enough. Don't look desperate. Don't be obnoxious. Take the time to come up with a visibility plan and then execute it over time.

▶ Take the time to understand who and what is driving a discussion before adding your comments.

Social Media Team

Connecting, Following, and Befriending

"He who hath many friends hath none."

—ARISTOTLE

Some people in social networking are there for purely personal reasons. They're not there to engage in conversation. They're there simply to collect followers and friends in order to have bragging rights every time they collect another thousand. It would be good if these people could find better uses of their bandwidth.

Some ways to connect with people make sense. On LinkedIn people cannot connect with other business people without both parties agreeing to the connection. One person has to send out an invitation to connect, and the other person has the option to accept that invitation or reject it. You can look up the person's profile before connecting, so it's easy to make sure you have common interests.

Connecting with everyone on the planet dilutes your pool of influence.

Every time you attend a business breakfast, other semi-social business events, or a business meeting ask those around you if they're on LinkedIn. Is so, ask them if you can send them an invite. Every time you finish working for a client and you've done a fantastic job, ask her if you can send a request for a recommendation. You'll never know what common interest might surface in the future.

Facebook works much the same way LinkedIn does. Each party has to agree to befriend the other before a connection is final. If your organization has a Facebook Fan page where you talk about your new products or services, remember that page is open to the public. Anyone can join and become a fan. Organizations love to be fans of their competitors so they can keep an eye them.

The Twitter community provides the least amount of resistance in gathering connections. Anyone can follow anyone else. Of course unwanted followers can be blocked from following. If you're looking for people to follow, MrTweet, Twellow, and WeFollow are good resources to see who's talking about what.

BE **STRATEGIC**

- ◗ Connect with and follow the influencers.
- ◗ Weekly/weekend: Check to see who's talking about new trends and connect.

Building solid relationships takes time and effort. Don't short-change your followers.

Social Media Team

Are You a Manic Depressive or Social Media Maniac?

"If we weren't all crazy, we'd just go insane."

—Jimmy Buffett

Clinically speaking, a manic depressive disorder is defined by the presence of one or more episodes of abnormally elevated mood. Some manic episodes include increased energy and activity, with rapid talking and thinking, followed by sustained periods of unusual, even bizarre behavior. That would accurately describe some social networking personalities representing companies (and individuals, too, of course). They don't post to their blog or text to their friends or colleagues for weeks at a time. They don't reply to messages sent to them nor do they participate in the community groups they joined with such enthusiasm. The company site looks like it has gone out of business. Then, without any warning, they're back . . . alive . . . and conversing. Was the organization's social networking person out of the country? Suffer a grave illness? Nope, just distracted, disorganized, sidetracked, or overworked. There's no method to the company's madness in being a social networking participant. It's on the social networking fringe. Not committed. No strategy. Its influence will never be felt. The competition will soon fill the void.

Whether the company is a one-person business or a large organization, the commitment to social networking should be consistent, compelling, and informative. The social networking community is a fragile, collaborative ecosystem. People will follow a trail of dependable, exciting, instructive news. But once the trail goes cold, they're gone and likely never to return.

But being a social media maniac isn't the right persona either. You know who we're talking about. You know who you are. These people can answer e-mails on their laptops with one hand while texting friends or colleagues on their iPhones with the other. They can't be looked in the eye when talking because their heads are always looking down at some screen. This behavior may be seen as good technology gone bad.

How about striking a balance somewhere in the middle. Avoid becoming a manic depressive or a social media maniac. Develop a social networking schedule that does not run your life but does keep you accountable. The sample social networking agenda below can be used as a springboard for designing one that suits your schedule and the community channels you've joined.

Sample Social Networking Agenda

Twice Daily Mornings/Afternoons
- Check Twitter via HootSuite. Respond when necessary. Follow the @replies that make sense.
- Check LinkedIn. Reply to e-mails and comments when appropriate.
- Scan Twitter followers for relevant conversations to join.
- Scan Google Alerts for brand and company mentions. Respond as appropriate.

Weekly/Weekends
- Build Twitter Lists to better organize ongoing discussions and special interest groups.
- Scan LinkedIn questions from network connections and respond when appropriate.

If a schedule is too restrictive then try a social "things-to-do" list. Work on the list during the week as time permits. Just make sure you finish all your social tasks by the end of business Friday.

- Catch up on LinkedIn group discussions. Add to discussion when appropriate.
- Check MrTweet and Twellow for new Twitter follow recommendations.
- Send LinkedIn invitations to connect with clients when beginning a new assignment.
- Ask for LinkedIn recommendation after successfully completing a project or engagement.
- Scan LinkedIn for new connections and send invitations when appropriate.
- Think of ways to repurpose this content and energy to reach a larger audience with the social networking gospel.
- Keep an eye open for new social networking venues, tools, and functionality that will make the social networking experience more enjoyable and easier to traverse.
- Identify new social networking influencers and build relationships where appropriate.

Ongoing
- Mondays. Schedule tweets through HootSuite to go out three times per day at eight-hour intervals.
- Mondays, Wednesdays, and Fridays. Join one hot trend conversation on Twitter, if appropriate.
- Tuesdays and Thursdays. Respond to blog comments.
- Fridays. Check traffic at your blog or website.

> ## BE **STRATEGIC**
>
> ▶ Be consistent. Stay the course for at least six months.
>
> ▶ Start out small and grow into your social networking persona.

Obviously, your daily social networking to-do list will be much different, given your available time and commitments. Just be sure to make the schedule livable. If it's not working, change it. Keep making modifications until it works for you.

Chapter 18

Social Networking and the Website

Social Media Team

"Do the right thing. It will gratify some people and astonish the rest."

—MARK TWAIN

MAKE THE COMPANY WEBSITE SOCIALLY ACCEPTABLE. SOME organizations have the best intentions when they start their social networking campaigns, but then everyone gets busy and the effort expended on social networking is one of the first causalities. When visitors come to the website expecting current blog and social networking channels, they find the blog posts are several weeks behind. It does not put the company in the best light. Prospects and customers are left wondering if the company is committed to hearing from them.

If the corporate website is not the right place to post your social media icons, then place them on the company blog.

FIGURE 18.1—A way to merge news happenings and community on a website

Company websites have long employed In the News, Events, and Press Release sections to keep customers and prospects abreast of company happenings. Now it's time to pull all of this information together in one easy-to-find spot on the corporate website by merging social networking with In the News, Events, and Press Releases into one location. Figure 18.1 shows an example of how this might be done.

Some companies hide the fact they're doing social networking. If you're going to do social networking, let people know. OK, maybe it would be best not to announce anything until the venture is up and running, everyone knows their assignments, the kinks have been worked out, and things are off to a good start. Then add the social networking icons to the website's homepage and start engaging your visitors.

BE **STRATEGIC**

▶ Don't use the Community section to advertise new product releases or announce the next trade show event.

▶ Ask provocative questions. Draw the reader into a discussion.

▶ Keep things current. This might not sound strategic but social networking is hard to restart once people think the company is not committed.

Letting People Know You're Out There

Social Media Team

"Confidence is contagious. So is lack of confidence."

—VINCE LOMBARDI

THE SOCIAL NETWORKING STRATOSPHERE IS A VIRAL COMMUNITY. Word spreads faster than a California brush fire being fanned by the Santa Ana winds. Why not leverage that enthusiasm by putting a signature at the bottom of all your e-mails to let people know where you congregate on the web.

Xeesm.com and WiseStamp.com offer an e-mail signature tool to inform people where they can find you online. I have one. Figure 19.1 shows my Xeesm e-mail signature. All someone has to do is click on the hyperlink "Where I hang out on the web," and a small window (shown in Figure 19.2) opens showing the communities, websites, and blogs where people can find me.

There's a photo. It's not really me. (Someone said he was dead, OMG!), a short description and a list of the places I hang out.

FIGURE 19.1—Viral signature at the end of an e-mail

The little stair steps to the right let people know where I'm most active.

There is also a My Groups tab to identify the Groups someone has joined and an Other Places tab so people can separate their locations on the web even further.

WiseStamp also offers a signature widget (Figure 19.3) with several dozen formats to choose from. It's easy to set up and it's configurable. You can add your photo, company logo, a handwritten signature, and personal feeds. WiseStamp lets you

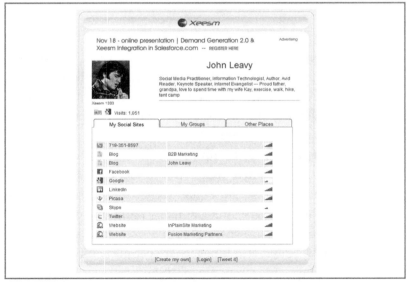

FIGURE 19.2—Xeesm viral signature popup

FIGURE 19.3—WiseStamp viral signature at the end of an e-mail

create personal as well as business signatures. It works with Gmail, Google Apps, *Yahoo!* Mail, Hotmail, and more.

BE **STRATEGIC**

▶ Make sure to add your signature to everything coming out of the company, such as newsletters, blog postings, and article submissions.

▶ Display your signatures on all social networking channels: LinkedIn, Facebook, Twitter, and so forth.

Chapter 20

Gaining Notoriety in the Social Networking Communities

Social Media Team

"I want to be famous everywhere."

—LUCIANO PAVAROTTI

Y OU NEED TO GAIN SOCIAL NETWORKING STREET CRED. STREET CRED is defined in *The Urban Dictionary* as "commanding a level of respect in an urban environment due to experience in or knowledge of issues affecting those environments" or "a person's coolness factor." Credibility is important in any business space. Without it, who's going to listen to the messenger?

Someone might think he has credibility in a certain marketplace because he has more than 10,000 followers on Twitter. But 10,000 followers do not mean they're hanging on every word that person texts.

Some people think social networking "street cred" is all about numbers and eyeballs.

Why work to convince thousands of followers they need a product or service when it would be much easier to talk with ten people who are already predisposed to your marketing message.

A truer metric for street cred is: Are the people listening, engaging. Are they taking action? Remember, social networking is not about page views or impressions. That was the strategy for banner ads. Social networking is all about engagement and action.

Don't let the pendulum swing too far in the other direction. There's nothing wrong with numbers. Numbers are meaningful to a degree. Numbers are just not the only metric that defines the success or failure of a social networking campaign, but marketing is a numbers game.

Consider this scenario: You have a Twitter account with 24 followers (Figure 20.1). You send out all kinds of tweets, follow people, and ask them to follow you back. One week later the number of followers jumps to over 4,000. What does that mean? It's too soon to tell. People have been attracted by the tweets sent out, but until engagement takes place, the real value of the 4,000 followers cannot be determined. You need to consider what drew these followers. Were the tweets sent out about a brand awareness

FIGURE 20.1—Twitter stats showing name, location, hashtags, and connections

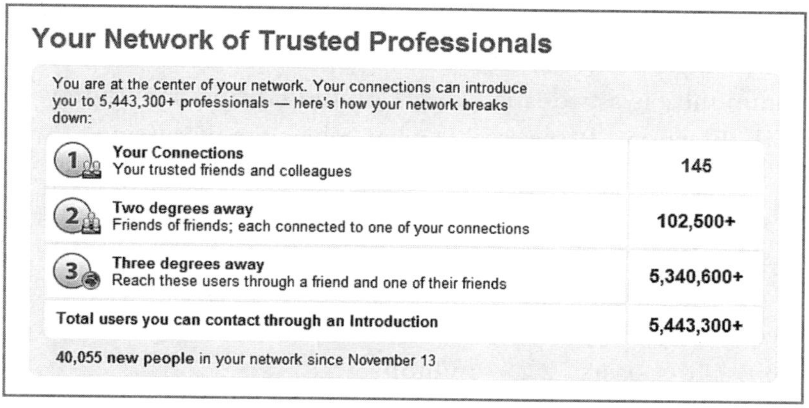

Your Network of Trusted Professionals

You are at the center of your network. Your connections can introduce you to 5,443,300+ professionals — here's how your network breaks down:

1	**Your Connections** Your trusted friends and colleagues	**145**
2	**Two degrees away** Friends of friends; each connected to one of your connections	**102,500+**
3	**Three degrees away** Reach these users through a friend and one of their friends	**5,340,600+**
	Total users you can contact through an Introduction	**5,443,300+**

40,055 new people in your network since November 13

FIGURE 20.2—LinkedIn stats showing network connections

campaign? Was a compelling offer made? Are the followers loyal customers already? Are they prospects looking for a solution? What action(s) are they willing to take? Are they ready to purchase or do they need more education?

Figure 20.2 gives another numbers example. Some pretty huge numbers are shown. You might say, "Wow, over 5 million connections!" The truth is most of the 5 million connections are unknown and can only be reached through the 145 first-level connections. The real useful number in this case is the 145 direct connections. These people are known friends, colleagues, or business associates. These people are more likely to take action on a request.

Now that you understand that numbers are not all that matters, let's look at a few metrics that will help you measure your effectiveness in gaining "street cred" in the social networking stratosphere.

In Twitter terms, if the number of followers is building slowly, if a percentage of tweets being sent out are compelling enough to be retweeted, and if the Twitter followers are taking some action—downloading an offer, joining a discussion, coming to a landing page—then it could be said that a credible Twitter campaign is being administrated. Keep in mind that the Twitter community is a two-lane street. Communication should flow in both directions. Retweet (RT) what others are discussing as well as send out your own messages. Join in discussions by replying (@) to what others are saying. Jump in group talks by replying to hashtag (#) discussions.

Being seen in all the right places also helps boost one's creditability. List your organization in the Twellow Pages (Twellow. com). It boasts 2.25 million followers with 15.6 million profiles on tap, from Aerospace and Aviation to Telecommunications and Textiles. Twellow is a great site to see who's listed in your business space. For instance, there are 1,337 profiles listed in 2B2 marketing. If your organization does B2B marketing, are you listed there?

Twellow is also a good place to find organizations and individuals to follow on the cutting edge in your business space. Following the right people also adds creditability.

> ## BE **STRATEGIC**
>
> ▶ Follow the influencers. Hopefully they'll return the action.
>
> ▶ Comment on trends and ask questions that make people think. Question conventional wisdom. Throw out thoughts and see if people agree with you or discount your perceptions.

Chapter 21

New Rules for
Social Networking

Social Media Team

"How can you squander even one more day not taking advantage of
the greatest shifts of our generation? How dare you settle for less
when the world has made it so easy for you to be remarkable?"

—SETH GODIN

NOW THAT YOU HAVE A BASIC UNDERSTANDING OF HOW SOCIAL MEDIA
works, let's develop an experiment to see if you can define
some goals to accomplish, build a plan of action, execute that
plan, and garner the desired results. What if you decided to use
social networking to let people know about this book: *Outcome-*
Based Marketing: New Rules for Marketing on the Web?

Your labor of love is over and the book manuscript is finally
complete. The next step in the process is to send it off to the
publisher. The publisher will now edit the manuscript, lay out
the pages, and design the book cover. Now it's time to begin your
awareness campaign.

How can you use social networking as a venue to raise
awareness, create excitement and land speaking opportunities?
Let's apply what we've learned:

The Social Media Inputs

The Inputs will be in the form of excerpts from the book, posted discussions and promotions on LinkedIn, and tweets sent out on Twitter. We'll also share information on upcoming speaking engagements.

The Social Media Activities

The LinkedIn Tactics
·   We'll share updates with our connections as we land speaking engagements, add blog posts, or secure locations for the book tour.
·   We'll use information from the book to start raising awareness for the book by starting discussions.
·   We'll add promotions about the book tour and upcoming cities.
·   We'll join specific groups and contribute to discussions where their interests are in line with the contents of the book.

The Facebook Tactics
·   On hold

The Twitter Tactics
·   Start by following the influencers.
·   Tweet about the discussion we start on LinkedIn.
·   Tweet about the speaking opportunities as they develop.
·   Tweet about posts as they relate to excerpts from the book.
·   Listen to conversations and follow those people where appropriate.
·   Keep an eye on trends as they relate to the subject matter in the book.

The Social Media Masses

Generally speaking, people tend to belong to several social communities at one time. They may listen in some communities and participate in others. They may have decided to separate their work colleagues from their family and friends.

What we need to understand about any community before we join it is whether our ideal prospects are there. If they're present we'll want to engage them. If not, we're wasting our efforts to sell the book in those venues.

Let's say we've decided our ideal prospects look likes this:

- They are a small business person or entrepreneur.
- The company size is less than 100 employees.
- They may already be on the web or contemplating the move to cyperspace.
- They're not afraid of technology.
- They love to learn and they're teachable.
- They're open to new ideas.
- They could be running a for-profit company or a not-for-profit organization.
- They read articles on web presence, lead generation, social media, and closing deals.

We could add more characteristics, but let's stop here for our exercise. Let's look at the LinkedIn and Twitter communities for this exercise.

The LinkedIn Community

LinkedIn is a community of professionals, some from one-horse, one-rider businesses and others from global conglomerates. Is every member of LinkedIn our ideal prospect? No, but many are excellent candidates. LinkedIn has a variety of ways we can reach people without being obnoxious. The focus of our campaigns will be three-fold. We'll focus on pain points, the remedies, and the benefits once the problems have been eliminated.

The Twitter Community

Twitter is the most diverse community of the two. We'll find ideal prospects for the book here and others that have no interest in talking business. The information stream in Twitter is constantly moving and it's harder to get people's attention or to be heard. Our marketing tactics will have to be more calculated.

The Social Media Leads

Remember leads are people that take some action to move the relationship forward. These people will be classified as leads:

· Those that sign up for the book announcement.
· Those that comment on our posts or discussions.
· Those that connect or follow us.
· Those that we connect with or follow. (potential leads)

The Social Media Outcome Targets

Defining Outcome Targets will keep us on track. Our goals might look like this:

· Create awareness of the book's eminent release.
· Provide an opportunity for people to sign up early to be notified when the book hits the bookstores.
· Look for speaking opportunities to promote the book.

We'll be doing marketing activities outside the social communities to promote the book; but for this exercise we'll concentrate on the social tactics. We only have so many hours each day for marketing. Our time and money should be spent wisely.

Let's convert our goals into numbers so we can track the outcomes.

1. Change the LinkedIn shared area once per week.
2. Post a promotion about the book in five groups per week.
3. Start new discussions in five different groups every two weeks.
4. Connect with 10 to 20 new LinkedIn members each month.

5. Have 10 to 15 LinkedIn members sign up for the book announcement each month.

6. Send out at least two new tweets per day three times per week.

7. Answer all replies within 24 hours.

8. Gain 100 new Twitter followers each month.

9. Have 5 to 10 Twitter followers sign up for the book announcement each month.

10. Try and connect with one to two influencers per week.

The Social Media Outcome Indicators

A positive outcome is what we're looking for to happen with our social media marketing campaigns. We've developed some baseline results with our goals. Now we can track those numbers to see if our projections are on the mark or way off base. Based on the numbers we can make adjustments to our prototype campaigns until we start receiving numbers that justify our efforts and investment.

Tracking LinkedIn Results

Tracking prospects in the LinkedIn community won't be so obvious. We cannot tell how many people read our promotions or discussion entries. We will know how many went to our blog or signed up to be notified of the book's release by looking at the analytics. It will be apparent how many people connect with us and how many we connect with as well.

Tracking Twitter Results

The results from the Twitter community will be similar. We won't know how many followers are listening to what we have to say, but we will notice those that take some action. The stats from Twitter will be gathered in the same manner as in LinkedIn.

As results come in we'll have to decide where to put our next efforts. LinkedIn may show more promise than Twitter. If that's the case, then it will make sense to dial down our efforts in Twitter and add more resources to the LinkedIn marketing.

Outcome-Based Marketing: Social Networking

· *Inputs.* Excerpts from the book along with LinkedIn discussions and promotional ads, plus Twitter messages.
· *Activities.* Change the LinkedIn shared area once per week. Post a promotion about the book in five groups per week. Start new discussions in five different groups every two weeks. Connect with 10 to 20 new LinkedIn members each month. Send out at least two new tweets per day three times per week. Answer all replies within 24 hours. Identify influencers.
· *Masses.* The LinkedIn and Twitter communities at large.
· *Leads.* Those that sign up for the book announcement, comment on our posts or discussions, connect or follow us, and those that we connect with or follow.
· *Outcome targets.* Connect with 10 to 20 new LinkedIn members each month. Have 10 to 15 LinkedIn members sign up for the book announcement each month. Have 5 to 10 Twitter followers sign up for the book announcement each month. Try and connect with one to two influencers per week.
· *Outcome indicators.* LinkedIn and Twitter results along with Google Analytics.

Take 5

Be Social on the Web

"However beautiful the strategy, you should occasionally look at the results."
—WINSTON CHURCHILL

The social media stratosphere is moving at lightspeed. Only apply this technology where and when it makes sense. Put a social media strategy together and then follow it to completion. Chatting is fine, but find time to do that with your firiends. From a business perspective there needs to be quantifiable reasons why the company is investing its time, talent, and invaluable resources in this technology.

Leveraging the Social Networking Stratosphere. Determine how to leverage social networking and then start out small. Either decide on a campaign to boost brand recognition or launch one to accelerate customer care. It will be hard to measure progress if several campaigns are started and compete for the customer or prospect's attention at the same time. If brand recognition and customer care are both social networking goals, then start one campaign by gathering metrics and wait for it to mature. Then start a second campaign. Make sure your ideal prospect or current customer base has a footprint in the social networking communities before expending resources.

The Roles People Play in the Social Networking Stratosphere. Remember, being involved in the social networking takes a "community" effort. Delegating the social networking responsibilities to one person in the organization will not work effectively. How can one person show the personality of the whole group? How can one person be abreast of all that's going on in the company? How can one person speak for all areas? How can one person be the subject matter expert in the whole the company? Pick a social networking team that can support each other and go for it!

Do You Really Have Time to Be Social? The first place to start in developing a social networking strategy is in listening to what's happening. Join LinkedIn, Facebook, and Twitter. Then listen to what people are talking about. Assess what conversations you can contribute to and then start conversing. If the conversations bear fruit, and you need to determine what that means, then become more involved based on the time constraints of everyone's calendars. Give the team assignments, develop a social networking syndication plan, and stick to it for six months.

Social Networking Parts and Pieces: Profiles, Friends, Groups, and Discussions. You'll find that different social networking outlets ask for various bits of personal information in creating your profiles. Give only what you believe the group needs to know. Some groups are more professional while others are more casual. Join groups that best suit the organization's goals. Follow the rock stars within the various communities. They're usually in the driver's seat and can tell you where the group is headed. Connect with people of like minds and common interests.

If You Don't Want to See It in Print Forever Then Don't Say It. Whatever is said or shared in the social networking stratosphere cannot be taken back. It will hang in the internet cloud forever. If it's juicy, insulting, or offensive you can bet people will spread the news around faster than if the Chicago Cubs were in the World Series. Keep things civil and professional. Remember, all of the people connected to you may not have the company's best interests or your career at heart.

Don't Drop Your Drawers on the Web. Some are relaxed after joining a social networking community. Somehow they believe Facebook, LinkedIn, or Twitter is guarding their every word. Their personal identify is safe, secure, locked up tight. The juvenile delinquents with time on their hands have already moved into the social networks to distribute their worms, trojans, and computer-hacking viruses. According to Ian Amit, director of research at Aladdin's Attack Intelligence Research Center, the potential damage for this new type of identity theft will be "devastating, both on the personal level by creating difficulties in employment, ruining social and professional connections, damaging reputations; as well as on a financial level, such as stealing customers, corporate data." Be careful what information you list in your profiles whether company or personal.

Create Different Social Networking Personas. LinkedIn is a business community while Twitter is more casual. To be successful in both it will take two different personas. One voice needs to be more formal while the other more relaxed. You'll find one community more open to discuss certain topics while another community might think such topics are out of bounds. Get to know the community before joining in the discussions.

Building Your Social Networking Strategy. Answering the twelve questions posed in this section gives any organization a good indication as to whether or not joining the social networking fray makes sense. A company cannot think it important to join because "everyone else" has. There needs to be achievable, measurable, quantifiable goals. There needs to be commitment by the entire organization. The social networking goals need to be in line with the company's marketing and communication objectives.

The 12 Ingredients of a Winning Social Network Marketing Plan. Have a good understanding of where your ideal prospects gather and what pain points motivate them the most. Take benchmarks before starting any campaign so the results can be measured. Put the plan on paper. Start out slowly and ramp up over time. Shut down the campaigns that are not producing the best results and shift the resources to the more successful efforts.

Send Someone Some Link Love. Don't under estimate the power of linking to other websites and to have those websites or blogs linking back to you. This process creates backlinks and backlinks help a website or blog's position in search listings and creates new visitor streams. Links also help expand the conversation and help educate. Information is what the internet is all about. Send people some link love and the love will come back to you.

Get Noticed in a Good Way. A small child has no trouble getting noticed in a food store when he does not get what he wants. This type of notoriety is not what organizations are seeking. The company wants to be seen as the expert in its field, the one company that has the best solution at the best price and can deliver the product or service in less time than any of its competitors. We're talking about credibility. Credibility will take time in the social networking community much like it takes time in any other venue.

Connecting, Following, and Befriending. Don't be a company that joins social networking communities just to make noise and extol the company's virtues, only to clog up the airwaves.

Connect and follow people who can be helpful to the organization and whom the organization can assist. Community means both parties benefit. The social networking stratosphere is more of a casual environment so have fun, find groups and people you enjoy.

Are You a Manic Depressive or Social Media Maniac? Consistency is everything when social networking. If time and resources are limited then limit the company's participation in the various groups. As time permits and resources loosen up, increase the company's level of commitment. Stay consistent. The other social networking members are not interested in listening to or following an organization that is indifferent. Put a social networking schedule together and stick to it.

Social Networking and the Website. The website and what's said elsewhere need to be in harmony. Consider creating a spot on the website where "community" can take place. Merge the news, events, press releases, and social networking hooks in one setting. Make sure the messaging is not identical.

Letting People Know You're Out There. Building a following in any social networking community takes time. Be as viral as possible. Keep track of the different social networking channels the organization has joined and also note the influencer's channels. Use every opportunity to tell people where you hang out on the web. They'll become aware of the common interests and start following.

Gaining Notoriety in the Social Networking Communities. There are a variety of tools, such as Twitterholic, TwitterAnalyzer, and Twinfluence that will help you gauge your participation level against your competitors if that's what you need to do. Blog on a regular basis and bookmark the postings to the social forums where your ideal prospects gather. The beauty of the social networking community is you can be unheard of one week and seen as a key contributor, a person-in-the-know, the next.

PART IV

GENERATE CLOSABLE OPPORTUNITIES

Leads are critical to the sales process, but talking about leads can be confusing because lots of terms are thrown around that may not mean the same thing to everyone. There are hot leads, warm leads, and cold leads; qualified leads and unqualified leads; A leads, B leads, and C leads. For discussion purposes here, a "lead" is defined as someone who has shown interest in or taken some action on an offer: a website visitor downloads a whitepaper, takes a free trial, subscribes to a newsletter, or joins a webinar. These are all examples of leads that could potentially turn into sales. But how do you move these leads through the sales process to create closable opportunities? Leads need to become prospects, and prospects in turn need to develop into opportunities.

> *"We are all faced with a series of great opportunities brilliantly disguised as impossible situations."*
>
> —CHARLES R. SWINDOLL

On the web, businesses need to know how prospects are searching for them. If the company sells coffee, are the searchers keying "whole bean coffee" or "coffee beans" into their browsers? These may not be the same search terms the business owner is thinking of using. Companies have to identify the key phrases potential visitors are using to find them. With that information in hand, businesses can synchronize their messaging and their content using those key phrases. If the business is using social channels, the messages going out need to include the company's key phrases as well. Everything needs to be in harmony: the key phrases, the company's brand promise, and messaging, along with all the organization's content. Any instrument out of tune could spell disaster for the marketing campaign.

Statistics tell us that only 3 to 5 percent of the visitors to a website are ready to make a purchase or commitment. What are we to do with the remaining 97 percent? This is where education and lead nurturing come into play. Companies need to move at the buyer's pace. Until the time of purchase, businesses need to build and foster relationships with those who are not ready or not sure they want to buy the company's product or service.

Chapter 22

Harmony Makes All the Difference

"There are two golden rules for an orchestra: start together and finish together. The public doesn't give a damn what goes on in between."

—Sir Thomas Beecham

BUSINESSES NEED TO COME TO GRIPS WITH THREE IMPORTANT FACTORS when trying to attract potential customers to their websites: key phrases, messaging, and content. It is critical that they be harmonized.

People search for products or services on the web by using key phrases. If you're looking for a "tax accountant," chances are good that's one of the key phrases you'll key into your favorite browser. If you live in Colorado Springs, Colorado, your search for an accountant might be "tax accountants colorado springs."

It follows then that businesses need to understand how their potential customers are looking for them. Businesses have to identify the best key phrases for their business space. Once they

On the web, it's important to say the same thing over and over.

go through that exercise, the next task is to make sure their website is optimized using those specific key phrases. In this way, when people search for "tax accountants colorado springs," their website should be listed in the search results.

The last step in this harmonizing process is to make sure the content on the website, all the social media chatter they generate and the company's collateral (whitepapers, webinars, and podcasts), resound with the same key terms.

Harmonizing the search phrases, messaging, and content not only keeps the story told to prospects and customers consistent, it positions you in the best possible stance for success.

Tuning Your Key Phrases

"Business is a combination of war and sport."

—Andre Maurois

Search engine optimization (SEO) is key to optimizing a website and its content. Recall from the discussion in Chapter 9 that search engine optimization is the process of placing important terms, keywords, or key phrases, in the headers, web page code, and content of your web pages. For example, a phrase such as "woodland park real estate" could be used if you list and sell homes in Woodland Park, Colorado.

These same keywords and phrases are located in places the visitor cannot see, but search engines can. SEO peppers the web pages with just the right words so people searching for a company's product or service will locate its web pages before its competition's pages. A good SEO campaign takes time and money for it to be successful because they can run from a few months to a year or more.

Today, people search the web for products or services using these key phrases in browsers. Say you're looking for an accountant in the area. You wouldn't key "accountants" into Google. More than 24 million pages would come up. It wouldn't help much to type in "small business accountants" either. There are more than 2 million small business accountant pages in that search. Try adding a geographic location to your search phrase, perhaps "small business accountants colorado springs." Finally, you can sift through the types of small business accountants until you find the right one. It's clear then that key phrases have to be as exact as possible. If you want to buy a new car, you would key in the type of car. No one walks into a car dealership and says, "I want to buy a car." People are more precise, "I'd like to test drive a 2011 Jeep Compass Sport."

Deciding on the best key phrases for your organization is helped by a three-step process that's proven successful over time.

1. Write down one or two dozen phrases that you believe prospects would use to locate your service or product on the web.

2. Visit the websites of your competitors to see what key phrases they have concentrated on.

3. Key both groups of terms into Google's Search-based Keyword Tool: Google.com/sktool. Notice when you key the terms in, Google displays derivatives of the keyed-in phrases. For instance, if you enter "coffee beans," Google displays phrases such as, "green coffee beans," "chocolate covered coffee beans," and "gourmet coffee beans." Soon you should have a list of key phrases that look something like in the terms in Figure 22.1

	A	B
1	coffee beans	165,000
2	wholesale coffee beans	4,400
3	types of coffee beans	1,900
4	roasting coffee beans	12,100
5	chocolate covered coffee beans	5,400
6	bulk coffee beans	2,400
7	arabica coffee beans	1,900
8	raw coffee beans	22,200
9	gourmet coffee beans	2,400
10	coffee bean	246,000
11	roasted coffee beans	9,900
12	coffee bean direct	2,400
13	best coffee beans	5,400
14	unroasted coffee beans	1,000
15	organic coffee beans	4,400
16	green coffee beans	22,200
17	espresso coffee beans	4,400
18	flavored coffee beans	1,600
19	sumatra coffee beans	480
20	buy coffee beans	4,400
21	whole coffee beans	6,600
22	peaberry coffee beans	390
23	kona coffee beans	1,600
24	coffee bean roaster	4,400

FIGURE 22.1—Spreadsheet of possible key phrases

The real art is in selecting the best search phrases for an organization. This is one place SEO experts earn their fees.

Tuning Your Messaging

"Carpe per diem—seize the check."

—ROBIN WILLIAMS

Three typical pieces of an organization's messaging platform are its tagline, shout out, and elevator pitch.

The Tagline:
"Creating Unstoppable Marketing and Sales Machines"

Taglines should be short and succinct, and should immediately tell readers what the company is all about. Many times the tagline is found below or included in a company's logo. Fusion Marketing Partners, an internet B2B marketing company, has a tagline that requires no guess work about what Fusion is all about: "creating unstoppable marketing and sales machines." Here are a few other popular company taglines:

- "You're in good hands."—Allstate
- "Don't leave home without it."—American Express
- "We bring good things to life."—General Electric
- "I've fallen and I can't get up."—LifeCall
- "Think outside the bun."—Taco Bell

The Shout Out

Think of a company's "shout out" like this: You're standing at a corner intersection waiting for the traffic light to change. You yell out to the fellow sitting in his car at the stoplight, "Hey bud, what does your company do?" As the light changes to green, he has about ten seconds to yell out his car window as he pulls away. Here's Fusion's shout out:

Fusion Marketing Partners uses the most effective strategies to help B2B companies generate more awareness, qualified leads, and revenue.

You can see how the tagline and shout out compliment each other. There are no mixed messages being sent. What does the unstoppable machine in the tagline do? Create more awareness, qualified leads, and revenue.

The Elevator Pitch

The elevator pitch is a shout out expanded enough for a short elevator ride. It should include three components: a statement of the business need, how the organization fulfills that need, and how the customer benefits. Fusion is spot-on in presenting its elevator pitch (which for clarity is separated into three parts).

"Increased revenue is the bottom-line priority for business. B2B organizations need to differentiate themselves in a crowded market and they need to bridge the gap between marketing and sales to optimize their performance."

"Fusion Marketing Partners offers deep strategic and tactical expertise in B2B marketing and sales. We deliver systematic and measurable improvements in marketing and sales performance to achieve strong, consistent revenue growth."

"FMP clients achieve an unstoppable marketing and sales machine that delivers large increases in brand awareness, qualified leads, and accelerated sales.

From these few pieces of its messaging platform, you can deduce some of Fusion's probable key phrases: B2B marketing, increased brand awareness, qualified leads, accelerate sales, increase revenue, improve sales performance, and grow revenue.

Having a written tagline, shout out and elevator pitch keeps your messaging focused and consistent.

The messaging sent out in press releases, webinars, social media, and other marketing channels should echo the same key phrases for consistency sake.

Tuning Your Content

"I don't know anything about music. In my line you don't have to."

—ELVIS PRESLEY

Suppose you had one set of key phrases in your search engine optimization and a second set of terms in your messaging? You can see how out of sync your efforts would be in attracting the right visitors to your website, blog, or landing pages. Your message needs to be consistent to the visitor as well as the search engines.

The process for optimizing content for a web page, a press release, or landing page does not differ. Go back to the coffee bean example. Suppose we had three key phrases (bulk coffee beans, storing coffee beans, and raw coffee beans) and we wanted to issue a press release. The title of the release should include the term we believe will bring the most visitors to our website. For example, say its bulk coffee beans. The body of the release should include the use of all three terms (bulk coffee beans, storing coffee beans, and raw coffee beans) more than once, but do not be excessive.

Use the same methodology when creating a web page, press release, landing page, or other collateral. Think of keeping a cheat sheet of your 20 or so key phrases by your side. Each time you create content for the website

BE **STRATEGIC**

- Make sure the key phrases you select are ones you can capture. It doesn't make sense to go after terms you can never win.
- Make sure you use past and present tense, singular and plural, as well as adding -ing to the verbs where it makes sense so your search terms get the best coverage.

or copy for a marketing campaign, take out your sheet of key phrases and include some key phrases when writing your copy.

Chapter 23

Keeping Your Eye
on the Prize

"Marketing is too important to be left to the marketing department."

—DAVID PACKARD

PLANNING IS AN IMPORTANT PART OF ANY SUCCESSFUL VENTURE. IT'S no different with marketing campaigns. Winning marketing campaigns don't just happen by chance.

First, you need to develop a winning marketing campaign strategy. This plan needs to: Define your goals, Outline the benefits to the consumer, Determine your audience, Choose your marketing weapons wisely, Know your company's niche, Define your company's personality, and Have a reasonable budget.

Second, included are three marketing plan examples. At times it may be easier to develop your own marketing plan once you review examples by others. In this section we cover three marketing plan examples: Plan A is a one-horse-one-rider design, a small one-person venture. Plan B looks at a small business, in no particular business space, of perhaps 10-50 employees. Plan C examines a larger company. Large businesses have their own set of problems. Learn from these approaches and develop your own marketing plan.

Third, part of any good strategy is boiling the details down and putting them on paper. A marketing calendar keeps track of key dates and marketing tactics. It can also record the good, the bad, and the ugly results of the marketing promotion. Learn how to use a marketing calendar to track your campaign results.

A Seven-Step Marketing Plan

"Unless commitment is made, there are only promises and hopes; but no plans."

—PETER DRUKER

Planning shows you're purposeful, ingenious, and determined to succeed and cannot be overlooked in the competitive web environment. Every organization is scrambling to be heard above the noise. Those that plan succeed; those that do not wander.

If you have the planning gene in your DNA, great, but what if that gene is not in your hereditary material? Where does one start?

Why do some people avoid planning like they resist a visit to the dentist for a root canal?

A Google search for the phrase "marketing plans" suggests there are Five Easy Steps, Nine Steps, Seven Steps, and Three Steps. Any could probably work. You just need to create a marketing plan template that covers all the bases, answering all the important questions relevant to your company goals.

Here a seven-step plan serves as a starting point. You can always add a step or two if you think your planning template needs to be a little more granular.

Jay Conrad Levinson developed his Seven-Step Marketing Plan some time ago, but it still rings true. Levinson had you answer these seven questions:

1. What's the goal of your marketing plan?
2. What benefits will your customer or client receive?
3. Who's your target audience?
4. What marketing weapons will you use?
5. What's your company's niche?
6. What's the personality of your company?
7. What will you budget for this plan?

The Goal of Your Marketing Plan

Every marketing plan needs focus. You need to ask yourself, "What is it we hope to accomplish with this marketing effort?" Your goals need to be as specific as possible—gain more visibility on the web, increase revenues, or draw more web traffic just won't do. Goals that are too general are hard to quantify. The following goals for four different marketing plans are exact and easier to measure:

- *Plan A.* Increase revenues by 5 to 15 percent by exploring opportunities for referral or follow-up business with existing clients.
- *Plan B.* Develop a webinar series to reach an audience of 1,000 and generate 100 new prospects in the next 90 days.
- *Plan C.* Generate 25 new leads per month through pay-per-click campaigns.
- *Plan D.* Increase website traffic by 1,000 unique visitors per month during the next 60 days through e-mail marketing. Generate 5 percent more new opportunities.

The Benefits the Customer or Client Receives

Customer benefits need to be real, not imaginary. They can't be feel-good benefits. For instance, you might offer a more durable product that requires less service and maintenance over the years.

Your software tracking system might allow field service people to make more service calls per week. If you have to convince the customer of the benefits, you're most likely on the wrong track. The payback needs to be explained in customer terms. How will their business profit? Will they be able to reach a larger audience, will their efforts generate more revenue, or will they gain more visibility/credibility in their primary business space? Our four plans have very specific benefits:

- *Plan A.* All customers will receive the direct benefits from our Rewarding Referral Program. New business opportunities can be generated from referrals. Customer care will be increased. Customer satisfaction can be measured. Problems that are brewing can be short-circuited. Upselling/upgrading can take place.
- *Plan B.* Two typical benefits of viewing a webinar are education and getting your questions answered. The material presented in a webinar may move prospects to opportunities or help seal the deal on purchasing the organization's product or service.
- *Plan C.* Pay-per-click campaigns force the messaging to be exact. Let's say they offer field service management software. The customer benefits could be in the form of "streamlined billing," "faster payment on invoices," or "more service calls being handled." The benefits have to be direct and explained in very few words. The prospect's pain points should be targeted.
- *Plan D.* The marketing tactic works, but it takes a good mailing list, knowledge of the pain points/benefits, compelling offers, and patience.

Who's the Target Audience?

The target audience, the ideal prospects, should be identified in as exact terms as possible.

If there are three distinct audiences, then develop and run three separate marketing campaigns. The four businesses take care in defining their ideal prospects.

· *Plan A.* The target audience is our existing customer base.
· *Plan B.* The company will purchase e-mail lists that fit the description of the ideal prospect and develop a double-opt-in e-mail campaign to solicit enrollment for the webinar series.
· *Plan C.* The targeted audience for a pay-per-click campaign can only be determined by the search phrases companies use in their advertising. For example, if the company has an e-commerce site that sells kitchen hardware, the search phrases might be terms such as cabinet hardware, kitchen cabinet hardware, cabinet knobs, drawer pulls, and cabinet pulls.
· *Plan D.* The e-mail list will be derived from three sources: past customers who have cancelled the service for some reason, prospects who signed up for a free trial but never started or finished the trial, and people who have visited the website and downloaded an offer but never become customers.

The broader the audience the wider their interest is in any product or service. The wider the interest, the more watered down the message needs to be to attract readers. This path can only spell disaster.

What Marketing Weapons Will the Company Use?

Jay Levinson and the guerilla marketing boys like to use battle lingo when talking about the types of marketing tactics a company might employ during a campaign. They liken tactics to weapons. Marketing weapons can be webinars, podcasts, e-mail blasts, landing pages, or pay-per-click campaigns. The four companies employ a variety of marketing weapons.

- *Plan A.* E-mail campaign followed up by phone calls. Mentions in the monthly newsletter along with postings on the website and blog.
- *Plan B.* A 50-minute webinar that will run live every other week and can be downloaded on demand. The webinar will focus on the prospect's' five pain points, the remedies, and the derived benefits. An education-based whitepaper will be offered at the end of the webinar.
- *Plan C.* Two AdWord campaigns will be developed, and A/B testing will be done to see what pain points strike a nerve and compel the potential prospects to respond. A landing page will be created offering an education-based whitepaper or free software demo.
- *Plan D.* Three e-mails will be developed around the top pain points. The e-mail subject lines will be tweaked to gain the most e-mail opens. The offers within the e-mails will be slanted to better the click-through rate. Specific landing pages will be designed and the content will be altered to gain the best possible response.

What's the Company's Niche?

Remember people do not like to hire generalists. Train your focus on one niche. Concentrate on the one thing that makes your business the most unique in the marketplace. Also make a list of your competition and highlight what they believe is their differentiation. Some would use the term "positioning." Next, use colleagues as a sounding board to make sure the unique quality is being expressed in understandable, practical, desirable terms. Example differentiators are terms such as faster service, less expensive, more reliable, more durable, better guarantee, or more proactive. The four companies follow these guidelines.

- *Plan A.* It runs a Software as a Service (SaaS) company and offers better report screens, comprehensive analytics, and a more robust dashboard than its competitors.
- *Plan B.* It's a field service management company and offers accelerated billing, in-field mobile access to account information, a full-featured customer portal, and integration to QuickBooks, Sage Peachtree, and AccountEdge.
- *Plan C.* It's a national kitchen hardware and accessories e-commerce site offering free shipping, deep discounts on brand names, and a 24-hour customer support chat service.
- *Plan D.* It's a mid-size real estate broker offering a new relocation service to families moving into and out of a certain area.

What's the Personality of the Company?

Companies, like people, have character traits. A company might be known for its strengths or weaknesses, values, culture, managing style, or work environment. The company's traits have to be desirable to the prospect. The four companies implement step six in various ways.

- *Plan A.* We are open, respectful, focused, and proactive.
- *Plan B.* We are high-tech, flexible, confident, goal-driven, and budget conscience.
- *Plan C.* We are logical, analytic, cause-and-effect driven, and experienced.
- *Plan D.* We are structured, organized, responsible, and quality-driven.

What Will Be Budgeted for This Plan?

Planning without an adequate budget does little to advance a business's goals. Money needs to be set aside for marketing.

Perhaps the marketing plan can be segmented and executed one step at a time. Maybe a portion of the project can be outsourced to save money. In any event, money is necessary for any marketing plan as the four companies show.

- *Plan A.* The company already has the e-mail addresses of their current customers. Say it decides to use an e-mail service such as ConstantContact. It will cost $50 per month to e-mail to 2,501 to 5,000 addresses and $75 per month to e-mail 5,001 to 10,000. The updates to the website and blog will be done internally, as will the phone calls.
- *Plan B.* Developing the webinar takes time and company resources if the project is kept inside the company. Outsourcing the project could cost $3,000 to $5,000. An outside contractor could develop the whitepaper for another $1,000.
- *Plan C.* The pay-per-click budget will run $8,000 to $12,000 per month. An AdWord expert requires 20 percent of the monthly spend to manage the ad campaigns. Another $800 is needed for designing the landing pages.
- *Plan D.* The cost and quality of e-mail lists vary greatly, and there are charlatans out there. A list of 500,000 names can cost as little as $400. Start small, measure the results of a few sample mailings, and then decide whether or not to ramp things up or choose another e-mail address vendor. Designing the three landing pages costs $1,200.

BE **STRATEGIC**

- It's important to keep refining the seven steps to ensure the best possible results.
- If you're going after more than one audience, launch multiple campaigns. Don't try to capture everyone at once. It will dilute your messaging.

As you can see marketing plans can have many moving parts, and all can vary. Take the time to outline a small marketing plan with just a few moving parts and measure the success rate. After launching some marketing plan prototypes, you should be ready to tweak things and also be able to gauge a success rate. You're on your way. Remember, your marketing plan should be in writing so you can go back and adjust what is not working.

Three Sample Marketing Plans

"A business absolutely devoted to service will have only one worry about profits. They will be embarrassingly large."

—Henry Ford

Many people learn best by example. It can be easier to develop your own marketing plan when you see someone else's ideas mapped out. The following three marketing plans are to be used in just that way. Choose among them. Then modify the best one to suit your company's individual needs. Components of the three plans can be combined to create your own unique plan.

Case Study A: One Horse, One Rider

This is a business run by one person or perhaps a few individuals. In businesses of this size it is not unusual for one person to tackle the marketing, sales, and technology duties.

Let's assume the business has a website. The site is OK, but the value proposition is not clear, the messaging is not very compelling, and the site lacks persuasive offers. The website is not search engine optimized. There is a blog on the website but it's been neglected. The first order of business is to generate revenue.

The other factors mentioned here do need attention, but not if the company goes out of business first.

The Marketing Plan

1. Develop a unique value proposition that includes a tagline, shout out, and elevator pitch.
2. Identify the ideal prospects and their gathering places on the web. Then rate those locations according to which will garner the best results.
3. Develop an e-mail campaign that focuses on pain points, remedies, and benefits to the prospects. Send the prospects to landing pages because this avoids having to update the website for the time being. Work on converting leads and opportunities.
4. Network. Network. Network. Don't run the business in a vacuum. Seek counsel and advice.
5. Collect e-mail addresses. Swap e-mail lists with colleagues.
6. Develop a consistent connection with current customers and prospects, and stay consistent.
7. Depending on the business space and audience, social media may work better than an e-mail campaign.

As time and resources permit, develop and execute a plan to attend to the aforementioned items (website, compelling content, attractive offers, SEO, and blog) that need attention.

Case Study B: A Small Business

The company has 5 to 50 people. In a business of this dimension, there may be a few people who can be tasked with the marketing and technology.

This small business recently launched a new website. It looks professional and has intuitive menu navigation. But the content on the web pages is not compelling, and there are no offers on the site to entice visitors to become more engaged. The website has not been optimized for the search engines. The company has been running Google AdWord campaigns for a year or so. Leads are being generated, and some are being converted into customers. Its monthly ad spend is between $12,000 and $15,000. It has been considering a newsletter for some time but the right resources have not yet been freed up to get the publication underway. The company opts to outsource some marketing activities to get things started more quickly.

The Marketing Plan

1. A search engine optimization strategy is undertaken. New key words and phrases are chosen. The web pages will be optimized and the content made more compelling over the next several months.

2. The AdWords campaigns are analyzed. Campaigns that are underperforming are turned off. The new search terms are added, and an A/B test is started to ensure the best possible results. Before, the PPC traffic was sent to the company's homepage. Now, landing pages are created with tailored messaging to generate more interest. Leads and conversions pick up. The ad spend drops to $8,000 per month. More leads and conversions are being generated for less money.

3. Offers are added to the website in the form of case studies and whitepapers. These additions generate more interest by visitors, and more leads and conversions are created.

4. The company had a blog that was not being fully utilized. An e-mail newsletter is started. Article excerpts are included in the e-mail. The full articles are posted on the company's blog. This generates traffic to the blog and interest in the company's products.

Case Study C: A Not-So-Small Business

Large organizations can pose a unique set of issues. Don't take things for granted. Remember the motto "First, do no harm." Move at a measured pace so that the current business processes are not thrown into turmoil. Let's say the business is successful, but growth has been flat for the last 18 months. The business space is quite competitive and crowded.

The company website is professional looking, optimized for the search engines with compelling content and attractive offers. It runs AdWord campaigns that produce good results, but not stellar ones. It has embarked on social media activities with little success. It does not have a customer retention plan in place and does not communicate with current customers on a regular basis. Its blog is stale.

The Marketing Plan

1. Perform marketing research to better understand the business space. Do a competitive analysis. Look for product or service gaps that can be leveraged. Plan a workshop to look over company messaging and adjust where necessary.
2. Do search term analysis to determine if a better set of key phrases can be found.
3. Stop AdWord campaigns that are not performing. Use new key phrases in campaigns to see if better results can be garnered.
4. Modify website content and offers to take advantage of new key phrases and gaps in product or service offerings.
5. Develop a social media strategy and execute if applicable.
6. Develop and deliver an e-mail/newsletter to current customers and prospects. Post full articles on the blog to drive readers to the website.
7. Have subject matter experts blog on some regular basis. Invite noncompeting authors to blog if appropriate.

Because of the complexity of large organizations, adjustments and prototyping will likely be an ongoing process.

Keep Marketing Tactics on Track with a Marketing Calendar

"Hitting is timing. Pitching is upsetting timing."

—WARREN SPAHN

The marketing calendar is an essential part of any successful marketing campaign. The calendar can be simple and just track the marketing activities and their timing. More complicated instruments might include who's responsible for each activity, the associated costs, and the estimated and actual results of each step. You may need to map your activities down to the week or day level, whatever suits your campaign model best. Try to record the information that is most useful, but don't tie yourself to the calendar and its updating.

Marketing calendars can track promotions, marketing campaigns, trade shows and other events, product releases, and more. You'll find a gaggle of software solutions to help you build and maintain your calendar. You need to decide how complicated you want the process to be. Figure 23.1 shows a simple marketing calendar.

It's hard to know if you have succeeded at your goals if you have no goals in mind. It's akin to driving aimlessly in any direction hoping to arrive home for dinner. Marketing plans do not have to be

> ## BE **STRATEGIC**
>
> ◗ Keep the different market segments on different timelines.
> ◗ Don't use the calendar like some cookie-cutter. Different prospect groups will react differently and need to be treated differently.

Marketing Calendar: Outcome-BasedMarketing.com/handouts

Marketing Calendar (January through June 2011)

Activities	Timing	Cost	Results	Comments
Newsletter	January, March, May	$500 per month		Add offers to bring past customers back
AdWords	January, February, march, April, May, June	$8,000 per month	20-25 leads per week.	20-25 new customers per month
Email	February, April, June	$3,000	300 new leads	15 new customers
SEO	January, February, March, April, May, June	$1,000 per month	25-30 leads per month	20-25 new customers per month
Webinars	February, April, June	$1,200	5-10 leads per event	12 new customers

FIGURE 23.1—Marketing Calendar

complex and overwhelming. Keep things simple, but follow the plan.

The Importance of Conversion Streams

"A business that makes nothing but money is a poor business."

—HENRY FORD

ONVERTING PROSPECTS INTO LEADS AND LEADS INTO OPPORTUNITIES are topics of many a marketing and sales meeting. Many companies that offer outsourced marketing tactics try to stay clear of this discussion, perhaps for fear of having their performance measured. They are also topics that many who offer search engine optimization or pay-per-click campaigns avoid discussing. These tech companies are in the business of bringing qualified visitors to the website. It's the job of the company that owns the websites to convert the prospects into leads and the leads into opportunities.

Conversion streams are about getting results from marketing, getting prospects and leads. They need to be a combination of information, soft and hard sells, pain points, remedies and benefits, and a dose of personality. Think of a conversion stream

Measuring a campaign's performance is not difficult. Getting the desired positive results from the campaign takes talent.

as a river of information that offers to entice a prospect to move the buying relationship to the next level. For instance, an e-mail marketing conversion stream might be a series of seven or eight e-mails sent out over two weeks. These e-mails provide information about a product's features and benefits coupled with a few soft- and hard-sell messages. Conversion streams are not the magic bullet that every marketing campaign is missing; they are just one of the tools that need to be employed to increase any marketing campaign's success rate.

Sample Conversion Streams

"Adopting the right attitude can convert a negative stress into a positive one."

—HANS SELYE

To help you understand some possible conversion streams, let's look at three typical streams that a business might employ.

A Free Trial Conversion Stream

A software company offers a 15-day free trial for prospects to try out its solution (Figure 24.1). The potential purchasers come from four venues—search engine optimization, Google AdWords campaigns, the company website, and the monthly eNews. During the trial the software company sends out seven e-mails while the trial is running and an eighth e-mail two days after the trial ends. Prospects can opt-out of the e-mail campaign at any time. They can also decide to purchase the software package and the e-mails will

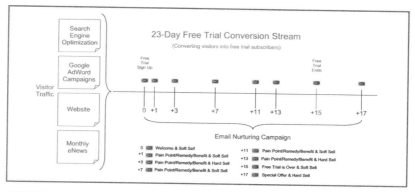

FIGURE 24.1—23-Day Free Trial Conversion Stream

stop. Each e-mail has a particular theme and focus. The first e-mail welcomes the potential customer and makes sure the company has their username and password. There is a soft-sell associated with the first e-mail. The third e-mail is quite different. It focuses on a pain point, a remedy, and the benefits the potential customer will receive. It also includes a hard-sell, something like: Sign up now!

A Webinar Conversion Stream

A marketing company offers a free webinar about the importance of branding (Figure 24.2). The potential clients are coming from four venues—search engine optimization, social media campaigns, the marketing company's website, and e-mail marketing campaigns. Twenty-one days before the webinar takes place the marketing wheels are set into motion. The marketing agency sends out its first e-mail to its prospect/past client database. Every member of the marketing team changes the Status Line on their LinkedIn account to announce the webinar. The Status Line steers people to a landing page where they can get more information and sign up in advance of the event. Members also create a promotional ad for each of their various Groups on LinkedIn. Fourteen days before the webinar a second e-mail is sent out to the e-mail list,

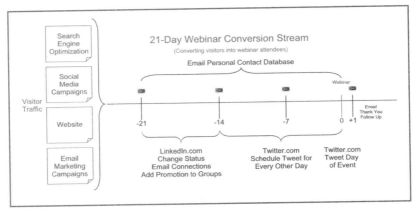

FIGURE 24.2—21-Day Webinar Conversion Stream

and the social media campaign kicks into gear. Compelling tweets are sent out to the agency's followers every other day. On the day of the webinar, a final tweet is sent out reminding everyone not to miss this exciting and informative event. The day after the webinar everyone who attended the event receives a thank-you note and a link to watch the webinar over on-demand. Viewers are also encouraged to pass the webinar along to any colleague they believe would find the information of value. The link is also sent out to all those that did not attend the event. Each e-mail and social text has a particular theme and focus. The first e-mail announces the webinar and talks about the value the recipient will receive. There is a hard-sell to sign up now. All messaging focuses on pain points, remedies, and benefits.

An E-mail Marketing Conversion Stream

In this second free webinar offer about the importance of branding (Figure 24.3), the webinar is recorded so people will be able to watch it at their convenience. This time the potential prospects (the masses) are coming from purchased e-mail lists. The marketing agency sends out the first e-mail. Let's not concentrate on the bounces or those that unsubscribe from the e-mail campaigns. Instead let's keep track of Non Responders, those people that do not open the e-mail. The people that open the e-mail but do not click through to the offer are the Opens. The people that read the e-mail and click-through to the landing page but do not take the offer are the Click-throughs. Those that take the offer and watch the webinar are the Leads. A week later a second e-mail is sent out to the Non Responders, the Opens, and the Click-throughs. The strategy will be to change the subject line of the second e-mail to see if the Non Responders will open it. The strategy with the Opens and Click-throughs is similar. For those two groups the goal is to make the e-mail content more compelling. A second offer, perhaps a whitepaper or a case study instead of a webinar, is also possible. Different people learn in various ways. Some people like to read while others like to view the information. The same tack will be used when sending out the third e-mail blast.

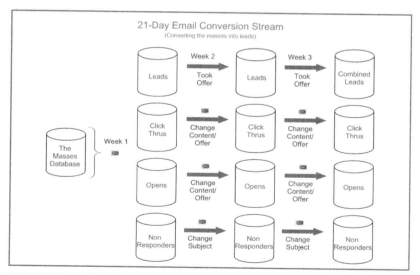

FIGURE 24.3—21-Day E-mail Marketing Conversion Stream

The Whole Enchilada

"You can't have everything. Where would you put it?"

—STEVEN WRIGHT

Now that you have a basic understanding of conversion streams, let's add a few more tactics to the marketing mix. Suppose you use the webinar and e-mail conversion streams to get attendees to your webinars, but you're looking for many more leads. What other actions can you take to increase your lead pool? You can add pay-per-click campaigns, search engine optimization, and social media.

Pay-per-Click Conversion Stream

Assume you have a product or service people are looking to acquire. The three basic components of any pay-per-click campaign are the search terms, the ads, and the landing page. Unlike the e-mail marketing campaigns, you won't get a second chance to try a different message on your potential prospects. If they're interested, they'll click on your ad. If not, they'll click on someone else's ad. That sale is likely lost.

The Search Terms

The search terms you choose will make or break your campaign success. If you choose the wrong terms, people may click on your ads, but only because they have a different interest than you think they do. Remember, the more vague the term, the larger the audience of searchers, and the larger the audience of searchers, the more diversified their interests. For example, if you chose the term "coffee," searchers might be looking for coffee shops, coffee beans, or coffee pots. You need to choose terms that are as specific as possible. Suppose you sell roasted coffee beans. More exact phrases that will garner better results are "Hazelnut coffee beans," "Columbian coffee beans," and "Roasted coffee beans."

The Ads

Your title might be "Wholesale Coffee Beans," "Gourmet Coffee Beans," or "Fresh Roasted Coffee." The title needs to grab the reader's attention. The content of the ad has to draw the potential customer further into the story. Suppose you say things like "Free Shipping," "Roasted Daily," or "40 Different Blends." Once the reader clicks on your ad, they're on their way to your landing page.

The Landing Page

The landing page serves only one function, to get the reader to act and act now. The headline and content of the landing page needs to convey the same message the ad communicated. If you have 40 different blends for sale, then mention the blends and their pricing. Don't try and sell coffee pots and espresso machines.

The Metrics

Of course, you're going to want to keep an eye on the statistics that are the most meaningful, such as Click Thru Rate (CTR), Average Position, Quality Score, Impressions Share, Bounce Rate, and Conversion Rate.

Search Engine Optimization Conversion Stream

The results from search engine optimization are not as immediate as pay-per-click. You don't switch search terms on a daily basis as you do with PPC. You have to go with what you thought were the top choices when you optimized your website. The other factors that enter into a conversion from SEO are the page the searcher lands on, the compelling content, and the call to action. From there you'll want to keep track of which search phrases bring the most visitors to the site and the search terms of those that converted into leads.

Metrics are extremely important in any optimization campaign. We need to know which search terms perform the best, not which search terms are in position 1 on page 1 of the search results. Being in position 1 does little good if those searchers

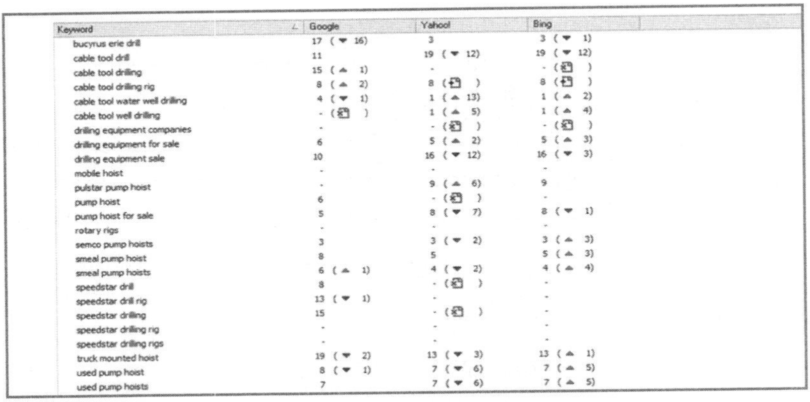

Keyword	Google	Yahoo!	Bing
bucyrus erie drill	17 (▼ 16)	3	3 (▼ 1)
cable tool drill	11	19 (▼ 12)	19 (▼ 12)
cable tool drilling	15 (▲ 1)	-	- ( )
cable tool drilling rig	8 (▲ 2)	8 ( )	8 ( )
cable tool water well drilling	4 (▼ 1)	1 (▲ 13)	1 (▲ 2)
cable tool well drilling	- ( )	1 (▲ 5)	1 (▲ 4)
drilling equipment companies	-	- ( )	- ( )
drilling equipment for sale	6	5 (▲ 2)	5 (▲ 3)
drilling equipment sale	10	16 (▼ 12)	16 (▼ 3)
mobile hoist	-	-	-
pulstar pump hoist	-	9 (▲ 6)	9
pump hoist	6	- ( )	-
pump hoist for sale	5	8 (▼ 7)	8 (▼ 1)
rotary rigs	-	-	-
semco pump hoists	3	3 (▼ 2)	3 (▲ 3)
smeal pump hoist	8	5	5 (▲ 3)
smeal pump hoists	6 (▲ 1)	4 (▼ 2)	4 (▲ 4)
speedstar drill	8	- ( )	-
speedstar drill rig	13 (▼ 1)	-	-
speedstar drilling	15	- ( )	-
speedstar drilling rig	-	-	-
speedstar drilling rigs	-	-	-
truck mounted hoist	19 (▼ 2)	13 (▼ 3)	13 (▲ 1)
used pump hoist	8 (▼ 1)	7 (▼ 6)	7 (▲ 5)
used pump hoists	7	7 (▼ 6)	7 (▲ 5)

FIGURE 24.4—WebCEO dashboard

never convert into leads. WebCEO has a nice optimization tool.

Social Media Conversion Stream

Firing up social media conversion streams takes more immediate action than other campaign models. You'll have to decide which communities have the best outlook for results. It may make more sense to stay with Facebook than launch campaigns on Twitter. It depends where your ideal prospects hangs out. Google Analytics will tell you which communities are generating the most/best traffic.

Conversion streams create our tactical battle map. They tell us what to do and when to do it. Each conversion stream may look quite different depending upon the desired results.

BE **STRATEGIC**

- Creating conversion streams is not a cookie-cutter process. One strategy will not fit all cases. The strategy that draws in webinar viewers will probably not work for your newsletter campaign.
- More than making the mechanics of the conversion stream work, the messaging needs to be educational and compelling. The contents of any communiqué should focus on pain points/remedies/benefits. The calls to action need to be a combination of soft and hard sells.

Chapter 25

Metrics and Analytics: Are You There Yet?

"Without the numbers you're just another person with an opinion."

—CARLY FIORINA

METRICS REVEAL THE HEALTH OF YOUR MARKETING CAMPAIGN. THE analytics highlight the areas where you're doing well and those that need additional tweaking. Businesses need to define the metrics that are most meaningful to their organization. Looking at some generalized "meaningful metrics" helps you build the metrics that are most useful.

Learn how to develop meaningful metrics that tell where the marketing campaign might need fine tuning or what processes need scrapping all together. Good metrics remove the gut-feeling and emotions from the equation. Good metrics never lie. The numbers cannot have a hidden agenda, and they're totally impartial.

There is no single set of metrics that will be meaningful to every organization.

Learn how reliable analytics help uncover weaknesses in the marketing campaign: timing problems, messaging, landing page bailouts, inconsistent search phrases, wrong prospect definitions, and flawed audiences.

Meaningful Metric Models

"Early numbers are always wrong."

—MARY CHENEY

The metrics most meaningful for your business are going to depend on the marketing tactics you're trying to measure. For instance, if you were running Google AdWords campaigns you would want to know a variety of statistics:

- *Click Thru Rate (CTR)*. The percentage of people that clicked on your advertisement. For example, a CTR of 5 percent means that five out of every 100 people that saw your ad clicked on it. An average CTR for e-commerce sites is 1 to 3 percent.
- *Average Position*. Tells you the placement of your ad in the search results. Most retailers find positions 3 through 5 have the best results.
- *Quality Score*. A measurement done by Google of your ad, landing page, and key phrases. This measurement also takes into account past performance, which gives the little guy who does a better job than a large company a chance of better placement for less cost. Seven to ten represents a decent Quality Score.
- *Impression Share*. Tells you how many times your ad displays per number of searches made on a particular search phrase. For instance, if your Impression Share was 50 percent, that

would tell you that your ad was displayed half the time. A strong Impression Share is 80 percent.

- *Bounce Rate.* Tells you the percentage of people that clicked on your ad, went to your landing page, but did not visit a second page. A Bounce Rate of 30 percent tells you that three out of ten people clicked on your ad, visited your landing page, and then left. The lower the Bounce Rate the better. A good Bounce Rate is 40 percent.
- *Conversion Rate.* Pulls everything together. Conversion Rate tells you the rate at which visitors are converted into buyers. Typically 1.25 percent is the low end for e-commerce sites.

Now suppose you want to look at some meaningful metrics when executing an e-mail campaign. The metric names are going to be different, but some of them tell you a similar story.

The most useful metrics of a typical e-mail marketing campaign are:

- *Opens.* Tell you how many recipients opened your e-mail
- *Clicks.* Let you know how many recipients clicked on your offers
- *Bounces.* Inform you of incorrect e-mail address
- *Unsubscribes.* Tell you the people that would like to be left alone
- *Non Responders.* Tells you the people that did not bother to open the e-mail
- *Forwards.* Notify you of how many people passed your e-mail along to a friend or colleague

Industry standard numbers you could use for comparison when running your own e-mail campaign can be useful. A few benchmark standards from MailChimp are:

- *Consulting.* Opens 29 percent, Clicks 8 percent, Bounces 6 percent, and Unsubscribe 0.35 percent

- *Health and Fitness.* Opens 21 percent, Clicks 6 percent, Bounces 6 percent, and Unsubscribe 0.30 percent
- *Professional Services.* Opens 20 percent, Clicks 4 percent, Bounces 4 percent, and Unsubscribe 0.45 percent
- *Retail.* Opens 18 percent, Clicks 4 percent, Bounces 1 percent, and Unsubscribe 0.24 percent
- *Software and Web Apps.* Opens 16 percent, Clicks 2 percent, Bounces 3 percent, and Unsubscribe 0.39 percent

You can also track visitor activity on a website, blog, or landing page. Google Analytics supplies great information at no cost. You can use some of those statistics along with a few other pieces of information from other sites on the web. All you need to do is create an analytics account at Google and then paste code on the pages you're interested in tracking. Some of those numbers are:

- *Total Visits.* The number of first-time and return visitors
- *Unique Visits.* The number of first-time visitors
- *Return Visits.* The number of return visitors
- *Leads.* The number of prospects that filled out a form or downloaded an offer
- *Popular Pages.* The pages most visited
- *Search Engine Key Phrases.* The top key phrases people used to reach the site/page
- *Geographic Locations.* People's geographic locations
- *Referring Websites.* The sites people came from instead of using a search engine to find the site/page
- *Page Rank.* A criteria created by Google and one of the determining factors of a web page's strength
- *Number of Inbound Links.* Links from other sites that point to another site/page
- *Bounces.* The percentage of visitors that left the site after viewing one page

- *Number of Key Phrases in Position 1 on Page 1.* No explanation necessary
- *Number of Key Phrases on Page 1.* No explanation necessary
- *Number of Key Phrases on Page 2.* No explanation necessary

You'd obviously want to create running totals month after month so you could see what areas are improving and where additional effort is needed. To put all this information together so that it makes sense, download the sample report at:

BE **STRATEGIC**

▶ If the metrics point to something that is not working, then stop doing it. Be flexible enough to adjust your strategy and push forward.

▶ The metrics ought to be tied somehow to revenue. Getting lots of action on your Twitter account and hordes of visitors to your website means very little as a final result.

Sample Metrics: Outcome-BasedMarketing.com/handouts

Then we'll talk. Done?

The key to gathering metrics that are meaningful is identifying if they show you're moving the ball. Are you making progress in the right direction? The metrics also show where your marketing campaigns are failing and need attention.

The Analysis of Analytics

"There are lies, damned lies and statistics."

—MARK TWAIN

Think of behavior as another word for analytics. When people talk about website analytics, they are interested in the behavior of

Sound analytics drive better business decisions.

website visitors: How did they arrive at the site, where did they go once arriving, and how long did they stay?

It's important to understand the conduct of visitors, whether to a web page, blog posting, or landing page. Visitors are typically looking for information. They're not interested, immediately anyway, in making a purchase. They want their questions answered first. Companies need to supply education-based materials to answer those concerns, and then potential sales follow later.

Website Analytics

There are probably more companies on the web launching analytic programs than you have time to consider. You can start with a free option from Piwik.com, an open-source, real-time web analytics PHP MySQL software program. You install the software where your website resides, copy some code onto all the web pages, and you're ready to go. Some of Piwik's features include: Last Visit Graph, Length of Visits, Visitor Countries, List of Keywords, Visitor Browsers, List of External Websites, Best Search Engines, and Visits by Server Time. You can also set up Visitor Goals to track the success of conversions. Figure 25.1 is a screenshot of the Piwik dashboard.

Blog Analytics

The folks over at HubSpot have a comprehensive blog analytics tool that lets you sort posts by authors, inbound links, comments, page grade, or visitors. You can also learn which posts are read the most and how you can turn your blog into a more powerful marketing tool. Figure 25.2 shows what the HubSpot Blog dashboard looks like.

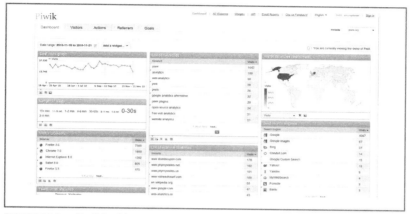

FIGURE 25.1—Piwik Dashboard

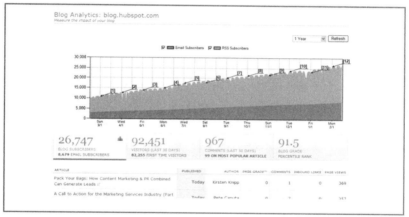

FIGURE 25.2—HubSpot Blog Analytics

E-Mail Analytics

VerticalResponse offers e-mail marketing on its site as does ConstantContact, MailChimp, and iContact. These e-mail marketing companies typically offer similar analytics:

· *Opens.* Tells you how many recipients opened your e-mail
· *Clicks.* Tallies how many recipients clicked on your offers
· *Bounces.* Informs you of incorrect e-mail addresses

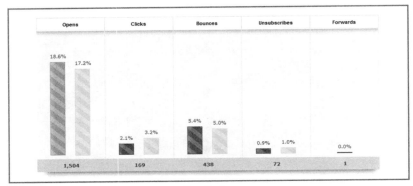

Opens	Clicks	Bounces	Unsubscribes	Forwards
18.6% 17.2%	2.1% 3.2%	5.4% 5.0%	0.9% 1.0%	0.0%
1,504	169	438	72	1

FIGURE 25.3—VerticalResponse e-mail analytics

- *Unsubscribes.* Lists the people that would like to be left alone
- *Non Responders.* Tells you who didn't open the e-mail
- *Forwards.* Notifies you of how many people passed your e-mail along to a friend or colleague

The Non Responder variable lets you know in no uncertain terms whether the audience that you are sending to wants your offering. If you're sending out a newsletter, as interesting and useful as it may be, it's time to try something else with these people. VerticalResponse also lets you see how well your latest campaign matches up against your lifetime campaign average. Figure 25.3 shows a typical graph.

Once you have your campaign tactics chosen, you can select the metrics that will be most telling and then choose the analytic tools that will help your efforts succeed.

Metrics and analytics will let you know how well your marketing campaign efforts are doing. They'll also signal what needs attention or change.

BE **STRATEGIC**

▶ When you choose an analytics tool make sure you understand how it is calculating its numbers.

▶ Look for industry averages you can benchmark to make sure you're getting the best possible results from your campaigns.

Chapter 26

Closing the Loop Between Marketing and Sales

"Many of life's failures are people who did not realize how close they were to success when they gave up."

—THOMAS A. EDISON

MARKETING AND SALES RARELY SHARE THEIR INFORMATION WITH each other, so both sides have an incomplete picture of the prospect. Neither side completely understands what constitutes a qualified lead. This lack of information sharing hinders the sales process.

Closing the loop between marketing and sales is an important step in generating closable opportunities. It means helping the information flow between what marketing and sales think constitute a qualified lead. With a "closed loop" system, information sharing takes place between the two sectors. Prospects can be tracked through the entire marketing and sales process. What motivates the prospect and how she likes to be sold are no longer restricted information.

eMarketing tracks such things as outreach and promotion activities, competitors, and market trends. Marketing has business intelligence and can alert sales to the low hanging fruit. Sales truly tracks pricing, what's selling and what's not, ordering history, what happened the last time it met with the prospect, and its all-important monthly quota.

Closed loop marketing tells the organization which marketing channels are the most profitable.

Rodney King uttered the immortal words "Can't we all just get along?" after riots broke out when LA police officers were acquitted of beating him. Marketing and sales might want to take these words to heart. A continuing point of contention between the two is what attributes determine a qualified lead. Marketing would say a prospect that takes an action and responds to an offer such as an e-mail campaign, attending a webinar, or downloading a whitepaper. In other words the prospect has done something to move the relationship to the next level.

The sales force has a much different view of the so-called lead. There are only so many hours in a day to make the monthly quota. It makes sense for sales to concentrate on the low hanging fruit, those deals that are the biggest and easiest to close. A salesperson may see no real value in calling someone just because he sat through a 50-minute product demo.

Is one party right or are both? Perhaps the solution is successful targeting brought on by a closed loop marketing system. With this system in place, both sides have a much clearer view of who the company's ideal prospects are and what motivates them to act. Enter customer relationship management (CRM) software solutions. Some of the leaders in the CRM market are Eloqua, Salesforce, SilverPop, Microsoft Dynamics, and Sage ACT. Most have platforms that sport the same features:

- *Campaign management.* Includes e-mail marketing, landing pages, and website forms
- *Lead management.* Comprises lead management and nurturing, as well as lead scoring and sales enablement
- *Contact management.* Takes in data profiling and management along with segmentation and preference management
- *Measuring instruments.* Consists of full-featured dashboards, reporting systems, analytics, and analysis

With CRM systems such as these, you can gather, report on, and track your prospects as they move through the sales funnel. You'll know what motivates them and their buying characteristics.

It's of paramount importance that the loop be closed between marketing and sales, even if you need to use a spreadsheet to track the activities of your prospects. Closed loop marketing will improve your close rate as will nurturing your prospects.

BE **STRATEGIC**

▶ Bang heads together if marketing and sales are not working together.

▶ Streamline the marketing and sales process as much as possible.

▶ Cherry-picking is great when the market is flush. When times are tight, it's going to take more effort to move the prospects down the sales funnel.

What to Do with the Other 97 Percent?

"It's not enough that we do our best; sometimes we have to do what's required."

—WINSTON CHURCHILL

NURTURING YOUR PROSPECTS WILL DOUBLE OR TRIPLE YOUR CONVERSION rate. Just consider: The average click-through rate for pay-per-click ads is 1 to 3 percent. The average click-through from an e-mail campaign is between 1 and 5 percent depending upon the industry. Most of the people arriving at a website are not ready to buy. These are people that are showing an interest in your product or service but not purchasing or signing up. You can expect to harvest between 3 and 5 percent of those that click-through. If 10,000 people click on your Google ad and 2 percent or 20 people click-through to your offer, only 2 percent, or four people will actually purchase your service or product. Four out of 10,000 is only a .0004 percent conversion rate. To get the conversion rate up, you should entice more of the audience of 10,000 that click through to purchase your product or service. Remember, there is not an unlimited supply of prospects interested in purchasing any product or service.

Lead Nurturing

"Either he's dead or my watch has stopped."

—GROUCHO MARX

So how do you entice and persuade more people to click-through and make a purchase? According to Forrester Research, companies that excel at lead nurturing are able to generate 50 percent more sales-ready leads at 33 percent lower cost-per-lead. Lead nurturing is a process by which unqualified leads are tracked and developed into sales-ready opportunities.

Lead nurturing keeps your company's products or services in the mind of the prospect until they are ready to buy.

The marketing tactics used to turn these unqualified leads into sales-ready opportunities could be webinars, podcasts, whitepapers and other education-based materials, blogging, free trials, newsletters, or e-mail campaigns.

Shaun Penny writes at HubSpot that you need to keep these five best practices in mind when developing a lead-nurturing campaign:

1. Thought leadership
2. Stay focused
3. Keep it short
4. Natural progression
5. Measurement

Thought leadership means you have to have something of value to say. Focus implies that each piece of collateral, whether an e-mail, blog post, or news article, needs to be centered around one specific pain point and include the remedy, benefit, and a strong call to action.

The subject line or story header needs to grab the reader's attention in five to eight seconds. Don't clutter the e-mail with extraneous links and other offers. Don't get off subject when writing the blog post or article. Stay on message.

Natural progression means don't rush the sale. Design an e-mail nurturing campaign or series of blog posts to take the prospect through a logical educational process. The nurturing campaign should be designed to cause prospects to move down the sales funnel at their own pace. The campaign should also be designed to cause the prospect to make a stronger commitment. For instance, at first the prospect gives her e-mail address. Later on during the nurturing campaign the prospect is asked for her company name, phone number, and a few pieces of information that will help qualify her as a potential buyer.

Measurement is the key to any successful inbound marketing campaign. Measurements give you the opportunity to fine-tune the calls to action, the offers, and the content, which in turn increases the click-through and conversion rates.

Keep in mind the difference between spam and nurturing. Spamming is when someone just compiles a list of names and e-mail addresses (who knows from where) and thinks there's some benefit to jamming his message down the recipient's throat. Nurturing a list of names means that those people have, in some way, touched the company in the past. Perhaps they took a free trial, signed up to receive a newsletter, or downloaded content (a case study or whitepaper) off the company's website.

Nurturing campaigns need to be timely and consistent. Run the campaign over weeks, not months.

Running an E-Mail Nurturing Campaign

"Invincibility lies in the defense; the possibility of victory in the attack."

—Sun Tzu

As an example, say you run a 17-day nurturing campaign while people are using a free trial of your software product. You'll send out eight e-mails focusing on pain points, remedies, and benefits and how they relate to your product. The 17 days could look like this:

- *E-mail 1.* Sent out upon subscribing to the free trial. Confirms they have signed up.
- *E-mail 2.* Sent out on Day 1. Welcomes them to the free trial process.
- *E-mail 3.* Sent out on Day 3. Focus on a pain point/the remedy/the benefit.
- *E-mail 4.* Sent out on Day 7. Focus on a pain point/the remedy/the benefit.
- *E-mail 5.* Sent out on Day 11. Focus on a pain point/the remedy/the benefit.
- *E-mail 6.* Sent out on Day 13. Focus on a pain point/the remedy/the benefit.
- *E-mail 7.* Sent out on Day 15. Lets people know their free trial is expiring.
- *E-mail 8.* Sent out on Day 17. Tells people about a special offer if they decide to purchase the product.

Using Your Blog to Nurture

"A satisfied customer is the best business strategy of all."

—Michael LeBoeuf

In this instance, you write your blog posts ahead of time and schedule the posts to be published as your nurturing campaign unfolds. The posts concentrate on pain points, remedies, and benefits. This nurturing campaign runs for 20 days. People that have subscribed to your RSS Feed will automatically be notified each time a new post is published. A campaign might be:

- *Day 1.* You write a post that gives prospects the 10,000-foot view of your online service.
- *Day 5.* You write a post about a pain point, remedy, and benefit.
- *Day 9.* You write a post about a pain point, remedy, and benefit.
- *Day 12.* You write a post about a pain point, remedy, and benefit.
- *Day 17.* You write a post about a pain point, remedy, and benefit.
- *Day 20.* You sweeten the pot by offering the first month of service free to those that sign up within the next 24 hours.

Using E-Mail, Telephone, and Direct Mail to Nurture

In this illustration, you design a nurturing campaign that takes place over 15 days. During that time the respondents receive a few e-mails and a direct mail piece followed up by a phone call and a final e-mail. It might look like this:

- *Day 1.* E-mail (focus on pain point/remedy/benefit)
- *Day 4.* E-mail (focus on pain point/remedy/benefit)
- *Day 9.* Direct mail piece (focus on pain point/remedy/benefit)
- *Day 12.* Phone call (sweeten the offer)
- *Day 15.* Final e-mail (recap the customer's two most important pain points/remedies/benefits)

Nurturing with Social Media

You could use Facebook or Twitter as the messaging vehicle to replace the e-mail portion in the previous example. Using Twitter, the same campaign could be scheduled with a social media tool called HootSuite (at HootSuite.com). You could use your 140-character social media message to direct prospects to customized landing pages or blog posts. Sending the messages out over time gives prospects time to think about what's being said and how it relates to their specific situation. It also gives them time to relax and not feel pressured. This time around, add a little more information in the pain point/remedy/benefit sections.

- *Day 1.* E-mail (focus on pain point: being out of touch with field reps/remedy: mobile access/benefit: timely reporting, more actuate records)
- *Day 4.* E-mail (focus on pain point: slow cash flow/ remedy: integration to major accounting systems/benefit: quicker invoicing/faster payment)
- *Day 9.* Direct mail piece (focus on pain point: scheduling issues/ remedy: job scheduling feature/ benefit: handle more service calls)
- *Day 12.* Phone call (sweeten the offer: waive the set-up fee)
- *Day 15.* Final e-mail (recap the customer's two most important pain points/remedies/benefits)

Nurturing campaigns need a back end to track things. So, whether you decide to use a full-featured customer relationship management solution such as SalesForce.com or a simple EXCEL spreadsheet, you need to know where each prospect is in the sales process.

It's easy to see now that nurturing takes time, patience, and consistency. The returns will be greater than starting over with a new batch of prospects. Remember to treat these prospects as perhaps interested but not ready to make a purchasing decision.

BE **STRATEGIC**

- Consistency is the key to any successful nurturing campaign. Many times companies stop right before they would be reaping the benefits of their efforts.
- Nurturing campaigns are all about education-based materials and building relationships. Don't push the sale process too quickly.

Chapter 28

Only Superman Can Leap Tall Buildings in a Single Bound

CEO

*"I thought I was bulletproof or Superman there for a while.
I thought I'd never run out of nerve. Never."*

—EVEL KNIEVEL

EVEN THOUGH YOU'D LIKE TO BE ABLE TO ACCOMPLISH EVERYTHING you set out to do, you are probably not talented in all the areas necessary to strategize, design, build, and launch every possible type of internet marketing campaign. Let the experts do what they do well; then you can concentrate on what you do well.

You should, if possible, outsource your weaknesses. Of course, it's hard, at times, to come to the realization that you need the assistance of others. When just starting a business or when times are tough and resources are tight people often come to the conclusion they should do everything by themselves. Is that the right conclusion in every situation? It's a tough decision to make.

With the advent of the web, there's free access to advice (good and bad, of course), instruction, information, and examples. The web has leveled the playing field for small companies battling against their larger foes. Every business has access to the best website design software and the finest blog templates. There are more free articles, blog postings, and books on marketing, wordsmithing, and messaging than a single person could read in ten lifetimes. The little guy can send out professional looking e-mail blasts using sites such as ConstantContact or iContact. There are both paid and free press release sites to get the company's message out in a professional looking form. All businesses have access to the analysis and analytic tools to make sure their website and collateral are appealing to the largest possible audience of prospects. Practical webinars and podcasts are being offered by the one-horse/one-rider businesses as well as the fat cats. People can no longer tell the size of a company by just visiting its website or blog.

The proof of a marketing company's prowess is now found in the metrics. Even though project execution, a company's deep pool of subject matter experts, and its success rate rank high, clients want to see evidence that the outcome desired and paid for will be reached.

A good place to start when contemplating an internet marketing campaign is to inventory the skills at the company and the available resources. Then decide what can and cannot be accomplished with the current staff. From there, some investigation and education may be in order. Some people can learn some things while they may struggle to become proficient at others. That's when outside help needs to be tapped. Networking groups are a great place to make contacts with other like-minded business associates. Who knows, you might be having breakfast with someone quite skilled at a talent you lack.

If you decide to hire some outside help, where do you start? "Word-of-mouth" is probably the best method of compiling sound references on companies that are practiced at internet marketing. Seek testimonials from your business contacts and colleagues.

The traditional marketing firm works with print: magazines, newspapers, direct mail, and such. Marketing firms that work over the web are very different. An internet marketing firm should be adept at:

- e-mail marketing
- viral marketing
- internet public relations
- multilevel, multitouch marketing
- writing compelling content
- developing eye-catching taglines
- developing decision-making paths that lead a website visitor down the sales funnel
- visitor conversions
- pay-per-click marketing
- internet press release outlets
- the blogosphere
- content syndication

It would be best to align yourself with a marketing firm that has these services in-house. The fewer cooks in the kitchen the better.

Web design has made leaps and bounds in the last few years. Make sure the web development firm you work with is not behind the curve.

1. Does it build sites in Web 2.0?
2. Does it build search-engine friendly websites?
3. Does it use very little scripting?

4. Is it conscious of typos and broken links on the site?

5. Is its hosting service impeccable?

Looking for a reliable search engine optimization company takes some investigation as well. Has it done for itself, its own website, and its clients what it purports to be able to do for you? Do not sign a contract. Do not accept any deal where the company takes your money now and shows you results in four to six months.

1. Can it show results from past engagements?

2. Does it understand your industry?

3. Does it understand your competitors?

In any subcontracting you do—web design, marketing, or SEO—make sure the firm:

1. Can show results.

2. Deliver projects on time and on budget.

3. Has a good reputation in the industry.

4. Is flexible with changes.

5. Employs "best practices."

Of course, these lists of characteristics for securing a marketing firm, web design company, or SEO expert are not exhaustive. Always be sure to get EVERYTHING in writing.

Say you decide to educate yourself before bringing on some outside contractors. To help jump-start your thinking, here are 50 websites worth visiting:

Helpful Websites and Blog Sites

· TemplateMonster.com

· OpenSourceWebDesign.org

· WordPress.org

· Blogger.com

- TypePad.com
- DIYthemes.com(Thesis themes)
- BlogSpot.com
- AddThis.com
- Images.Google.com

Helpful Social Media Sites

- LinkedIn.com
- Twitter.com
- Facebook.com

Helpful Community Sites

- Digg.com
- Sphinn.com
- Reddit.com
- StumbleUpon.com
- Delicious.com

Helpful Analytic Sites

- Grader.com
- SEOTools.com
- Compete.com
- CrazyEgg.com

Helpful Virtual Meeting and Webinar Sites

- DimDim.com
- GoToMeeting.com
- GoToWebinar.com

Helpful Visitor Statistic Sites

- StatCounter.com
- VisiStat.com

- Google.com/Analytics

Helpful Search Term Analysis Sites
- SEOP.com
- SEOChat.com
- SEOmoz.org
- Google.com/AdWords

Helpful Business, Web, Technology, and Marketing Sites
- Mashable.com
- gMarketing.com (Guerrilla Marketing)
- DuctTapeMarketing.com
- HubSpot.com

Helpful Web Luminaries
- ChrisBrogan.com
- SethGodin.com
- DavidMeermanScott.com

Helpful Reads
- Entrepreneur.com
- FastCompany.com
- Wired.com
- Inc.com
- B2BMarketingZone.com
- CustomerThink.com

Helpful E-mail Marketing Sites
- ConstantContact.com
- iContact.com
- MailChimp.com

Helpful Survey Tool Sites
- SurveyMonkey.com

The Pros and Cons of Outsourcing Your Weaknesses	
Pros	**Cons**
• Contractor may be able to react quicker	• Loss of control
• Contractor adds depth to the staff	• Loss of market research for project
• Project deadlines can be accelerated	• Loss of knowledge gained
• Costs may be lower	• Dependency on outsource company
• Quality may be better	• Outsource company may go out of business
• Advantages of new blood/new ideas	• You may lose people no longer involved in the outsourced process
• The company may lack left-brain analytics	• You know your clients better than the outsourced company does
• Terminating a contractor is easier than firing an employee	• Customer relations may suffer
• Hiring a contractor is all about results, not excuses	• Outsourced company may not understand company goals and values
• Fixed costs turn into variable costs	

- ZoomerRang.com
- SurveyGizmo.com

Note: Listing these sites does not imply endorsement. The sites are not listed in any order of preference. You're on your own on this one.

Set aside pride and outsource the talents your organization is lacking. The benefits will vastly out weigh the valiant efforts put in by an untrained staff.

BE **STRATEGIC**

- Don't assume anything when interviewing potential subcontractors.
- Ask for bids by at least two candidates. Don't hire the first company that looks like it can do the project.
- You may want to talk with business colleagues to see if they regret not outsourcing their weaknesses.

Chapter 29

Miscellaneous Marketing Matters

"Many a small thing has been made large by the right kind of advertising."

—MARK TWAIN

THIS CHAPTER DEALS WITH MARKETING ITEMS TOO VALUABLE TO overlook. They just didn't seem to fit into any of the other sections in *Outcome-Based Marketing*.

· Outbound marketing vs. inbound marketing
· It's not all about you.
· Are you targeting the indecision-maker
· Draw a bead on your target markets
· Tell me, don't sell me
· Don't push the sale
· Viral marketing

Some marketing agencies use outbound marketing tactics to sell a company's wares while other marketing firms use inbound marketing. You'll have to decide which works best in your business space. It may be one or the other or it may be a combination of both. Some prospects will respond to the delivery of a piece of direct mail, responding to a radio commercial or answering a magazine ad (outbound methods). Still other prospects prefer the product or service hunt. Inbound methods include blogs, websites, social networking, webinars, or virtual events.

This statement may be hard for some to accept but "the sale" is not all about you. Prospects are more interested in hearing how a product or service eliminates the problem they are facing. Later in the sales cycle they will become interested in the company selling the solution. Answer all the prospect's concerns first then give them an introduction to who you are and how long you have been in business.

Remember, when selling, the focus is always on the customer and not the company. Don't waste your time focusing on the indecision makers in an organization. If you are unable to avoid the gatekeeper and get the right person on the phone, then it may be time to storm the gates. Try a more aggressive approach.

Target one marketing segment at a time; don't dilute your efforts. Go to where your ideal prospects already gather instead of trying to pull them back to the company website. Tell the prospect, don't sell him. Don't push the sale too hard because then it may be lost. Use viral marketing whenever possible.

Outbound Marketing vs. Inbound Marketing

"The aim of marketing is to know and understand the customer so well the product or service fits him and sells itself."

—Peter Drucker

There was a time when a housewife relished the thought of a salesman knocking at the front door so she could see the latest technology for cleaning floors. People actually enjoyed watching commercials when they first appeared at the beginning or end of their favorite TV shows. (Commercials never appeared during the actual show.) Those days are long gone. Perhaps they're so far in the past that many readers cannot even relate.

It's no wonder Caller ID, spam filtering, and DVRs are so popular. People are finding ever more creative ways to shelter themselves from the assault of interruption marketing.

Outbound methods include spam, junk mail, cold calls, postcards, trade shows, and radio spots.

The Pros of Outbound Marketing
- reaches the masses
- measurable results
- tried-and-true outcome
- familiarity with methods

The Cons of Outbound Marketing
- costly
- low conversation rates
- harder to get prospects to listen
- interruption method
- less trustful
- does not build a relationship

Today, the average person is mugged by more than 2,000 outbound marketing messages per day.

You have to ask yourself, does it make sense to try to convince someone (bend someone's arm) to buy a product or service or should the company sell to those already on the hunt for what the company has to offer? The latter seems to be more reasonable, less costly, and garners better results.

Inbound marketing is all about going to where your prospects already hang out on the web, engaging them in a conversation and sharing information—information they care about, on their terms, on their time.

Inbound Marketing includes blogs, landing pages, articles, newsletters, social networking, webinars, websites, videos, podcasts, virtual events, Facebook, Twitter, et al. The prospects are in charge of these venues. They go where they want, when they want, and read about what they are most interested in.

The Pros of Inbound Marketing

- less expensive
- effective for large and small businesses
- quicker return on investment
- levels the playing field
- reaches targeted, predisposed prospects
- measurable results

The Cons of Inbound Marketing

- time consuming
- learning curve
- can be costly if mismanaged
- may tie up internal resources

Many organizations produce good results with a mixture of inbound and outbound marketing, usually with less outbound. Push marketing methods (outbound) are employed when it appears the business' ideal prospect cannot be reached or wooed with normal inbound methods.

Take the time to develop some inbound and outbound prototype campaigns, and then measure the results to see which ones work best for those you're trying to reach.

Be prepared to change or drop campaigns that have been successful in the past. Successful campaigns do not last forever.

Things change, times change, prospects change. Good ideas only last so long. Then more good ideas need to be developed.

It's Not All About You

"Every experiment, by multitudes or by individuals, that has a sensual and selfish aim, will fail."

—RALPH WALDO EMERSON

Sorry to be the one to break the bad news. Yes, mom did pack your lunch in the morning, button your coat, and walk you to the bus stop each morning for school. But now you're selling products and services that other people need. It's time to change your focus.

A quick way to improve your website, from the buyer's perspective, in just 15 minutes is to remove every occurrence of "we," "us," and "our." The buyer is not interested in you at first, it's all about them. They will eventually care about your experience, how long you've been in business, and your other credentials. But in the beginning they're more interested in how you can solve their problem at hand.

Even the About Us page on a website can talk from the buyers' point of view. You can talk about how your past experiences will be a key part in being able to remove their pain. Your About Us content can reassure them that you're the best choice to solve their issues.

We already talked about not building the website so visitors can just wander. The website should continually talk about the buyer's pain, how you can remedy that pain, and what the benefits will be after the pain is removed.

Are You Targeting the Indecision Maker?

"Indecision and delays are the parents of failure."

—GEORGE CANNING

Qualified leads are individuals who are displaying both the intent and the capacity to make a buying decision in a reasonable time frame. Sometimes we seek the path of least resistance, which in turn leads us to the indecision makers in the company. Those are people that love to be educated, love to have lunch, love to ponder the existence of black holes in our solar system, the tire-kickers. Many of us have wasted a considerable amount of time with these corporate black holes.

Let's parse the first sentence you read in this section, "Qualified leads are individuals who display both the intent and the capacity to make a buying decision in a reasonable time frame." Qualified leads are those we should be focusing on in our marketing efforts. Other words for "qualify" are restrict, limit, and reduce. We're not going to sell to everyone on this planet. Another key phrase in the sentence is "displaying intent." This means potential buyers are making overtures in your direction. They have displayed "interest" in your product or service in some manner. Perhaps they have attended a webinar, downloaded some collateral from your website, or signed up for a free trial. They have taken some action.

The question many salespeople avoid is "Can you make the buying decision?" Does it make sense when trying to close a deal to spend your time talking to those in a business that do not have the capacity to purchase? No. You should be off to find the decision maker in the organization. Your last key ingredient in the sentence is, "a reasonable time frame." You're not talking about a time frame such as the next time Halley's Comet appears, which by the way, is in 2161, give or take a few months. Granted, the sale does take longer now because the timeline is in the prospect's hands. But "reasonable time frame" does not mean you should bird-dog someone for the foreseeable future. If the prospect is not clearly demonstrating interest by her actions, then be on your way.

Draw a Bead on Your Target Markets

"Aim for the highest."

—ANDREW CARNEGIE

The shotgun approach works great for ducks and pheasants, but not for lead generation. All the prospects in one market segment will not respond to the same message in the same way. They all have different pain points. Let's say you're a software company that offers web-based information governance solutions. The solution covers four areas: retention management, security, privacy, and inventory management. Even though the companies involved with information governance are all in the same business sector, they all deal with different issues at various times. The people focused on privacy will respond better to privacy messaging while those dealing with retention management issues will respond favorably to messages about that topic.

Even though people purchase the same product, they all have different needs. Then how should you break down your prospects into market segments? Think of separating the people groups by geographic location, demographics, or behavior. People could be divided by age, gender, income, occupation, education, or nationality. Candidates could be further split up by activities, interests, opinions, attitudes, or values. You could also separate potential opportunities by company size, industry, and purchase criteria.

Whether your market is large or small, you need to do market segmentation. Put like-minded people into similar groups. That way you can direct your messaging right at their common pain points. You can create specific e-mail campaigns, social media messaging, tailored landing pages, and blog posts.

Tell Me, Don't Sell Me

*"Sales are contingent upon the attitude of the salesman—not
the attitude of the prospect."*

—W. CLEMENT STONE

Whether you're sending out a newsletter, doing a blog post, or creating a webinar, stick with these three message components: pain points, remedies, and benefits. Don't fixate on the software's features or the product's functions. Potential buyers won't mind hearing about features or functions as long as they remove pain, remedy problems, and give great payback. Keep the focus on why the buyer should purchase your product and not someone else's. Continue to talk about value, quality, ease of use, seamless integration, safety, service, control, and support. Tell people how your product or service helps them.

There will be plenty of time to sell once you find out if the person is really interested in what you have to offer.

Don't Push the Sale

"Remember, you only have to succeed the last time."

—BRIAN TRACY

Every business person wants things to happen faster than they do. Pushing the sale, more often than not, causes the prospect to back away.

There are ways you can tell if you're pushing too hard. Let's says you have a form people need to fill out to attend your free webinar—asking for their name, company, title, phone, address, and e-mail. When you look at the statistics for your landing page, you notice the Bounce Rate is extremely high. Remember the Bounce Rate has to do with people that arrive at a landing page but then decide to leave without filling out the information form. Perhaps you're asking for too much information too early in the relationship. Now you launch a landing page that only asks for a person's name and e-mail. After you run stats on this landing page, you note the Bounce Rate is much lower. You haven't changed anything else. What conclusion can you draw from this exercise? Were you asking for too much information at the beginning of the relationship?

The same exercise can be done with e-mail campaigns. Launch a few e-mail campaigns that include hard sells and measure the response rate. Then send out a few more batches with soft sells, and see if the response gets better. It doesn't have to be a mystery why people are not responding to your marketing message. It just takes some investigation on your part to understand which pieces are working well and which pieces need tuning.

MKT   SLS

Turn Others into Your Willing Marketing Staff

"If the internet can be described as a giant human consciousness,
then viral marketing is the illusion of free will."

—GEORGE PENDLE

When first hearing the term "viral marketing," you might want to start running in the other direction. The phrase does not sound friendly at first blush. If one thinks of how a virus spreads, the expression starts to make more sense. A virus does not reach its unsuspecting prey without some help from the unwilling "carrier." So viral marketing is the act of encouraging people to pass along your marketing message.

Here's a brief list of what's involved in the viral marketing process:

- Gives away products or services
- Provides for effortless transfer to others
- Scales easily from small to very large
- Exploits common motivations and behaviors
- Utilizes existing communication/social networks
- Takes advantage of others' resources

Sounds a little like how chicken pox or strep throat works its way through an elementary school population, especially, "Provides for effortless transfer to others" and "Scales easily from small to very large." The "very large" would be the unsuspecting parents at home. Yep, that works.

People really aren't talking among themselves, but they are transferring information between each other by passing along a hyperlink to a page they think their circle of friends or colleagues might be interested in reading. YouTube is perhaps the biggest and best example of successful viral marketing today. A humorous video (Figure 29.1) can be passed along to hundreds of thousands of viewers in mere minutes, a marketer's fantasy come true. Business and marketing videos spread a mite slower.

Viral marketing is much like digital word-of-mouth.

Hotmail put viral marketing on the map. The company, founded by Sabeer Bhatia and Jack Smith in 1995, was commercially launched on July 4, 1996, to give people

Mad TV Bob Newhart Skit - Mo Collins - Stop it

FIGURE 29.1—YouTube viral video

access to e-mail via the web from a computer anywhere in the world. By December 1997, Hotmail reported more than 8.5 million subscribers and was sold later that month to Microsoft for a reported ("whopping," "astounding," "shocking") $400 million. Nice ROI. Hotmail, supporting 36 languages, is still the world's second largest webmail provider with 343 million users.

Hotmail's Six-step Strategy was:

1. Give away free e-mail addresses and services.
2. Attach a simple tag at the bottom of every free message sent out: "Get your private, free e-mail at Hotmail."
3. Stand back while people e-mail to their own network of friends and associates.
4. Some will see the free message and ignore it.
5. A number of people will see the message and sign up for their own free e-mail service.
6. These new signups will propel the message still wider to their own ever-increasing circles of friends and associates.

Attaching a simple message to the end of every e-mail that any Hotmail owner sent out was what started the epidemic. Satisfied customers spread the word near and far. If you sign up for a Hotmail account, this is what it's up to these days. Here's what the viral marketing tag says at the bottom of every message sent out today:

Hotmail: Powerful Free email with security by Microsoft. Get it now.

Viral marketing can be used to inform people about a new product line or enlist their help in spreading the word. Today, businesses have seven media types at their disposal to use as viral marketing outlets: print, recordings, cinema, radio, TV, the web, and mobile devices. Mobile devices prove to have more conversion influence than the other media types. Key Pousttchi and Dietmer G. Wiedemann did a multicase study that outlines the viral marketing success factors when employing mobile media:

- Perceived usefulness by recipient
- Reward for communicator
- Perceived ease of use
- Free mobile viral content
- Initial contacts
- First mover's advantage
- Critical mass
- Scalability

Remember, mobile devices are the first media type people have on them at all times. It's always on and has a built-in payment mechanism.

How might you make a newsletter viral?

- Create a newsletter that has timely, useful information. No sales rants.
- Keep the newsletter to a one-page e-mail. Send it out each month. Introduce each subject with one or two sentences.

At the end of each subject, add a "Rest of the Story" link back to your website or blog where the reader can take in only those news stories he is interested in reading.

· Each story should have a "Send this page to a friend" or "Share this" link.

· Give people a chance to bookmark the newsletter page.

· Keep an archive of past articles so people come back and reread them later.

· Add "calls to action" to read those insightful articles in the signature at the end of every e-mail.

How might you make your website or blog viral?

· Write short articles about the collateral (case studies, whitepapers, data sheets, etc.) on your site and post them on your blog or free article sites to create cross-traffic opportunities.

· Take the same short articles and create News items or Discussion topics on LinkedIn.

· Send out tweets about the collateral topics and direct visitors to your website or blog.

· Make it easy for people to stay up on what the business is up to by adding an RSS Feed.

· Make the pages on your website and blog easy for people to share with their circle of friends.

· Crosslink the pages of your website with the posts on your blog.

If the website collateral, web page, or blog post is beneficial to readers, they are bound to send it to friends or colleagues they believe will profit from it as well.

Viral is all about giveaways, effortless transfer, scalability, exploiting behavior, utilizing existing communication channels, and making use of other's resources.

The Pros and Cons of Viral Marketing

Pros	Cons
• Unlimited tools at your disposal	• You don't control the market
• Inexpensive	• You may not have control of the results
• Immediate response	• Results may be hard to pin down
• Less intrusive	• Can cost a lot
• Spread by friends and friends of friends	• Bad humor or poor taste may have unintended consequences
• Tends to break through the noise	
• Builds equity	
• Differentiates from competitors	
• Market could be exponential	
• Find out more about prospects	
• Improve brand awareness	

Take 5

Generate Closable Opportunities

"It doesn't mean they can't win. It means it's uphill."

—DENNIS SIMON

Generating closable opportunities is what business is all about on the web. The opportunities might be a partnership with a not-for-profit organization that brings clean water to third-world countries, a marketing agency looking to help companies generate more revenue, or a software company looking to generate more sales. Take the time now to review the topics covered in this last part of *Outcome-Based Marketing*.

Tuning Your Key Phrases, Messaging, and Content. Covering harmonizing the key phrases, messaging, and content is important. Companies must understand how prospects are searching for them on the web. With that information in hand, AKA the key phrases, they can then go to work on wordsmithing their messaging and tuning their content. Web pages, press releases, social chatter, webinar, and podcasts are content examples.

A Seven-Step Marketing Plan. Gives you an overview of a simple seven-step marketing plan that anyone can develop and execute in a single day. The plan includes the marketing goals, benefits, target audience, marketing tactics employed, company's niche and personality, and the budget constraints.

Three Sample Marketing Plans. Many people learn best by example. To that end, Outcome-based Marketing gives three marketing plan examples in this section, a one-horse, one-rider business; a small business; and a not-so-small business. Take one of these example plans and adjust it to suit your company's needs.

Keep Marketing Tactics on Track with a Marketing Calendar. Marketing calendars are easy to build and help keep your marketing campaigns on schedule. You can make a simple plan and track dates, tactics, people involved, cost, and projected results. After the campaign ends, add the actual results and match those against the projected outcome.

Sample Conversion Streams. Conversion streams are not a cookie-cutter process. Each conversion stream is meant for very different campaigns. The conversion stream that works for webinars may not work for building a free-trial audience. Each conversion stream has to be strategically thought out and implemented. As the campaign develops, the stream will need adjusting to gain the maximum results.

Meaningful Metric Models. For some reason people don't want to know how good or bad things are going. Measuring marketing campaigns are no different, but the reality is marketing tactics need to be measured. Those that are working need to be turned up, and the ones that are failing need to be turned off. Metrics take the emotion and gut feelings out of the decision.

The Analysis of Analytics. There are new analytic tools coming on the scene each week. Look for ones that are not too complicated and give you the information you believe valuable to your marketing efforts. Analytics, along with sound metrics, can aid in tuning the marketing campaign for maximum, positive impact.

Closing the Loop Between Marketing and Sales. Closing the gap between marketing and sales is critical. In this day of tough competition, which will only get tougher, everyone has to work for the common good of the company and the client. Differences need to be put aside, and information and connections must be shared. Closed loop marketing provides that information-sharing, "can't we all get along" opportunity.

Lead Nurturing. Most visitors to a website—97 percent—are not ready to commit. These undecided people need to be routed through a series of programs that educate them and give them the opportunity to gain a better understanding of the benefits derived from the company's offerings.

Only Superman Can Leap Tall Buildings in a Single Bound. Perhaps this is a no brainer, but there are times when people believe they can do anything. The advances in technologies are making it harder for those supermen or superwomen to survive. Everyone needs help at one time or another. Choose the parts of a project that your team can do well. Farm out the balance of the tasks to experts.

Miscellaneous Marketing Matters. Keep the focus on the client or prospect; forget the in-decision makers; focus on your target market; go to where your ideal prospects gather; tell me, don't sell me; and don't push the sale.

Chapter 30

Some Assembly Required

"Most people run a race to see who is fastest. I run
a race to see who has the most guts."

—STEVE PREFONTAINE

WHENEVER YOU FINISH A NEW BOOK, DO YOU JUMP RIGHT IN AND start implementing what you've read? Or do you need time to contemplate what the writer has said? Do more questions than actionable tactics seem to flood your mind at those times? Do questions crop up: What insights did I gain? What new ideas were presented? Does what I read apply to me? Do the ideas make sense? Are they practical to employ? What concepts in the book really grabbed my attention?

A good cup of tea is not made by simply pouring boiling water over a tea bag in your favorite cup or mug. The water must be brought to a full boil and then left to sit for 30 to 60 seconds. This process allows the water to cool so it does not cook the tea. Green tea (one of my favorites) needs to steep, or bathe, in the hot water for one to two minutes. Steeping the tea longer than recommended causes the tea to become bitter. Perhaps your thought process is much the same. After reading a good book or hearing a thought-provoking discussion or presentation, you need time to ponder, mull over, or consider the information. Later on you're ready to jump into action.

Outcome-Based Marketing, So What?

"Business has only two functions—marketing and innovation."

—Milan Kundera

Businesses have been getting results from their marketing efforts from the beginning. But have the results been positive or negative? Did the results move the company forward or backward? Did the results increase the company's bottom line? Did they result in more market share? These are all important questions.

Businesses continue to spend millions of dollars on strengthening their web presence. They're doing everything within their power to gain visibility in all the right places on the web. They are investigating social media and wondering how it can be leveraged to deliver better customer care, increase their brand's awareness, and generate new revenue streams. Most of all, companies are putting in Herculean efforts to generate more closable opportunities. The problem is that their efforts are not producing the desired results. *Outcome-Based Marketing: New Rules for Marketing on the Web* delivers on all these topics.

The tenets of outcome-based marketing are easy to understand and apply.

- *Inputs.* Materials and resources used during the marketing activities. The materials could be case studies, whitepapers, as well as other collateral pieces. The resources might be people, time, and money.

· *Activities.* Processes the business executes during the marketing campaign. Processes such as e-mail blasts, webinars, blog postings, or podcasts.

· *Masses.* People made aware of the marketing promotion.

· *Leads.* The number of people that took some action as a result of the marketing campaign. For instance, the number of people that subscribed to the blog after reading it or the number of prospects that downloaded a whitepaper after watching a webinar.

· *Outcome targets.* For example, the stated outcome might be 1,000 new attendees to the next webinar series or a 15 percent increase in visitor traffic to the company website over the next three months.

· *Outcome indicators.* Observable and measureable milestones toward the outcome target. For instance, a marketing campaign is launched, and it generates a 5 percent increase in visitor traffic in the first month. Then it is likely the visitor traffic will increase by 15 percent after the third month. The outcome indicators let you know if the outcome targets are realistic and achievable or if other activities need to be added to reach the marketing goal.

Before you start the planning process for your next marketing campaign here are five important takeaways from each of the major sections within *Outcome-Based Marketing*:

Building a Strong Web Presence
1. Grab a website visitor's attention in the first eight seconds.
2. Develop decision-making paths for your homepage.
3. Win over audiences with compelling content.
4. Develop and execute a content repurpose strategy.
5. Persuade your website visitors to take action.

Be Seen in All the Right Places on the Web

1. Identify your ideal prospect.
2. Maximize your online presence.
3. Attract new web visitors in droves.
4. Develop and execute dozens of online strategies that directly impact your business.
5. Get noticed and grow your business on the web.

Being Social on the Web

1. Leverage social media.
2. Incorporate efficient and effective ways to stay in touch and build relationships.
3. Build and execute a social media strategy.
4. Develop social media best practices.
5. Create a believable social networking presence.

Generate Closable Opportunities

1. Be found by search engines and those people doing the searching.
2. Measure sitewide success as well as online marketing campaigns.
3. Write a seven-step marketing plan.
4. Build a conversion stream to improve your close rates.
5. Develop analytics and metrics to measure your marketing campaign's success.

Hopefully, one of the most important takeaways from this book is that you can raise the bar without busting the company budget. Outcome-based marketing is a method that can be adopted over time without upsetting all a company already has in place. Remember, be strategic. Put into practice what you believe makes the most sense for your organization. Keep retooling your marketing tactics until they produce the best possible results.

Where to Start?

"Without passion, you don't have energy; without energy, you have nothing. Nothing great in the world has been accomplished without passion."

—Donald Trump

This is the last question to tackle together. Can you just jump in anywhere in this book and get started? Many business books seem to give that advice today. That approach won't work for *Outcome-Based Marketing*. You're not going to run a marathon and finish without starting with 5 and 10K runs first. A great website with lousy content will not close any new business. Spending time and resources on social media without a strategy in place is a waste of time. *Outcome-Based Marketing* works much the way constructing a house might take place. The book starts out by laying a solid foundation with "Building a Strong Web Presence." It then discusses "Being Found in All the Right Places on the Web." Let's call that section putting up the outside walls. The third part of the book, "Being Social on the Web," is akin to putting on a well-sealed roof. The final section, "Generating Closable Opportunities," might be seen as finishing the insides of the structure. First the foundation, then the walls followed by the roof with the inside being completed last. *Outcome-Based Marketing* needs to be followed in the same way.

Here's hoping all your future marketing outcomes are positive ones.

Glossary

Aggregation. A website or computer software that aggregates syndicated web content.

alt tag. The alt attribute is used in HTML and XHTML documents to specify alternative text (alt text) that is to be rendered when the element to which it is applied cannot be rendered. (Wikipedia)

Analytics. Generates detailed stats about website visitors.

Atom format. The Atom format was developed as an alternative to RSS.

Attraction marketing. See *Pull marketing*.

Average position. Average position tells you the placement of your ad in the search results. Most retailers find positions three through five have the best results.

B2B marketing (B2B). Business-to-business marketing.

B2C marketing (B2C). Business-to-consumer marketing.

Backlink. Hyperlink from another website or web page. See *Themed backlink*.

Blog post. A short article written on a blog.

Blogosphere. A collected community of blogs and their individual connections.

Blogroll. A blogger's list of other blogs of interest.

Bookmark. See *Social bookmarking*.

Bookmarking. See *Social bookmarking*.

Bounce rate. Bounce rate tells you the percentage of people that clicked on your ad, went to your landing page, but did not visit a second page. A bounce rate of 30 percent tells you that only three out of 10 people clicked on your ad, visited your landing page, and then left. The lower the bounce rate the better. A good bounce rate is 40 percent.

Brand promise. A statement made to customers that outlines what they should expect for all interactions with your people, products, or service.

Call to action. A call to action tells the website visitor to take some immediate action; "Call Now!," "Download Now!," or "Sign-up Today!"

Cascading Style Sheets (CSS). A style sheet language used to describe the presentation semantics (the look and formatting) of a document written in a markup language. (Wikipedia)

Click Thru Rate (CTR). Click Thru Rate is the percentage of people that clicked on your advertisement. For example, a CTR of 5 percent means that 5 out of every 100 people that saw your ad clicked on it. An average CTR for e-commerce sites is 1 to 3 percent.

Closable opportunity. A sales lead that has taken action(s) to move the relationship along the sales funnel and has shown considerable interest in purchasing a product or service.

Closed loop marketing. Talks about healing the information flow between what marketing and sales each think constitutes a qualified lead.

Collateral. Marketing materials.

Content Management System (CMS). A software system used to control web pages, documents, materials, and other forms of media residing on a website.

Content map. See *Website Content Map*.

Content repurpose strategy. A strategy to repurpose or reuse marketing materials in various forms outside its original intent.

Conversion rate. The conversion rate pulls everything together. Conversion rate tells you the rate at which visitors are converted into buyers. Typically 1.25 percent is the low end for e-commerce sites.

Conversion stream. Conversion streams outline marketing tactics in a linear form so you can see the pace of the campaign, who's involved at what step, what methods work, and what needs improvement. A conversion stream can be a simple diagram that shows when e-mails are sent out, to whom they are sent, and what offers are being made and taken advantage of during the mailing process.

Crawls. The process a search engine uses to read, or crawl, a web page.

Customer Relationship Management (CRM). A company's strategy for mapping the company's interactions between customers, prospects, and sales prospects. (Wikipedia)

Data sheet. A spec sheet summarizing the performance and other technical characteristics of a product or service.

Decision-making path. Decision-making paths are mechanisms to guide and educate those website visitors through the web pages until they are ready to make a decision "to buy" or "not to buy."

Direct Message (DM). On Twitter, you can send a follower a private, direct message.

Elevator pitch. A business's 30-second pitch stating the business need, how the organization fulfills that need, and how the customer benefits.

E-mail blast. See *E-mail marketing*.

E-mail marketing. A form of direct mail over the web using electronic mail as the means of communication.

Geotag. A geographical identification.

Google AdSense. Offers a contextual advertising solution to web publishers. Delivers text-based Google AdWords ads that are relevant to site content pages. (Google's words.)

Google AdWords. Sponsored ads in the Sponsored Links section next to search results to boost website traffic and sales. (Google's words.)

Google Alerts. Google Alerts are e-mails sent to you when Google finds new results—such as web pages, newspaper articles, or blogs—that match specific search terms. (Google's words.)

Google Analytics. Google Analytics (GA) is a free service offered by Google that generates detailed statistics about the visitors to a website. (Wikipedia)

Hashtag. A tag embedded in a message posted on a microblogging service, consisting of a word within the message prefixed with a hash sign. (Wikipedia)

Heat map. A graphical representation of visitor data points on a webpage or blog. Colors delineate the most popular areas.

Ideal prospect. A quantifiable description of a business' perfect consumer or client.

Impression share. Impression share tells you how many times your ad displays per the number of searches made on a particular search phrase. For instance if your impression share was 50 percent, your ad was displayed half the time. A strong Impression Share is 80 percent.

Inbound marketing. See *Pull marketing*.

Influencer. A person on the web that has a huge following, perhaps a blogger or someone who has prominence in the social media communities.

Internet road map. A map describing a business's planned marketing activities on the web.

Key phrase. A select word or phrase used to better position a web page in search results.

Key term. See *Key phrase*.

Landing page. A web page designed with a marketing message asking the visitors to take one specific action.

Lead. A person that answers a specific call to action, moving the sales relationship to the next level.

Lead management. A business practice describing the marketing methods and practices used to generate new potential business opportunities.

Lead nurturing. A process that looks after and/or educates a prospect or lead while in the sales funnel.

Link love. A hyperlink from one website page or blog posting to another website page or blog posting.

Livecasting. Similar to podcasting only the broadcast is live.

Marketing calendar. A calendar of marketing events.

Mention. A mention is any Twitter update that contains @username in the body of the tweet.

Metadata. Information or data about data.

Metrics. A system of measuring the deciding factors in a marketing campaign.

Micro-blogging. See *Tweet*.

Multilevel, multitouch marketing. An approach that attempts to reach prospects with a variety of marketing tactics several times or more.

Natural search. Search results that are listed on search engine results pages because of their relevance to the search term.

Nurturing. See *Lead nurturing*.

Offer. A bid (trial demo, whitepaper, podcast, or webinar) to attract a prospect.

Off-page optimization. Deals with the number and relevance of websites linking to your website.

Online virtual meeting. See *Webinar*.

On-page optimization. On-page factors such as website structure, navigation, the use of meta tags, keywords, phrases, and content, along with other aspects.

Organic search. See *Natural search*.

Organic search marketing. See *Search Engine Optimization* and *Pay-per-Click*.

Outbound marketing. See *Push marketing*.

Outcome-based marketing. A philosophy that centers on empirically measuring the progress and results of marketing campaigns.

Outcome-based marketing activities. Processes the business executes during the marketing campaign. Processes such as e-mail blasts, webinars, blog postings, or podcasts.

Outcome-based marketing indicators. Observable and measureable milestones toward the outcome target. For instance, if a marketing campaign is launched and it generates a 5 percent increase in visitor traffic in the first month and everything remains the same, then it is likely the visitor traffic will increase by 15 percent after the third month. The outcome indicators let you know if the outcome targets are realistic and achievable or if other activities need to be added to reach the marketing goal.

Outcome-based marketing inputs. Materials and resources used during the marketing activities. The materials could be case studies, whitepapers, as well as other collateral pieces. The resources might be people, time, and money.

Outcome-based marketing leads. The number of people that took some action as a result of the marketing campaign. For instance, the number of people that subscribed to the blog after reading it or the number of prospects who downloaded a whitepaper after watching a webinar.

Outcome-based marketing masses. People made aware of the marketing promotion.

Outcome-based marketing targets. The number and percentage of leads that you need to achieve the stated outcome. For example, the stated outcome might be 1,000 new attendees to the next webinar series or a 15 percent increase in visitor traffic to the company website over the next three months.

Paid search. See *Pay-per-Click (PPC)*.

Page Rank™. A link analysis algorithm, named after Larry Page, used by Google that assigns a numerical weighting to each element of a hyperlinked set of documents, such as the World Wide Web, with the purpose of measuring its relative importance within the set. (Wikipedia)

Pay-per-Click (PPC). An advertising model on the web where advertisers pay a host to show their ads in specific search results.

Plug-in. A software component that adds special functionality to a larger program. Plug-ins are popular add-ons in the blogosphere to add functionality to blogs.

Podcast. A podcast (or nonstreamed webcast) is a series of digital media files (either audio or video) that are released episodically and often downloaded through web syndication. (Wikipedia)

Podcast directories. Websites that specialize in housing the best-of-the-best in video and audio podcasts.

Pop-up. Small windows that pop up on your screen, usually an advertisement.

Positioning. In marketing, positioning has come to mean the process by which marketers try to create an image or identity in the minds of their target market for their product, brand, or organization. (Wikipedia)

Profile. An area where personal information is stored and which identifies a member of a social community.

Prospect universe. The sum of all your ideal prospects found on the web.

Pull marketing. Refers to the process of pulling a prospect toward you by means of being found in all the right places; locations such as an optimized website, blog, social media, or landing page.

Push marketing. Refers to a marketing method used to push a message out by sending direct mail, certain types of advertising (commercials, billboards), and sometimes spam.

Quality score. Quality score is a measurement by Google of your ad, landing page, and key phrases. This measurement also takes into account past performance. This gives the little guy who does a better job than a large company a better chance of placement for less cost. Seven to ten represents a decent quality score.

@reply. Any Twitter update that begins with @username.

Retweet. The process of sending a Twitter users favorite post, tweet, or link.

RSS feed. Real Simple Syndication. It's one of the coolest ways to pass information along to your blog subscribers.

Sales funnel. A systematic sales method used to track the process of selling a product or service.

Search Engine Marketing (SEM). A form of web marketing that seeks to promote a website's visibility by increasing its position in search engine results.

Search Engine Optimization (SEO). The process of placing important terms, keywords, or key phrases, in the headers, web page code, and content of your web pages to improve placement in search results.

Shout out. Think of it like this: You're standing at a corner intersection waiting for the traffic light to change. You yell out to the fellow sitting in his car at the stop light, "Hey bud, what does your company do?" As the light changes to green, he has about ten seconds to yell out his car window as he pulls away.

Site map. A web page that lists all the pages that comprise a website.

Social bookmarking. A method for internet users to organize, store, manage, and search for bookmarks of resources online.

Social channel. A social community of members such as Facebook, Twitter, LinkedIn, or MySpace.

Social media. Social media is media designed to be shared through social interaction.

Social media netiquette. In any community civility, should be championed. Everyone needs to have equal rights and to coexist for the community to stay together and survive. People that cannot keep their negative personal attacks to themselves will find themselves on the outside of the community looking in.

Social networking. Social networking is linking people together in some way.

Social networking ecosystem. A social networking community and its associated tools and web applications.

Social networking stratosphere. See *Social networking ecosystem*.

Social site. See *Social channel*.

Sticky. Relates to how much time someone might spend viewing a web page or blog page, or watching a slide presentation or web demo.

Street cred. Short for street credibility. The Urban Dictionary defines street cred as "Commanding a level of respect in an urban environment due to experience in or knowledge of issues affecting those environments" or "A person's coolness factor." Credibility is important in any business space; without it, who's going to listen to the messenger?

Style guide. A set of standards for writing or designing a newsletter, website, whitepaper, or blog.

Tagline. Six to eight words, fewer if possible, that create a memorable message in the mind of a consumer. Taglines are usually associated with a company's logo.

Themed backlink. Also known as relevant backlinks, these are backlinks from sites in the same business space. For instance, an architectural firm might target an architectural, construction, and engineering consortium for "themed" backlinks.

Tweet. 140-character message sent out across the Twitter network.

Twitter follower. A Twitter member who decides to follow, or listen to, another Twitter member.

Vertical. A specific market segment. For instance, education, health care, pharmaceutical, finance, and government.

Video blog (vlog). A collection of video podcasts.

Viral marketing. A marketing tactic that causes others to use their resources and connections to help spread a marketing message.

Virtual event. An event or conference delivered over the web in which attendees stay at their offices and view the activities on their laptop or desktop computer.

Visitor conversion. A visitor to a website or blog that takes some action to move the relationship from stranger to prospect, lead, opportunity, or consumer.

Visitor traffic. The number of people that visit a website or blog for some time interval.

vlog. See *Video blog*.

Watering holes. The places (forums, social communities, or blogs) where like-minded people gather on the web.

Web 2.0. The term Web 2.0 is commonly associated with web applications that facilitate interactive information sharing, interoperability, user-centered design, and collaboration on the World Wide Web. (Wikipedia)

Web conference. A software toolset used to conduct meetings, training, or presentations over the web.

Web presence. A company or organization's visibility or prominence on the web.

Webcast. Similar to TV broadcasts, they may be live or prerecorded. The program can be sent to an unlimited audience. The attendees experience a high-end, branded meeting. Webcasts are usually viewed with your browser and Windows Media Player or RealPlayer.

Webinar. A two-way web conference presented by a speaker to an audience.

Website content map. Content maps hold much more information than a website's site map. A content map might show what web pages hold offers, which are maintained by whom, which are up-to-date, and which need revision.

Whitepaper. A document or paper that has a distinctive purpose, audience, and format.

Acknowledgments

DURING THE LAST YEAR I HAVE HAD THE PLEASURE OF WORKING with and for some terrific people and organizations. I've learned plenty—more than I can put into practice. When thanking people, there's always the danger of forgetting one person's name you believe had a positive effect on the way you conduct business, but I'll take my chances.

Dave Bellandi, a black belt in marketing, helped strengthen my resolve to always measure every marketing activity for results. Sometimes we get so busy with the marketing activities and launching the next tactical volley that we forget what we're striving for in the end: Results! Dave's gang, The Bellandi Group, wouldn't be who they are without Ami, Gina, Laura, and Sunny. I've learned valuable lessons from all of you.

Fusion Marketing Partners, Chris, Myron, Jim, and Gail, are wonderful to work alongside. Everyone always has the other person's back when times get tough and project deadlines loom overhead. I've never worked with a better group of lead-generation specialists and marketing professionals.

I developed a fast friendship this last year with a fellow I hope to spend time with for many years to come, Bill Petro. Bill is a marketing professional extraordinaire. He offered so much good advice and direction as this writing project got off the ground. Many thanks, brother.

This project, like all the other crazy ideas I convince my wife Kay are worthy, would not be a reality without her support, editing, good intuition, and love. Honey, I owe you big time!

Six months ago I approached Entrepreneur Press with this project, and the people there went for it. I couldn't believe my good fortune in landing the best darn publishing house in the entrepreneur/small business market and consummate professionals all. Many thanks go to Jere Calmes, publisher; Leanne Harvey, director of marketing; Jillian McTigue, and everyone at the Irvine, California, offices. Thanks also go out to Karen Billipp for riding herd on this project.

Much appreciation also goes out to Chris Brogan for writing the Foreword to this book. I love Chris' focus on the person running the business and not just on the business's bottom line. Chris has loads of high-quality information to share. Stop by his site at ChrisBrogan. com. Sign up for his newsletter. You never know what Chris will share, but it's always worth the read.

I hope *Outcome-Based Marketing: New Rules for Marketing on the Web* becomes a mainstay in your office. Enjoy.

About the Author

J OHN LEAVY IS FOUNDER AND OWNER OF INPLAINSITE MARKETING, LLC, a Colorado-based web marketing firm specializing in creating massive awareness, increasing leads, and generating closable opportunities for its clients.

John has spent decades developing and delivering top-notch Internet Presence Management strategies such as: strategic marketing, lead generation, social media, branding, web design, and search engine optimization. Some of Mr. Leavy's satisfied clients include: Oracle, SAP, Kennedy Space Center, Mobil Oil Corporation, Steelcase, Army Corps of Engineers, General Motors, Delco Products, City of Chicago, New York State Legislature, Chrysler Corporation, Ford Motor Company, Bose, the Department of Defense, the Departments of the Army, Navy, and Air Force, United States Air Forces in Europe, Aviano Air Base (Italy), Ramstein Air Base (Germany), the Central Intelligence Agency, and Federal Bureau of Investigation.

John is an in-demand presenter and keynote speaker at national and international events. Mr. Leavy is a best-selling author and regularly contributes articles to leading publications and content to web portals and blogs.

John lives in the Rocky Mountains of Colorado near Colorado Springs with his wife and best friend Kay. They have three adult children: Doug, Daniel, and Sei. They also have five grandchildren: Caleb, Hannah, Isaac, Becca, and Tessa Bella.

Index